JOURNEY TO OBLIVION

To my parents

JOURNEY TO OBLIVION

The End of the East European Yiddish and German Worlds in the Mirror of Literature

PETER STENBERG

UNIVERSITY OF TORONTO PRESS
Toronto Buffalo London

ISBN 0-8020-5861-2

∞

Printed on acid-free paper

Canadian Cataloguing in Publication Data
Stenberg, Peter, 1942–
  Journey to oblivion

  Includes bibliographical references.
  ISBN 0-8020-5861-2

  1. Holocaust, Jewish (1939–1945), in literature.
  2. Deportation in literature.   3. Yiddish fiction –
  20th century – History and criticism.   4. German
  fiction – 20th century – History and criticism.
  5. German fiction – Jewish authors – History and
  criticism.   6. Jews – Europe, Eastern – History.
  7. Germans – Europe, Eastern – History.
  8. Language and culture – Europe, Eastern.   I. Title.

  PT772.S86 1991   833'.9109358   C90-094507-9

This book has been published with the help of a grant from the Canadian
Federation for the Humanities, using funds provided by the Social Sciences
and Humanities Research Council of Canada.

Contents

vi Contents

Acknowledgments

Several old friends have been very generous with their time and thoughts in helping me to find a way through the vast landscape covered in this work. My first thanks must go to Richard Swartz, East Central European correspondent for *Svenska Dagbladet*, who gave me many perceptive suggestions, brought me into contact with numerous crucial sources of information, and finally did me the deeply appreciated favor of reading the rough draft and suggesting what should go and what should stay. Nobody knows Central Europe better than Richard and his influence and experience is reflected throughout this work. My colleague Marketa Goetz-Stankiewicz has brought a great knowledge of the German, Slavic, and Jewish cultures of Central Europe with her to North America and has passed much of it on to me during many exhilarating trips into the wilderness of British Columbia. The idea for a book on this topic undoubtedly was born on the trail or around a campfire at a magnificent place like Cape Scott, Carmanah Creek, or the Forbidden Plateau, a spectacular place of genesis for such a disturbing story. Hartmut Heuser's abundant supply of information about wartime Germany and the immediate postwar years was crucial to the formation of the relevant chapters. He and his wife, Lilo, also helped make Munich a second home for me and my family. Walter Dillenz has been discussing this topic with me for a quarter-century in places as different as Tofino and Budapest. My wife, Rosa Levyne Stenberg, has been a part of the conversation for just as long and has played a major role in the formation of the work from beginning to end. Never has work been such pleasure as during the many hours of discussions with them.

I should also like to thank a number of people whose ideas and insights have filtered down into this manuscript throughout. Kati and Rudolf Vögelin-Meyer, Birgit Weidinger, Jan Röge, and Walter and Ursula Kolbinger have all made significant contributions with their thoughts while simultaneously making our European years so pleasant. Ron Beaumont, Jack Stewart, and Howard Schulman did the same in British Columbia. I am also very grateful to Fred and Maria-Luise Neufeld for their help with the section on the Mennonites in Russia, and to Laurence Kitching for dragging me into the computer age. Kate Harrison was indispensable at the keyboard, and Marcus Waldmann in the photo laboratory. A special thanks to the late Lydia Burton, whose commentary was all that an author could wish for from a superb copy editor.

I must also thank various authors, who contributed their time and insights, in particular Edgar Hilsenrath. One of the great pleasures in writing this work has been to get to know Edgar, who has provided me with much valuable material, and has gone far out of his way to help me in any way possible. I also would like to single out the contribution of Martin Pollack, who helped convince me to look eastward from Vienna. In addition, Horst Bienek, Herta Müller, Nikolaus Berwanger, Stefan Heym, Rudolf Vrba, Claudio Magris, and Ota Filip have all been most helpful in conversations and correspondence.

I would like to acknowledge, with gratitude, permission to use parts of an article, which I first published in the *Deutsche Vierteljahrsschrift*, June 1982, and which has been integrated into chapter 4 here.

Translations appearing in the text are mine, unless the work quoted has been published in English (see bibliography).

This work was written with the support of a two-year research grant from the Alexander von Humboldt Foundation. I am eternally grateful to them for their generosity, as I am to the Universität

Augsburg, President Josef Becker, and Professor Helmut Koopmann of that university for their continuing encouragement and advice. In addition I thank the German Exchange Service (DAAD) for a short-term grant which allowed me to finish the revisions in Germany in the historic spring of 1990.

The distribution of ethnic Germans in Europe: the view from Germany in 1934, according to Paul Blankenburg and Max Dreyer in *Nationalsozialistischer Wirtschafts-aufbau und seine Grundlagen* (*National Socialist Economic Structure and Its Basis*). The map shows the number of ethnic Germans outside the boundaries of Germany. (Published Berlin: 1934 [no publisher given]; reprinted: Hilgemann, *Atlas zur deutschen Zeitgeschichte*)

German and Yiddish language areas in Eastern Europe in 1910:
post–Second World War political boundaries

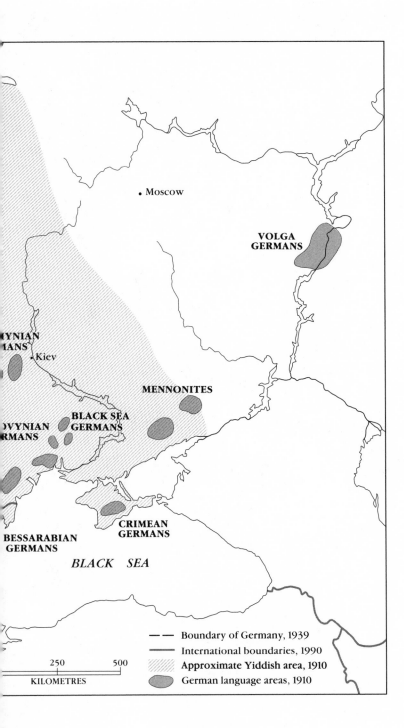

Moscow

VOLGA
GERMANS

YNIAN
IANS
Kiev

MENNONITES

BLACK SEA
GERMANS

VYNIAN
RMANS

CRIMEAN
GERMANS

BESSARABIAN
GERMANS

BLACK   SEA

— — Boundary of Germany, 1939
——— International boundaries, 1990
Approximate Yiddish area, 1910
German language areas, 1910

250   500

KILOMETRES

The family of Heinrich Toews in the Mennonite settlement of Waldheim, Molotschna, Ukraine, 1906. Toews owned a large farm and the machine factory of Waldheim. In 1924, both Mr and Mrs Toews were murdered and the surviving children fled to Canada. (Peter J. Koop)

A street scene from the Polish shtetl of Zabludow, northeast of Warsaw, in 1916. Today, there is nothing left of this heartland of the East European Jewish world other than neglected cemeteries. (YIVO Institute for Jewish Research, New York)

The trek: Attempting to keep ahead of the advancing Red Army, a German wagon train struggles with the mud and the cold of the approaching Russian winter. (Mennonite Heritage Centre Archives 294 USSR, Winnipeg)

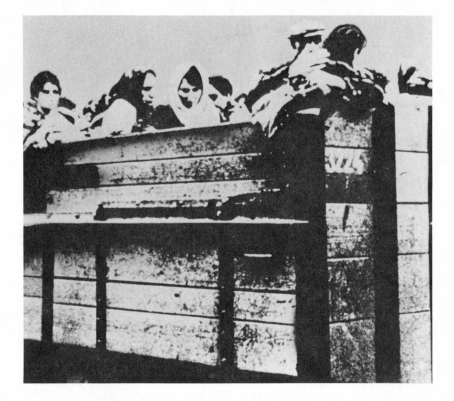

1939–45: As it was strictly forbidden to photograph the Jews on their way to the killing centers, there are few such photos. This one shows Polish Jews in an open cattle car on the way to Auschwitz. (Süddeutscher Verlag Archive)

28 May 1942, train station, Hanau. This photo is one of the very rare original documentations of the deportations of the German Jews to the extermination centers. Here the last Jews of Hanau board the trains for Theresienstadt. Of the 600 Jews in Hanau, 3 survived. (Süddeutscher Verlag Archive)

The flight of the Mennonites from Ukraine in the fall of 1943. In this scene from Einlage near the Dnieper River, a cow and an ox have been harnessed to a cart carrying the remaining possessions of the fleeing family. (Mennonite Heritage Centre Archives 113; Heinz Hindorf, photographer)

The Eastern Front, winter 1945. With the beginning of the great Russian drive on 12 January 1945, the endless treks of the ethnic German civilian population in East Central Europe filled the icy roads in the often futile attempt to reach safety ahead of the Red Army. (Süddeutscher Verlag Archive)

A street scene from a German settlement near Timisoara, Romania, in 1982. By the time of the revolution of December 1989, which began with a bloodbath in Timisoara, much of the last viable East European German world had been abandoned as the Romanian Germans fled to the West. (Richard Swartz)

JOURNEY TO OBLIVION

Introduction

This is the story of the end of two closely related European languages in Eastern Europe and of the people who spoke them. The larger linguistic group, moving east in search of land and racial purity, annihilated the smaller one at a moment in history when cultural and linguistic assimilation seemed more likely; it was in turn driven out by victorious counterattacking forces moving west. The Yiddish-speakers of Eastern Europe were destroyed by the murderous henchmen of an efficient German bureaucracy that organized the slaughter of the European Jews. The German-speakers of Eastern Europe were virtually eliminated as a result of a violent expulsion carried out by their former neighbors and the Red Army, and sanctioned by the decision of the Allies to remove them from their centuries-old homelands. This double destruction of two large, long-standing, and linguistically kindred cultures transpired within the extraordinary period of less than one decade. It has resulted in a radically different linguistic, cultural, and national map of Europe, whose borders remain a contentious issue for West Germany even after almost fifty years of existence.

The first of these events, the carefully organized destruction by Nazi Germany of the Yiddish-speaking East European Jews and the elimination of them from their homelands of more than half a millennium, has become a landmark event for the Western historical consciousness. This event has been granted a linguistic term, the Holocaust, which conjures up in all Western languages the murder of approximately six million people and visions of utmost depravity and horror. The reasons for this response seem clear: a prominent religious and cultural group, which survives in significant numbers outside the area of destruction, suffered, through no fault of its own, the horrifying fate of mass extermination.

The second occurrence, the violent expulsion of the Germans of Eastern Europe, has made little impression on those not immediately involved. The words used in connection with it – 'Die Vertreibung' ('the expulsion') and 'Heimatvertriebene' ('those driven from their homeland') – have no understood connotations except in German. Yet even Germans rarely comprehend that these words refer to the forced deportation of an estimated 12–15 million ethnic German civilians to the west, or in far smaller numbers to the Asian Soviet Union, with a disputed death toll that must be well in excess of 1 million.[1] The reasons for this response are probably also clear: for non-Germans, these refugees, belonging to the linguistic and ethnic group that organized the Holocaust, received a suitable punishment, the personal or cultural consequences of which are thus of little interest. Whatever might have happened to them, this argument would run, is minimal compared to what they did, or allowed to be done, to their former non-German neighbors. For West Germans, these former refugees are a nagging reminder of what Germany has lost in terms of geographical space and cultural and political influence in Eastern Europe (and indeed in the world) as a result of the war, and they also would rather not listen to their story.

Taken together, these two historical events of the 1940s constitute not only one of the great tragedies of history, but also the largest forced movement of populations, for which the word 'Völkerwanderung' would be appropriate, a term usually employed to describe tribal movements in early European history. For the Jews who survived, the desperate journey often took them as far as Palestine or the Americas. For the great majority of the East European Germans, the chaotic trek involved moving west until the Polish, Czech, or Hungarian border had been left behind.

In literature, the catastrophic end of these two worlds has provided the backdrop against which grand epics have been placed. The tragedy of the Holocaust has provided source material for major works in many languages. It now has become such familiar territory that a debate has ensued regarding the appropriateness of using such a 'private' cultural calamity in a 'public' fictional sense, particularly if the author does not belong to the victimized culture.[2] In addition, since the 1970s, a convincing selection of critical works has appeared, mainly in English, which has become (along with Hebrew) the major language of the survivors. These works are dedicated to an analysis of the content of what has become known as 'Holocaust Literature,' and attempt to set up the generic boundaries for writings dealing with the historical events. The Holocaust story has been most difficult to tell in an effective and creative literary way in German, but in recent years such iconoclastic writers as Jakov Lind, Edgar Hilsenrath, Jurek Becker, and Udo Steinke have written powerful and moving works of fiction that do not merely rely on the narrative strength inherent in the story of a reconstructed horror almost beyond imagination.

Several decades after the event, the expulsion of the Germans has also become a milestone event through which judgment is being passed in fictional form on the catastrophe of twentieth-century German history. Such prominent German writers as Siegfried Lenz, Christa Wolf, and Horst Bienek have used the desperate flight of the Germans at war's end as the epic material for major works. These writings contain an assessment of the reasons why the German populations had such a dramatic and brutal fate forced upon them. Inevitably, the difficult and almost taboo question of a possible injustice inflicted upon the East European German community (or at least on many individuals in it) as a result of forced mass expulsion based exclusively on ethnic and linguistic background is raised in such novels.

These works of fiction, describing the merciless destruction in Eastern Europe of the Jews during the war and of the vengeful expulsion of the Germans after it, offer a powerful and consistent body of literature showing how the ancient German/Jewish symbiosis continued on gruesomely into its violent disintegration. The aims of this study are, first, to place the Yiddish- and German-speaking worlds of what we now call Eastern Europe[3] into a context determined by their historic interdependence; and, second, to use landmark works of fiction by Yiddish- and/or German-speaking authors (with particular focus on those from Yiddish communities who chose to demonstrate their desire to assimilate by writing in German) as guides through the fearful decades of the twentieth century that led to the catastrophic decimation of both linguistic communities in this area.

After sketching the historical spread of the two sister languages into East Central Europe and Russia, I turn to works describing the East European Yiddish world during the period preceding and including the First World War, when that world began to show signs of a relatively gradual deterioration. The reader should not expect here an extensive analysis of Yiddish literature: the emphasis shifts from writers describing the world of East European Jewry in Yiddish to authors from that same world writing in German to demonstrate their mastery of the related Western cultural language. In the Yiddish shtetl, the decline begins relatively gently. The seductiveness of neighboring 'modern' cultures (particularly by means of the easily available linguistic assimilation into German) begins to tear at the isolated Jewish society. It leads to the breakup of families that had provided the foundation of Jewish society for centuries. The violence of the First World War and the Russian Revolution then provide a foretaste of the final scenes of this centuries-long drama. The orchestrated horror that ended the world of the East European Jews in its entirety begins to gather momentum in the political and social chaos of the between-the-wars period.

In the case of the Germans of Eastern Europe, this study will be dealing with an area that has become terra incognita. The outside world has forgotten, for the most part, the fact that many millions of Germans lived east of the current German-language states before the Second World War. For the more than 1 million German subjects of the Russian czar, the Bolshevik Revolution was the violent beginning of a bloody process that would see them removed entirely from the European Soviet Union within twenty-five years. By looking at works from the periphery of German colonial expansion – the eastern Baltic in the north and eastern Ukraine in the south – I will trace the first events in the developments that would culminate in the expulsion of almost all East European Germans at the conclusion of the Second

World War. As a guide to these final events in the history of the eastern drive of the Germans, I have chosen novels that tell the story of both the expulsion and the events preceding it. These works make more understandable the reasons why once multicultural East Central Europe has been turned into a series of largely monocultural, monolingual states.

Any attempt to approach such monumental historical events through a small selection of subjectively chosen works is, of course, open to attack because, of necessity, it does not include many other important works relevant to the topic. My defense is simply that I am attempting to put under the covers of one reasonably sized book an immense story, and I have chosen the guidebooks to that story as best I can. In particular, it may seem regrettable that so many important creative works dealing with the story of the Holocaust are not here, not the great poetry of Paul Celan, nor indeed any of the extraordinary lyrics enclosed in what is, to my mind, one of the most powerful and moving books published in German since the war, Heinz Seydel (ed.), *Welch Wort in die Kälte gerufen* (What Words Called into the Cold, 1968), an anthology of the poetic responses in the German language to the Nazi persecution of the Jews. The reason is simply that the inclusion of lyrics would have greatly interfered with the epic voice I have tried to maintain in my narration. I also reluctantly concluded that I could not include works from languages other than Yiddish and German, even when they dealt with relevant historical material on a high literary level, without straying from my original intention. Thus, there is no discussion of novels by such important writers as Primo Levi, André Schwarz-Bart, or even the native German-speaker from Czernowitz, Aharon Appelfeld, because the inclusion of Italian, French, or Hebrew works would have made the sketching process uncontrollable. There is a substantial amount of recent literary criticism dealing with the literature of the Holocaust in many languages and from many perspectives; readers are urged to turn to such works if they wish to follow the story beyond the perimeters of German and Yiddish.

I feel that the authors whose works I have chosen form a powerful cross-section of those who have experienced and described the end of these two worlds of the Jews and the Germans of Eastern Europe.

They include the well known and the unknown, fundamentalist Christians and orthodox Jews, skeptics and atheists, natives of all parts of that Europe from which German and Yiddish have been eliminated. These writers with West German, East German, Austrian, Polish, Russian, Ukrainian, Israeli, Canadian, and U.S. passports – Sholom Aleichem, Karl Emil Franzos, Alexander Granach, Joseph Roth, Siegfried von Vegesack, Dietrich Neufeld, Jurek Becker, Edgar Hilsenrath, Isaac Bashevis Singer, Udo Steinke, Johannes Bobrowski, Siegfried Lenz, Horst Bienek, Christa Wolf – have told the tale of this monumental tragedy with the sustained narrative power that it demands.

The intention of this work, therefore, is to present the haunting shadow journeys of two kindred languages by using epic works of literature. These languages rose and fell together in Eastern Europe; their speakers were eliminated almost simultaneously from a vast area they had coinhabited for centuries. This study does not attempt to provide a cultural history of either the Yiddish or German speakers of Eastern Europe; rather it traces the parallel routes of the two cultures as revealed in key works of their literature. As such, it has unusual goals for a work of scholarly research. It does not aim at the reader who is looking for more detailed examination of either the Yiddish-speaking communities of Galicia or the German-speaking ones on the Volga River. Such examinations would duplicate numerous studies that are readily available. Instead, I attempt to step back from the trees and look at the forest: to see the interrelationship between these two linguistically related cultures that shared the same general area for more than half a millennium and were terminated together in a macabre historical dance of death.

Chapter One
German and Yiddish
A Case of Awkward
Family Relations

The statistics of population sizes of minority linguistic, ethnic, and religious groups in Eastern Europe before the establishment of its current national and demographic makeup are somewhat vague and are very much likely to remain so. Political boundaries changed and census figures concerning ethnic background and mother language were in any case unreliable. For example, minority groups interpreted their ancestry flexibly to avoid trouble, and Yiddish was often not included as a language choice. Finally, the complete chaos of the first half of the 1940s for the Yiddish-speaking population and of the second half for the German-speaking population makes it impossible to determine today exactly how many native speakers of the sister Germanic languages – German and Yiddish – lived in the areas east of the current German-speaking states before Hitler's invasion of Poland in September 1939. However, it is possible to estimate roughly that there must have been somewhere near 25 million native German and/or Yiddish speakers in a vast geographical space in which both languages exist today only in scattered isolation.

The estimated 7.5 million Yiddish speakers of Europe in 1921 have been reduced now to perhaps 700,000 mostly aging speakers, very few of whom live in the former heartland of Poland. A language that at the end of the First World War had more speakers in Europe than did Portuguese, Czech, or Greek now has fewer speakers than does Estonian, Basque, or Bakirisch. No other major European language has had any loss approaching the 90 percent drop in numbers of speakers since the First World War that Yiddish shows.[1] The 'final solution' of the Nazis, as it turned out, involved the proposed extermination of all European Jews, but in practice it was the Yiddish-speaking East European Jews who bore the brunt of the slaughter in the few years in which Nazi troops controlled Eastern Europe. The ultimate result was that, as a consequence of this organized extermination and to a much lesser extent through emigration, 6 to 7 million Yiddish speakers were eliminated from the population of Eastern Europe between 1940 and 1945. In a potentially viable sense, all that is left of this population is a declining group in the Soviet Union of perhaps 400,000 people.

The situation with regard to numbers of native German speakers in this same area is somewhat more complicated because of the number of national states involved and the position of the various German minorities within them. But approximately 10 million German speakers (so-called Reichsdeutsche, national Germans) lived in the eastern parts of the German Empire which were given to Poland and the Soviet Union at the end of the Second World War. Another 8–10 million (so-called Volksdeutsche, ethnic Germans) were inhabitants of the East Central European states and the Soviet Union – with populations in the millions in Czechoslovakia, Poland, and the Soviet Union.

Unlike Yiddish, the German language was not devastated by the catastrophe of the Second World War; the numbers of native German speakers actually increased by 14 percent (from 80.5 to 92 million) in the same period when Yiddish speakers declined by 90 percent, but that population has been shifted dramatically to the west (Haarmann, 1975, 17). As a result of the forced population movements at the end of the war, the number of German speakers fell precipitously throughout Europe east of the German-language states, where Yiddish had been virtually eliminated during the war (Haarmann, p. 22). What was left were small, aging, isolated German-speaking populations with few or no language rights in Czechoslovakia, Yugoslavia,

Hungary, and Poland, most of whom would eventually try to emigrate, and the only potentially viable East European cultural entity in Romania. The Romanian-German population, however, had been drastically reduced to little more than 200,000 people by the time of the revolution of December 1989, as the ethnic Germans left Europe's most repressive land as fast as West Germany was allowed to pay for their exit visas. All indications are that the open borders of the 1990s and the liberal immigration policy of West Germany will result in the emigration of almost all ethnic Germans left in Eastern Europe.[2] West German official statistics from 1959 suggest that of a rough total of 18–20 million Germans from areas east of the contemporary German-language states, 8 million had fled to West Germany, 4 million had gone to East Germany and half a million to Austria and other countries, 4.5 million were missing, and 2 million had remained in their homelands.[3] It now can be estimated that by the mid 1990s more than 16 million Germans will have left Eastern Europe, with 12–14 million of them eventually settling in West Germany.

For the purposes of this study, the estimated numbers will suffice; the linguistic and demographic map of Europe changed dramatically within a few years and the long-range effects on Germany's position as a world power have been radical. The result has been three relatively small rump states of the former German and Austrian empires (plus a stable German population in Switzerland). Perhaps even more important in a cultural context, there has been a greatly reduced sphere of influence for the German language. Germany, a military power capable of threatening all of Europe only fifty years ago, may not have been as dramatically reduced in political, economic, and military strength after the Second World War as was Austria after the First World War. But West Germany, the largest exporting nation in the world in 1988, is surely having some trouble accepting the idea that it is merely a middle-sized power permanently set within narrow geographical confines, and that its language is of lesser importance in an international sense than those of its main European rivals of former times, England and France, both of which have far fewer native speakers in Europe. The imminent union of the two Germanies in the 1990s only adds to this feeling of unease. The Yiddish language is almost entirely gone and can only be found today in certain major cities of the Americas and Israel, as well as indigenously in the Soviet Union. But it is threatened with extinction everywhere and is hardly extant in East Central Europe where it once flourished alongside German, which now also seems likely to disappear as a significant minority language in all that area by the early part of the next century.

The ultimate result, therefore, of Hitler's attempt to gain territory for Germany in Slavic Europe has been the creation of the exact opposite: an Eastern Europe with little German cultural input and with an insignificant native Germanic linguistic presence, except for an isolated and evaporating population in parts of Romania, which is best discussed culturally as the final remnants of the Austrian Empire. Thus, a combination of the near realization of one major Nazi objective – the elimination of the East European Jews – and the total failure of a second – the creation of German 'Lebensraum' ('room to live') in Eastern Europe – ultimately culminated in the most drastic setback in the history of the German nation and the most devastating loss of geographical space in the history of the Germanic languages.

In order to understand what was lost, we must now discuss what was there, how it got there, and what the relationship was between the German and Yiddish populations of Central and Eastern Europe. Critical works dealing with the literature of the Holocaust in the English language (in particular from North American critics) have been relatively numerous, qualitatively excellent, and perceptive in the last decade, but they have tended to treat the literature in isolation. In the beginning were the Nazis, in the end was the problem of silence: Theodore Adorno's provocative suggestion that there could be no poetry after Auschwitz plays a central role as a focus for discussion. The object for these critics thus becomes the attempt to grapple with the fictional works that ignore Adorno and describe in words the indescribable events of the Holocaust. Lawrence Langer begins with Adorno (in *The Holocaust and the Literary Imagination*, 1975) and Auschwitz (in *Visions of Survival*, 1982); Alvin Rosenfeld (in *A Double Dying*, 1980), with Adorno and George Steiner, who also originally suggested that the proper response was silence; Sidra Edrahi (in *By Words Alone*, 1980), with the founding of the killing centers; Edward Alexander (in *The Resonance of Dust*, 1979), with Lionel Trilling; and Hamida Bosmajian (in *Metaphors of Evil*, 1979), with the 'prophetic' stories of Franz Kafka. Only *Against the Apoca-lypse* (1984), David Roskies's exhaustive study of the Jewish response to disaster, covers the long historical developments that led to the ultimate catastrophe of the twentieth century, but Roskies's study does not extend beyond Jewish writings in many languages. It is significant that none of these critical works on Holocaust literature attempts to trace the historical and literary threads that have run in broadly parallel and often intertwining lines for more than half a millennium between the sister language cultures before exploding in the period with which these critical works are concerned. Their atten-tion is focused clearly on the extremely complex and difficult problem of the fictional description of the catastrophe that engulfed the Euro-pean Jews and on attempts to find a proper narrative voice in which to speak about the unspeakable evil of the Nazi period.

Critical works dealing with Yiddish literature also tend to function in isolation and to move with the emigrations of the twentieth century from Eastern Europe to North America and, most frequently, to New York. Thus, the fascinating search by Ruth Wisse for the heroic qualities of the Jewish fool (*The Schlemiel as Modern Hero*, 1971) begins briefly with the oral traditions of the Yiddish East European Jews; it stops in the world of Mendele Mocher Sforim and Sholom Aleichem and continues on to the new world of Isaac Bashevis Singer and his English-writing heirs, Mordecai Richler, Saul Bellow, Bernard Malamud, and Philip Roth. Along the way there is only one brief glance at that extraordinary figure, who seems to straddle all worlds, depending on your peephole: Franz Kafka. He made one of his few public appearances to deliver a speech in praise of Yiddish, but he couldn't speak it himself and wrote solely in German. There is no mention of such figures as Karl Emil Franzos, Joseph Roth, Alexander Granach, Jurek Becker, or Edgar Hilsenrath, who could have added so much to the richness of the topic of heroic fools, but whose works were written in German. Similarly Sol Gittleman's *From Shtetl to Suburbia* (1978) concentrates totally on the depiction of the family in the Yiddish literature of the old world (Sholom Aleichem in particu-lar) and its transformation in the heirs of the new world (Bellow, Roth, Malamud and, of course, the world-straddler I.B. Singer). Once again one can regret in particular the exclusion of a major novelist like Joseph Roth, who structured some of his major novels around the breakdowns of Yiddish-speaking families, but who wrote in German.

One of the aims of this study is to trace the complex relationship of these two often mutually comprehensible languages and to show how the often intertwining fates of their speakers are reflected in their literatures. The horrors of the Second World War with regard to the meetings between German and Yiddish speakers have removed recollections of the sometimes pleasant meetings between the German-speaking soldiers of the First World War and the Yiddish-speaking populations of the areas of conflict.

In her memoirs, Ida Kaminska, the grand old lady of the Yiddish theater in Poland and later in America, recalls the boon for the Yiddish theater of Warsaw when the occupying German troops arrived:

> My father, meanwhile, was very busy, hurriedly organizing performances in Yiddish in his theater. There was a feeling in town that one could become rich from the Yiddish theater. The reasoning was that since the Germans had money and liked theater but did not understand Polish, they would go to the Yiddish theater. Hence several Yiddish theaters opened in Warsaw. Everyone rushed about grabbing Yiddish actors and trying to open up his theater the sooner ... On posters all over town the title was printed in Yiddish and German, because the Germans – as expected – frequently attended the Yiddish theater ... Yes, these were Germans of the First World War. My popularity, with both the Jews and the Germans, grew from day to day. Jews greeted me, and German soldiers saluted as they met me.[4]

The German and Austrian soldiers, for their part, were apparently often pleasantly surprised that there was a native population in the areas of Slavic conflict with whom they could converse.[5] What these armies had met was a population in the millions still speaking a Germanic language that had not changed so drastically from that of their ancestors who had emigrated eastward from Germany more than 500 years before. This linguistic group would be systematically annihilated one generation later by the second meeting with German-speaking soldiers from the west.

The history of the Jewish presence in Germany reaches back into the period of Roman settlement. However, the fate of these first Roman camp followers becomes obscure in the Dark Ages that followed. It is only during the tenth century that the documentation of Jewish settlers on the Danube, the Mosel, and, in particular, the Rhine becomes certain. The historical events, which resulted in the introduction of a German language into Slavic Europe, where it would flourish for a period of more than half a millennium, reach back into the Middle Ages in Germany. For the development of the Yiddish language in the centuries that followed it is significant that the Rhineland and, through subsequent migrations, middle and eastern Germany (but not the north) provided the German dialect spoken by the Jewish inhabitants; at the time it did not differ greatly from the dialect spoken by Germans of the same areas. Historically, the wandering Jews had traditionally adopted the languages of each new host culture in the Diaspora, whether Arabic, French, or Spanish; they used it for everyday life while employing the original Semitic language, Hebrew, for sacred matters. Thus, the development in Germany of a bilingual society in which business was run in the common language of the neighbors and religion in the private language of the initiates was completely within the historical pattern.

For our purposes, it is significant that the special relationship between Yiddish and German gives the Yiddish language, on the one hand, its strange familiarity to German speakers, and, on the other, its total incomprehensibility to German readers. For in Germany, too, the Jewish settlers maintained their centuries-old tradition of employing the twenty-two basic letters of the Hebrew alphabet in the written form of the adopted immigrant language. This Hebrew-script German began its existence at about the same time that German was developing into a major independent literary language in the twelfth and thirteenth centuries and offered a totally different and for Germans totally foreign written version of the cultural developments of their language. Written from right to left and employing a script that remained completely undecipherable even to the scholars of the classical European languages, stories written in 'Judendeutsch' ('Jewish-German'), as it was originally and occasionally still is called, served as a source of both entertainment and religious information for Jewish women, who did not have access to sacred Hebrew texts.

There are certain significant conclusions to be drawn from the documentation available from the beginnings of the Yiddish language. A comparison with Icelandic, the European language that has a documented period of existence similar to that for Yiddish and also shares a close relationship with a mother language (in its case Norwegian), may underline the peculiarities of the history of Yiddish. In both cases, the mother languages, Norwegian and German, changed greatly over the centuries, while Icelandic and Yiddish remained relatively stable. A present-day Norwegian probably has more trouble understanding an Icelander, who is speaking a language only moderately different from that of the Norwegian's ancestors a thousand years ago, than a German does understanding Yiddish, which has changed from the medieval German of about six hundred years ago largely through the addition of Hebrew and Slavic vocabulary to make up about 25 percent of the words. In written form, however, Icelandic is accessible to the modern Scandinavian, although it demands some grammatical study, while Yiddish remains completely unreadable to any German who has not learned Hebrew script.

A comparison with Icelandic is also illuminating with regard to the literature, for it is in the Icelandic language that many of the major works of medieval Germanic literature were written down. Thus, in any study of medieval European literatures, the Icelandic manuscripts play a crucial role, offering the most important works of poetic theory (Poetic Edda), the source books of Germanic myths (Elder Edda), the most thorough historic documentation of any culture of the period (Landnamnsbok), and the first great flowering of fictional prose writing (the family sagas). For the Icelanders, their private language was (and still is) the carrying cultural force of history, myth, poetry, storytelling, and imagination.[6] For the European Jews of the same period and for centuries after, the Yiddish language was nothing of the sort. Until comparatively recent times, there were no Yiddish works of poetic theory or of original poetry, of history or myth, and works of entertainment, while written in Yiddish, were borrowed from the neighboring culture. Yiddish was the language of everyday unimportant matters and of business; all important matters were dealt with in Hebrew, for all important matters came from liturgical texts. Yiddish was to be taken seriously only insofar as it served as a teacher of the serious script.

The texts used to practice this Hebrew script were often the same texts that were providing the basis for the flowering of German literature. Thus, some of the first written works that have been found in the Yiddish language are versions of medieval German classics, including the Gudrun saga, the Nibelungenlied, and even Minnesang. At the same time there are no works of original literature in Yiddish and would not be for centuries. By the late thirteenth century, even after the ghettoization of the German Jews as a result of the anti-Semitic edicts of the Lateran Council of 1215, such popular Germanic heroes as Arthur and Dietrich were well established as the entertainment figures of Yiddish writing as well.

This ghettoization of the Jewish populations had at least two important effects on the development of the Yiddish language and literature. The separation of the Jewish community from the neighboring German one, despite its menacing foreshadowing of the events of 700 years later, allowed the language and the culture of the ghettos to develop in relative isolation for 500 years, until the sudden abandonment of the Yiddish language by the German Jews with their linguistic assimilation into German beginning in the late eighteenth century. But the increasingly unpleasant position of the ghettoized Jews of Germany led the majority of them to leave, to move east into the then welcoming lands of the Polish aristocracy, who sought a trading class to serve as intermediaries between themselves and the general population. The immigrating Jews brought with them business experience with the dominant German neighbor and an easy access to the German language as well. Thus, paradoxically, the anti-Semitic developments in Germany, which in later centuries were to find more virulent form in the Slavic lands, led to the solidification and enrichment of the language of those confined to the ghetto, and to the solid establishment of a Germanic language in vast areas of Eastern Europe.

If the Yiddish language had followed the route of previous Jewish secular languages and been replaced by the everyday languages of the new homelands, it would be only a curiosity today and would play no role in the discussion of modern European literatures. But this time the wandering Jews maintained the original language in the new exile, and Yiddish, instead of shrinking away into the declining ghettos of Jewish Germany, expanded its territory throughout Eastern Europe, making it for several centuries the most widespread European language. Within two centuries the center of Yiddish activities had moved to Eastern Europe, but the language had in the same process become the lingua franca of the great majority of the Jews of Europe.

In the half-millennium after the Lateran Council of 1215, Yiddish led a double existence, growing rapidly in Eastern Europe as the majority of the Jewish population became established there, but remaining the everyday language of the Western Jews as well. Dialect differences between Eastern and Western Yiddish became more and more evident in the spoken language as Eastern Yiddish picked up vocabulary and expressions from the neighboring Slavic languages. Within Eastern Yiddish as well, completely different neighboring languages had varying impacts on the local Yiddish. But the written language remained unified for readers throughout Europe. The literature written during this period basically maintains its original aims of providing entertainment as well as basic liturgical information for the women. Thus two of the most popular works of Yiddish literature from this period are fantastic chivalric tales of Elijah Levita (1469–1549) from the early sixteenth century, Yiddish adaptations of Renaissance romances, and an introduction to Jewish learning, written in the late sixteenth century by Jacob Azhkenazi (1550–1628). This last consists of translations of appropriate parts of the sacred scripts with explanations and moral commentary, and provides a basic primer for those not involved with the serious study of these texts.[7] Such works, and many others which were written for similar reasons, provide the rule for the Yiddish literature of these centuries.

The first significant Yiddish work describing the world in which the author lived and its everyday problems was written in the early eighteenth century by a Western Yiddish woman, Glückel of Hameln (1646–1724). Glückel's biographical reminiscences, undertaken, she declares, to help her deal with the death of her first husband, offer a unique window on the world of the German Yiddish-speaking Jews. The work is unique because the Jewish world is not discussed in any serious sense in the German writing of the time and because the role of educated Jews did not involve writing down in Yiddish the problems of everyday life.[8] Hebrew, in contrast, had long since petrified into a language that could only be used to deal with liturgical material.

It did not even have the vocabulary to describe the comings and goings of businessmen and relatives, of sickness and death, of birth and childhood, all of which was the material of Glückel's story (along with a substantial amount of anecdotal and religious moralizing).

In hindsight, with our knowledge of the subject matter of 'modern' Jewish writing in Yiddish, German, and English, the most striking aspect of Glückel's story may well be the depiction of family life in general, and the rather stormy relationship between husband and wife with regard to business on the one hand and the quality of relatives on the other. In Glückel's Hamburg, and later Metz, we find the clearly identifiable ancestors of figures such as Singer's *Magician of Lublin* (1960), and his world of itinerant travelers, more or less successful businessmen (whose money is never secure), home-dominating wives, and often rather suspect relatives. What one does not find there, is a topic that is often near the center of Singer's universe: evidence of the breakdown of the Jewish world through loss of belief or through the seduction of assimilation. For Glückel of Hameln, in the late seventeenth and early eighteenth century, the world is full of danger and deceit, as well as happiness and security, but it is also absolutely full of the certainty of the Jewish way of life in every event that we witness. Despite the insecurity of the vaguely threatened communal outsider that is often felt in these memoirs, there is an even more powerful sense of serenity based on religious certainty throughout. For Glückel the question of whether it would not be wiser to disappear into the safer neighboring German community is never even raised on the furthest horizon.

By employing Yiddish to describe this certainty, Glückel sets a historical landmark that can be marked against the German-Jewish literature of less than a century later, when Yiddish and, in some ways the traditional Jewish way of life itself, had begun the fast process of disintegration in Germany. Ironically this unique glimpse into the everyday world of the Yiddish speakers of the post-Renaissance world comes from the West, from the branch of the Yiddish language that would not survive the ideas of the Enlightenment. In the East there is no such document from the same period; there is no such look into a world that would survive, probably with minimal change, into a period when Yiddish literature would quite suddenly begin an existence as an independent carrier of the stories of a culture, and, without great change, carry on into the time when it would be able to tell the tale of its own destruction.

For the Jews of Western Europe the history of their language begins to come to an end with the ideas of the Enlightenment in the second half of the eighteenth century. The gradual granting of civil rights to the Jews of France and Germany, accelerating during the Napoleonic years, brought apparent historical affirmation of the ideas of tolerance propagated in such German Enlightenment works as Lessing's *Nathan der Weise* (1779). This most famous dramatic plea for religious tolerance and freedom does not take place among the Germans and the Jews of eighteenth-century Germany but in the exotic world of the Crusaders in the Near East. Nevertheless, its message of tolerance is easily understandable within the context of the contemporary situation. In Nathan's climactic narration of the parable of the ring, in which Christianity, Judaism, and Mohammedanism are found to be equally true, a signal was given that suggested that the less-than-equal status of the Jews might be reconsidered by the Christian majority. It was a sign of hope for a German-Jewish society, which, for the first time, felt the possibility that it could become accepted as a normal part of the social fabric. One of the first major steps this society could undertake on its own to facilitate the process of equalization was to jettison the language that set it apart from the majority culture surrounding it and identified its members as outsiders.

Only fifty years after the death of Glückel of Hameln, the language in which she set down her biographical reminiscences was well on its way to extinction in the West. Yiddish was, according to the leading proponent of Jewish assimilation, Lessing's friend Moses Mendelssohn (1729–86), 'the jargon that has made no small contribution to the immorality of the common man, and [I] am quite convinced that the recently increasing use of the pure dialect [High German] among my brethren will have a very good effect.'[9] The history of the Jews in Germany over the next century and a half involves a complex and subtle struggle among assimilationists, intent on becoming part of German culture, if need be at the expense of their religious traditions; political activists, most prominently represented by Karl Marx; Zionists, seeking a return to the Holy Land; and a small percentage of orthodox Jews, attempting to carry on in the old way despite the encroachments of a new world. But by the mid-nineteenth century one aspect of their lives united them all. They all spoke German; Western Yiddish had ceased to exist. In many ways the history of the Jews in nineteenth- and early-twentieth-century Germany is best seen within the context of this successful attempt to abandon the language of the outsiders and become completely at home in the language of the majority insiders.

Figures as different as Rahel Varnhagen (1771–1833), Heinrich Heine (1797–1856), Karl Marx (1818–83), Albert Einstein (1879–1955), and Hannah Arendt (1906–75) all spoke a language that was indistinguishable from that of their German neighbors. Yiddish was gone forever from the German Empire, France, Bohemia, and western Austria. In a matter of two generations, a language that had existed for more than 500 years was abandoned on its home soil. At this point the histories of the West European and East European Jews separate dramatically. One of the tragedies of the history of the German Jews was the (in hindsight) extraordinary naïveté of so many of them during the 1920s and 1930s in assuming that the Nazis made a distinction between West European and East European Jews. In anti-Semitic tirades the Nazis must have been talking about someone else, they thought, not about the German-speaking Jews who had apparently settled into such a 'normal' role in German society, but rather about the 'Ostjuden,' the ragamuffins from the east, who still spoke the jargon, Yiddish, and who often represented family members whom the German Jews wished would not come for dinner.

In various novels, Aharon Appelfeld has portrayed this position: 'It's not flattering because it was an assimilated society. The assimilated Jews were denying themselves. They were denying their identity. They were trying to escape from themselves. That is psychologically a dangerous process and culturally an ugly process ... For the Austrian Jews, the Ostjuden – the East European Jews – were a symbol of a primitive, ugly, non-cultured, superstitious, anachronistic society.'[10] The Yiddish-speaking Orthodox Jews' way of life was so alien to the dominating assimilated liberal Jews in those border outposts, such as Königsberg, where they coexisted that there was, according to the

Königsberg-born journalist Immanuel Birnbaum, 'practically no spiritual connection between the educated Jews, brought up on the German classics and philosophers, and the Yiddish-speaking sect.'[11] Thus in the border areas between Eastern and Western Europe we find two solitudes within the Jewish community itself.

For the East European Jews few of the developments associated with the West had occurred. The reason was relatively simple: the ideas of the Enlightenment, in particular the concept of religious tolerance, did not find fertile ground in Eastern Europe, where the often desperate struggle for an independent political identity usually magnetized (and still does) around a national grouping that was determined by a common language and religion. By the early twentieth century some assimilation of the Jews into Polish and Russian life and language had occurred in the large urban areas; and in such eastern Austrian outposts as Bukovyna, German-language assimilation was taking place; but the great majority of East European Jews spoke Yiddish. The original Yiddish-speaking emigrants from Germany had found a landscape that was, in comparison to the West at that time, relatively tolerant of their religion, and welcoming to their professional talents. In the thirteenth century, it was possible for the incoming Jews to form self-governing communities and even to establish colonies, an extraordinary sign of freedom at a time when the German Jews were in ghettos and the English and Spanish Jews were either about to be or had already been deported. Originally an example of the tolerance of the Slavic aristocracy, this would eventually lead to the misery of the shtetl and the urban ghetto, where so many of the victims of the Holocaust made their homes, and where most East European Jews, for almost 400 years, lived in a combination of religious devotion and political persecution. One aspect of this life had, however, remained constant for the entire period of the Jewish diaspora in Eastern Europe: the domination of the Yiddish language.

In the shtetls and ghettos of Hungary, Romania, Slovakia, Poland, Russia, Ukraine, and Lithuania, and even in Vilna, where the Western Enlightenment had made its strongest inroads, Yiddish was the dominant language. All business between Jews was run in it, and it was the daily language of the home; Jews traveling over the thousands of kilometers from northern Russia to the southeastern Austrian Empire could be certain they would find a common language with other Jews, even though the Slavic language of their home district, which they would probably speak, would be virtually useless on the route. Even emigrating Jews, who would number in the millions by the early twentieth century, would bring their language with them and new-world cities like New York, Montreal, or Buenos Aires would by 1935 boast a combined Yiddish-speaking population of nearly 3 million, almost half the population numbers in Eastern Europe. Thus Yiddish would remain, at least for a generation or two, a transatlantic business language. In Eastern Europe, Yiddish created a Germanic-language base, which was complemented by the more erratic settlements of the German colonialists in much the same geographical space.

Otto Best, in his 1973 German introduction to Yiddish, identifies the following areas as those where Yiddish was mother language of the majority of the Jewish population until the Second World War: 'Poland, in the boundaries before 1918 (excluding areas previously belonging to Germany or Austrian Silesia), Slovakia, Austrian Burgenland, northern Hungary and Romania, Estonia, Latvia, Lithuania, White Russia, Ukraine, and Moldavia. In the east it is bordered by a line drawn from Leningrad to Rostow, with Yiddish settlements in the more eastern cities of Moscow, Saratow, Rostow, Tiflis and Baku.'[12] There are several aspects of this linguistic map that are of special interest. First, it is a very large geographical area throughout which the German language also had established a minority linguistic presence. Second, in the areas bordering Germany and Austria on the east, there were pressures on Yiddish from German similar to those that had been experienced by the Yiddish population of Germany in the eighteenth century. There was the definite lure of a very similar language that offered entry into the cultural world of the West, in particular of Vienna and Berlin, and a passport out of the narrowness of Eastern European Jewish life. In effect, the developments of the Western European Enlightenment were beginning to have a serious impact on the East European Jewish world over a century after they had permanently altered the linguistic makeup of West European Jewry. Third, in the course of a decade, from 1938 to 1948, this language spoken by approximately seven million people in Eastern Europe was almost completely eliminated from that entire geographical space. It carries on its existence only among the exiles in the Americas and, to a certain extent, in the Soviet Union. Thus, for the second time in its history, Yiddish suffered a stunning and catastrophic blow to its existence: after the extraordinarily fast extinction of Western Yiddish through the gentle process of voluntary linguistic assimilation came the extraordinarily sudden near-destruction of Eastern Yiddish through the savage process of mass murder of the speakers.

The Yiddish speakers went to Eastern Europe as part of the millennia-old process of wandering in the Diaspora. Once again the Jews had moved on, in search of a better resting place on the road to the ultimate goal of the return to the Holy Land. Once again they would find out that their welcome was temporary and that ultimately the majority neighbors would turn against them, would force them to live in ghettos, and would allow uncontrolled forces to do with these ghettos as they pleased. This time there was no further wandering, however, except the forced wanderings demanded by the local authorities. The effect was to concentrate nearly all the Jews of Russia in the narrow Pale of Settlement and most of the Jews of Poland and Eastern Austria in the innumerable miserable towns of the countryside or in the large cities. This meant that the Jews had not been forcibly expelled from their temporary homelands, as they had been from England in the thirteenth century and from Portugal and Spain in the fifteenth. But it also meant that they were concentrated in settlements that remained substantially intact well into the twentieth century, even after almost half the population had immigrated to the new world in order to escape the poverty and the pogroms that had made their existence so tentative for centuries. This concentrated minority culture – viewed with suspicion by the religious majority, dominated by the prescripts of religious writings set down more than two thousand years before, and using a sacred language unknown to the outsiders and a daily language that came from Germany – was an easy prey when an enemy came with whom no one had really reckoned.

For finally it was not the geographical neighbors who would administer, after centuries of harassment, one final blow to the outsiders, but the linguistic relatives – the Germans – whom they had moved eastward to escape. Centuries later they discovered that an enlightened

Germany was apparently far more tolerant of outsiders than an unenlightened Russia or Poland. But only apparently, for when anti-Semitism moved from the latent to the active form in Germany it would take on proportions that went beyond the worst nightmares of the European Jews. No longer content with making life difficult for the apparently assimilated German Jews, it finally took upon itself the extermination of all European Jews, both within and beyond its borders, whose property the Germans would claim for their own, whose land the Germans would claim for their future, and whose bodies the Germans would claim for their killing centers. That historical event has provided the tragic background for stories of unparalleled historical catastrophe for writers in many languages. It has been hardest to tell in German.

When the Nazi troops swept through Poland, White Russia, Hungary, Romania, and Ukraine on their march deep into the Soviet Union, they were met not only by the stunned almost-German-speaking Jews (who would be rounded up and murdered) but also by for the most part jubilant German-speaking populations who were delighted to have finally been called 'Heim ins Reich' – back into the homeland – or at least to have the homeland and its armies come to them. Their period in the Reich would be measured by a few years, in some areas only by a matter of months, and then they would be driven forever from their settlements by a furiously counterattacking and revengeful enemy. Even those East European Germans who had wished that the Nazis had never left their West European birthplace were to be treated as the enemy and driven from the land. Our story now turns to them, for in a strange way they provide a shadowy counterpart and share a grotesquely similar history to that of the Yiddish speakers. Their reasons for being in Eastern Europe were different, and their expulsion was a direct consequence of the aggressive German invasion, but they, too, are now almost completely gone. Their final chapter has also provided contemporary German literature with a tragic epic sweep, which would only find an appropriate literary form, and then with great difficulty, decades after the events.

For Jewish literature the story of the Holocaust will remain almost a sacred topic. Jewish writers will rework it endlessly, as its tales of destruction seem endless, and ultimately the masterpieces, some of which are already discernible, will be sifted from the reminiscences and the clichés. This process of identification is already well under way, particularly in English, while German critics tend to shy away from literary judgments in this sensitive area. In German literature the story of the East European Germans and their expulsion has proved to be taboo in a very different way. It is a tale that mainstream German historians and critics would rather forget, as it immediately suggests the possibility of potential German victims at the end of a catastrophic German-initiated war. Those victims would be better left talking to themselves – the basic fate of the 'Heimatvertriebenen' ('those driven from their homelands') and their literature – or even better, not talking at all.

Who were these millions of Germans waiting to be called 'Heim ins Reich'? What were they doing in areas the postwar world has come to understand as Slavic spheres of interest in Eastern Europe where German language and culture play no substantial role? The answers to these questions involve the discussion of eastward migrations that are more complex and cover a longer period of time than do those of the Yiddish-speaking population. But in the broad sense there is a remarkable similarity with regard to the spread of the two Germanic languages into Eastern Europe. The movement of the German language from its earliest historically established base between the Rhine and the Elbe eastward into areas that still remain German-speaking – large parts of Austria and current East Germany – goes back to the centuries after the withdrawal of the Romans, the end of the westward surge of the Slavs in the seventh century, and the reign of Charlemagne, and does not as such interest us here.

The spread of German into those areas east of the contemporary German-language states, however, is central to our story. German begins its drive into Eastern Europe at about the same time as Yiddish does, moves into approximately the same territory, eventually finding a home in much the same geographical space, and comes to a historical end at almost exactly the same time. Thus roughly speaking, the two sister Germanic languages travel eastward together (though in isolation from each other), spend approximately 750 years in this newly won linguistic territory, establish populations numbering in the millions in generally the same area, become the mother languages of large minority populations in great parts of Eastern Europe, and virtually cease to exist in these areas within a decade of each other.

In sketching the history of the migration of the Yiddish-speaking Jews, it was hardly necessary to differentiate greatly among the various geographical settlements. From Lithuania in the north to Romania in the south, the basic historical reasons for the presence of Jews speaking a Germanic language were quite similar. It is only south of the Danube in the Sephardic regions of the Balkans and Turkey that one must discuss the different historical background of Ladino, the Spanish-based Jewish language.[13] Such historical similarities, however, do not apply to the Germans of Eastern Europe. The history of the 'Germanization' of the Baltic coast is completely different from that of the German settlements of Silesia, the Sudetenland, or Poland; likewise there are different reasons for the spread of German into Hungary, Romania, or Ukraine. It cannot be the aim of this work to describe in detail the historical background of the various successful and occasionally failed attempts of the Germans to find living space, or in some cases religious breathing space (much like the Jews), in Eastern Europe. This background often involves well-documented stories of settlements of homogenous groups from specific western locales. Books have been written on virtually every reasonably sized German colony of Eastern Europe, and the historical work is still under way in the West, as those expelled attempt to set down for posterity the history of their roots, which even they are beginning to suspect may have been sawed off forever. However, it must be an aim of this work to offer a rough sketch of the differing histories of some of the German settlements in certain areas – the Baltic states, Silesia, East Prussia, Ukraine, Romania – because ultimately the imaginative works describing the catastrophic end of these worlds (which in the case of Romania is taking place at the moment) will, as a matter of course, reflect the varying reasons for the presence of the Germans, and imply reasons for their expulsion.

As we have seen, the thirteenth and fourteenth centuries were pivotal in the history of the expansion of the Yiddish language. The anti-Semitic decrees of the Lateran Council of 1215 convinced most German Jews that it was the right moment to continue their wanderings, this time into the Polish lands east of the Oder River. It was also a period of German-language expansion to the east. What the Jewish and German settlers found there were lands that since the tenth century had been governed by the Poles, whose westward migration had come to a stop at the borders of German concentration. The somewhat forced official Christianization of Poland, with the conversion of Miezko I in 966 under pressure from German eastward expansion, contained the seeds of two developments that occupy Poland to the present day. First, it established the central position of the Roman Catholic Church in Poland, which led to both a spiritual connection with Western Europe and a source of conflict in post-war 'East Bloc' Warsaw. (Much the same can be said of Prague and Budapest: capital cities that were traditionally part of middle Europe were expected to play an 'Eastern' role that is alien to their history and their culture.) Second, it suggests a German-Polish antagonism almost from the moment when language first began to record the history of Poland.

It is neither historically accurate nor fair to force a power struggle between an offensive eastward-looking Germany and a defensive Poland to the center of Polish-German relations from the beginnings through to the present day. Nevertheless, such an oversimplified explanation of the dynamics between the two largest neighboring groups of Germans and Slavs does highlight a situation of conflict that characterized, to some extent, their relations for centuries. This conflict found its ultimate release in the Second World War and its aftermath. The dynamics of this struggle also provides a convenient historical pattern that would generally be relevant to the histories of Germany and its eastern neighbors from the Baltic to the Balkans. Germany's linguistic (and political) western boundaries were basically set many centuries ago, but everywhere in the East there was a migration of German settlers into the neighboring states, in many cases far into the heartland of non-German peoples. On German frontiers in the west there was no such movement, and linguistic struggles there have been limited to such immediately contiguous areas as the Saar, Schleswig-Holstein, or Alsace. Nor was there any significant westward movement of the Slavic languages. The many Polish, Czech, or Russian exiles, who at the turn of the century made German cities like Munich or Berlin into centers of Russian art or who make present-day Vienna an important outpost of Czech literature, have no permanent linguistic influence in the German-speaking territories. The exiles remain exiles; their language dies with them in the West.

But the pressure from the German populations moving east was constant from the tenth century on, reaching a temporary high point during the twelfth, thirteenth, and fourteenth centuries, before ebbing for several hundred years and flowing again in the eighteenth century and, of course, finding its most aggressive form in the twentieth. During this millennium there are certainly long periods of stagnation, when, for reasons of politics, economics, or natural catastrophe, little or no eastward German expansion occurs. During this period there is also very little retreat of the German language from areas once established, and assimilation of Germans into the home language of Slavic neighbors is less than might be expected. In effect, the pattern is very similar to that of Yiddish expansion. The German language is maintained, even at the price of isolation and estrangement from neighbors, the main reason surely being the attempt to hold on to a familiar culture in an unfamiliar territory. In a few areas, such as East Prussia, the German language would become completely dominant, but in most of Eastern Europe, German would become established as a minority language, much like Yiddish.

In the twelfth and thirteenth centuries, from the Baltic to Hungary, there was an eastern migration of German peasants, leading to the settlement by German immigrants of significant parts of what is now Poland, Moravia, Bohemia, Slovakia, western Hungary, and even Transylvania in Romania. Each of these areas of settlement would come to play a crucial role during the Nazi march into Eastern Europe. Beginning with the Czechoslovak Sudetenland, and continuing on into Poland with the start of the Second World War, the settlements founded more than half a millennium before were called 'Heim ins Reich.' It should be emphasized that this expansion had not been of a political colonial nature when it took place, and that German political control did not necessarily move eastward with the German migrations. Thus, many of these Germans were in reality being called back into an empire to which neither they nor their ancestors had ever belonged. But the groundwork for a German cultural and linguistic presence in Eastern Europe was securely established by the migrations of Germans to newly founded Baltic cities as well as, somewhat later, to other major East Central European urban centers, and also by the establishment of German-speaking rural settlements throughout East Central Europe and eventually in Russia itself.

For the most part the Slavic nobility did not oppose the influx of the German population, whose farming and commercial expertise could play a major role in developing an already established agricultural base, and could help to found new urban centers. Along the Baltic coast, the merchant experience of the Hanseatic League, which was heavily, although not exclusively, German, became the determining factor in the development of urban shipping centers. In general, such migrations proceeded by mutual consent and in an orderly and peaceful fashion. Often the political relationships between Slavs and Germans were determined by intermarriage of the nobility; everywhere, except in the northeast Baltic, there was the common church, and similar economic and agricultural interests. In addition there was the shared need to find workers to develop such resources as the mines of Silesia, which drew in so many German workers that Silesia had abandoned its political relationship with Poland by the mid-fourteenth century and would remain German in a political sense for almost six centuries. German law often followed settlers into Slavic lands, sometimes eventually establishing itself even in areas without a German majority.

The history of Poland in the next several centuries would become extremely complex and be dominated by its attempts, after its union with the Lithuanians in the fourteenth century, to preserve a national unity in the face of growing political powers on all sides. By the late eighteenth century, after the Russians, the Germans, and the Austrians had taken turns picking apart the body of Poland, there was nothing left. But throughout this time, and well into the twentieth century, the population of the original Polish-ruled territories would be characterized by large minorities of Germans and Jews who for hundreds of years maintained their Germanic languages of settlement.

At the same time that this German movement into Poland was taking place in orderly fashion in the early thirteenth century, events were transpiring on the eastern border of Poland that would have profound effects on German-Polish and German-Russian relations to the present day. It is perhaps significant that these events were brought into motion at the request of a Polish duke, Conrad of Masovia, for German help in conquering recalcitrant heathen Prussians along his eastern frontier. The Germans he called upon, the religious Order of Teutonic Knights, were just licking their wounds from a failed attempt to secure secular political power in the German settlement in Transylvania and were only too ready to try again along the Baltic. This Polish request for German aid on its eastern Baltic frontier would bring about a German political presence east of Poland, and its militaristic characteristics would create a lasting negative image of Germans in all of Eastern Europe.

These warrior monks, sworn to celibacy and to the conversion of heathens to Christianity at any cost, belonged to a crusader order, set up in 1198, whose main function was meant to be the winning of the Holy Land for Christianity. In fact, they had also been active there along with other Christian crusaders, but their place in history would be more clearly drawn by the role they played in establishing a German presence along the Baltic and across the Russian frontier. In effect, their actions on behalf of Christianity in Jerusalem belong to the essentially short-lived and ineffective adventurous forays of the crusaders. But their engagement in the Christianization of the eastern Baltic would be so successful that it would dominate the politics and culture of that area into the twentieth century. By the turn of the twelfth century, Europe was formally Christianized virtually everywhere except along the northeast Baltic coast. For the Order of Teutonic Knights, the heathen lands directly to the east of areas where Germans had successfully and peacefully settled among the Poles offered the possibility of religious, territorial, and political triumphs that could never be achieved in the Holy Land. In 1226 the order had received what it needed in order to achieve these triumphs: in the Golden Bull of Rimini, the framework of a political state was established where the Teutonic Knights would have control of all the Baltic lands where they had converted heathens.

With the Vistula as the western bulwark and with massive fortresses built in the five years following the Golden Bull, at Thorn, Kulm, and Marienwerder, these northeast European crusaders began the process of military control, conversion, and governing along the Baltic coast. By 1255 this process had been achieved to the extent that German merchants and traders felt secure enough to work together with the order in the founding of new settlements at the mouths of the major rivers flowing into the Baltic: Braunsberg (approximately 1250), Memel (1253), Königsberg (1255). The formal conversion and conquering of all the lands and peoples between the Vistula and Memel would take a few more decades, but with the founding of Königsberg, the eventual capital city, and Memel, one of the first places to be annexed (from Lithuania) by the Third Reich, the heart and the eastern boundary of the future state of East Prussia had been firmly placed in German hands.

In the wake of the Teutonic Order's conversion of heathen Prussia into a German-run state east of Poland, and with the founding of the Baltic seaports, came the German peasant population, first to settle around the fortresses and outposts and later to populate the new ports and surrounding countryside. With these events, the seeds of German-Slavic rivalry for land and power, which would flourish to the present day, were being sown. But for the immediate future, Prussia would enjoy a relatively peaceful period of development. In the thirteenth century, the lands were settled more and more heavily from the German west or, increasingly, from German Silesia. The native Prussians and their non-German language were pushed into the backcountry and into a completely secondary role. This section of the Baltic coast had thus become Germanized to such an extent that, in large sections of the formerly completely non-German areas east of the Vistula, German would be the overwhelmingly dominant language until 1945. The movement of the Germans to the northeast under the banner of the Teutonic Order did not, however, stop at Königsberg or even at the Memel. To the northeast of the Memel were Kurland (Courland) and Livland (Livonia); in these lands the Teutonic Order undertook a second crusading mission even before it had finished converting Prussia.

While the Teutonic Order never successfully subjugated neighboring Lithuania, despite repeated attempts throughout the thirteenth and fourteenth centuries, it succeeded in setting up a German-run state northeast of there that reached near Lake Peipus to the Russian frontier, which would be breached by Germans only in the twentieth century. Thus, we have, in the course of the thirteenth and fourteenth centuries, developments in Livland and Kurland that are to some extent (but only in a limited sense) parallel to those in Prussia. German coastal merchants, under the protection of the administrative military order of the Teutonic Order, helped found the cities of Riga (together with Hanseatic Scandinavians), Dorpat (Estonian Tartu), and Reval (Estonian Tallinn); they established a ruling German presence that would make German the dominant administrative language of Riga, the capital city of Latvia, until quite recently.

With the founding of the northeast Baltic coastal cities and the subsequent migration of relatively small numbers of professional and administrative support populations, the ability of the German language to expand in northeastern Europe had reached its limits. A subsequent settlement of peasants and the large immigrant population that went along with the general Germanization of large parts of Prussia did not occur. Partly this lack of settlement was because truculent Lithuania interrupted a contiguous German presence along the Baltic coast, but surely it was also partly because the barrenness of the landscape and the life in the harsh climate and unyielding forests so close to the Russian border offered little allure for the German peasant. Thus the Germans in the northeast Baltic remained as an elite ruling class, providing little of the support power, which was left to the native Baltic populations; they in turn were granted virtually no access to positions of administration or power. Needless to say, as this situation continued on into the twentieth century, the seeds of discontent had been germinating for centuries as a ruling ethnic class tried to control a resentful native population. In addition, the Germans in the Baltic areas had found themselves under 'foreign' governments (particularly Sweden) after the decline of the Teutonic Order in the fifteenth century. Eventually they would be compelled to swear allegiance (an event of real consequence to an essentially elite and somewhat militaristic population group) to the Russian czars upon the rise of Peter the Great and the founding of St Petersburg, only 400 kilometers up the coast from Reval, during the early part of the eighteenth century.

In one of the most powerful and extraordinary sequences ever filmed, Sergei Eisenstein, in his 1938 anti-German propaganda film *Alexander Nevsky,* chose the moment of catastrophe for German eastward expansion under the banner of the military crusaders of the thirteenth century to predict to his audience the fate of the eastward-looking Germans of the twentieth century. For the first time, in April 1242, German and Russian armies met in battle on Lake Peipus, on the Russian frontier. In Eisenstein's re-creation of this battle, the army of German crusaders in full armor sinks into Lake Peipus, as the ice cracks and breaks beneath them. Eisenstein's message to his Russian audience was clear: the first German invasion into Russia ended in total defeat in the face of the Russian winter and the superior Russian general, Alexander Nevsky, and another potential German invasion from the west would meet the same fate. As a matter of fact, almost exactly 700 years later, the Nazi attack on the Soviet Union in the north would be stopped slightly to the east of Lake Peipus and the invaders driven out.

Eisenstein, in his version of the first martial meeting between Germans and Russians, was surely more interested in dramatic spectacle and propagandistic power than in an accurate portrayal of historical events, but his choice of this battle was based on careful historical consideration. It was not a piece of fiction, although the setting was so extravagantly handled that it might seem the fantasy of a master expressionistic filmmaker. The extraordinary visual sequences of the sinking crusaders and their horses create an unforgettable metaphorical image of the warlike Germans, storming through Eastern Europe in search of new territory.

In essence, however, this brilliant work of art by Eisenstein visualized an essentially misleading concept of the Germans in Eastern Europe. It may be an effective image of the Germans in Russia in the mid-thirteenth and twentieth centuries, but the great part of German expansion into Eastern Europe was accomplished in far more peaceable ways. Only in the last heathen strongholds of Europe along the Baltic, east of the Vistula and west of Russia, were armed Christian knights, such as we see in *Alexander Nevsky,* sent forth to do battle with the enemy. And even there they would quickly be joined by German traders and merchants who were busy populating the coast for economic reasons. Alexander Nevsky met with the furthest wanderers of these armed missionaries, who had passed over into Russian-Orthodox territory.

The activities of the Teutonic Order brought about two consequential developments for the history of the German language. One was the settling of a German ruling class, made up largely of the nobility or successful merchants, in the northeastern Baltic bordering upon Russia. The other was the apparently permanent establishment of the German language in large areas east of the Vistula (East Prussia) and the founding of large coastal cities, which would be either substantially or almost totally German speaking until the end of the Second World War. These two populations would have greatly differing histories. The Baltic Germans would hang on to an increasingly tentative existence under Russian control, gradually losing their administrative powers and eventually becoming pawns in political negotiations between East and West, while the Germans of Prussia would play a leading role in the rise of Germany as a unified world power, beginning with the formation of the Second German Empire in 1871. In the end, however, the German populations of both areas would share the same fate – the expulsion from the homeland – although in the Baltic states it occurred as a result of the nonaggression pact between the Nazis and Soviets of 1939, while in Prussia it happened by military force at the end of the war.

Further south, the expansion of the German language eastward during the Middle Ages brought about a similar linguistic mixture to the one it had along the eastern Baltic: a large German minority language group arose in non-Slavic lands, which themselves made a definitive break in the contiguity of Slavic territories. The languages of the Baltic states (Latvia, Lithuania, and Estonia) were spoken by relatively small populations in confined geographical spaces, which had independent political status for only slightly more than two decades in modern times (1918–40). The non-Slavic languages to the east of the German-speaking Austrians (Hungarian and Romanian), however, contributed a relatively large and powerful presence that effectively split the north Slavic and south Slavic language groups. In particular the Hungarians provided a force to be reckoned with after the ninth century, when their westward migrations stopped in the area east of Austria along the Danube. (The linguistic kinship of

Hungarian to Estonian and Finnish suggests a unity of these peoples in prehistoric times, with the eventual separation into three distinct branches, the largest of which settled in Hungary.)

Although the relationship between Germans and Hungarians became problematic within the context of the declining Austro-Hungarian Empire, the movement of German-speaking settlers into Hungary took place peacefully over an extended period of time. The presence of a major German-speaking urban center in Vienna and the willingness of the Hungarian nobility to bring German settlers to Hungarian territory made this movement possible. By the late twelfth century the eastward expansion of German resulted in substantial German populations in border areas of western Hungary and the establishment of a relatively solid German settlement in the mining areas of Hungarian Slovakia on the north side of the Danube (the Zips). By 1271 these German settlements had been granted special status by the Hungarian king. In the late twelfth century German settlers had also been welcomed into the furthest eastern frontiers of Hungary to populate an almost uninhabited territory that was to serve as a bulwark against the Turks. There, in Transylvania, German culture and language established its strongest presence in southeastern Europe, an importance verified by its special status of an independent crown colony of Hungary. By the end of the fourteenth century the population of Transylvania was so well established that colonialists could begin to move out from cities like Hermannstadt into Bukovyna, where they would help form, in centers like Czernowitz, a very fruitful multicultural, multilingual center, which lasted until the Second World War.

In the twelfth century, the Hungarian-ruled areas southeast of Vienna, partly in present-day Yugoslavia, also received an influx of German-speaking settlers. Eventually this area would become one of the most ethnically and linguistically diverse provinces of the Austro-Hungarian Empire. The German-speaking settlements of the Balkans would feel the earth shake under them in June 1914, when just to their south the First World War began its inexorable course with the assassination of the Austrian crown prince in Sarajevo. (It is also only here, in the northernmost outposts of south-Slavic languages in the Slovenian-speaking sections of Austrian Carinthia, that a contemporary German-language state has to deal with a substantial native Slavic linguistic minority and continues to have great problems in doing so.) After this hectic activity of the late Middle Ages, it is not until the eighteenth century that the Germanization of Eastern Europe in a cultural and linguistic sense finds new impulses. In the centuries in between – while the Yiddish language was spreading from its Polish base with further Jewish wanderings into Ukraine, Russia, Romania, and along the Baltic – the German language maintained its established presence but did not greatly expand its geographical base.

In the eighteenth century, the last peaceful migration of Germans into Eastern Europe began. It was a migration that would be instigated for the most part by the desire of Russian and Austrian rulers to utilize potentially productive agricultural areas that had in effect never been cultivated. By the late seventeenth century, before the rise to power of Peter the Great, it is estimated that there were only 18,000 Germans living in Russia, most of them in the capital city of Moscow, where they formed by far the largest group of foreigners in a city of 200,000.[14] Thus, one could speak of a certain German presence in the main city, but hardly of a population of settlers. Along the Baltic the Swedes maintained control of the territories they had conquered earlier in the century. The Baltic had become a Swedish sea as a result of military forays by the suddenly powerful and expansionary Scandinavian state, which had gained colonies as far away as Bremen-Verden on the North Sea and Pomerania on the Baltic, and which had sent armies far into Central Europe. In the northeast Baltic the Swedes had become masters of the old territories of the Teutonic Order, and they had the general support of the established German aristocratic and merchant population. The peasant population remained Latvian or Estonian, and the German elite class was willing to accept political control from a Swedish kingdom, which shared its religion and made no attempts to replace its language. On the contrary, the closeness of the two Germanic languages led to an interchange of cultural and linguistic influences that lasted until the twentieth century. Thus Dorpat (Tartu), which became the major university city of the eastern Baltic, is considered an important cultural landmark by the Swedes, the Germans, and the Estonians.

There was no Russian city up the coast east of Reval but only the final Hanseatic outpost at Narva and then swampland, which stretched around Ingermanland at the eastern end of the Baltic to the Swedish territories in Karelia in present-day Finland. Thus, when Peter the Great was born in 1689, one can speak of a significant German presence in the eastern Baltic on Swedish territory (which had once been German) but hardly of a significant presence in Russia. By the time Peter died in 1725, at the age of only 46, all this had changed.

Through military strategy he had won control of the Baltic by routing the Swedes from the eastern Baltic in a twenty-year war (1700–21), which resulted in the destruction of the Swedish fleet and the end of Sweden's period as a great military power. Suddenly a long-established economic and cultural German elite class had become subject to the czar of Russia; for this class, it was quite a different proposition from being subject to the king of Sweden. As a result, the German population of the easternmost Slavic nation increased radically, and continued to grow as the czar brought in skilled German craftsmen and professionals to build his new capital in the swamps at the eastern end of the Baltic. St Petersburg, the new city which had as its closest urban neighbor the 'German' cities of Reval and Riga, established a powerful Russian dominance over the easternmost Germans, who now had to swear allegiance to the czar and were rewarded with linguistic and cultural rights for doing so. At the same time, the city symbolized the establishment of a new westward-looking Russia, which in the decades to follow would welcome German settlers into its heartland instead of defending its borders against them with military power.

By the time of the rise to power of Catherine the Great of Russia (1729–96) in 1762, Germans were established in most of the major cities of Russia, in numbers that ranged from a few hundred to ten thousand in Odessa, twenty thousand in Moscow, and more than forty thousand in St Petersburg.[15] In addition, of course, Germans dominated the urban life and ruled the countryside of the recently conquered Baltic territories and it is fair to speak of a significant German input into the cultural life of urban Russia in this period. What had not happened, however, was a substantial settlement of rural population. There was not a base population of Germans out on the land that could potentially grow into a contiguous whole as it had done four centuries earlier in Prussia, Pomerania, and Silesia, or into sizable linguistic islands, as had happened in parts of Poland, Hungary, and Transylvania. In effect, the situation was similar, although certainly less marked, to that in the Baltic states. The German population of Russia was urban, professional, or aristocratic and represented something of an elite class. There were virtually no German peasants. Certainly Germans did not dominate the cultural life of Odessa or Moscow as they did that of Riga, but their social position in the urban order was similar. Perhaps it is worth recalling at this point that the only Germanic language in Russia used by the lower class was Yiddish, which would come to be spoken by a significant population in cities like Odessa and Moscow, but even in the late nineteenth century was still largely the language of the shtetl.

The situation with regard to German would change dramatically almost immediately upon the coronation of Catherine II, later called Catherine the Great, who was born Sophie von Anhalt-Zerbst in Stettin. One of her first major acts as the ruler of Russia was to invite her German countrymen into the uncultivated but fertile lands along the Volga River in the heart of European Russia, far to the east of the borders that had been defended by Alexander Nevsky. These Volga Germans, as they would come to be called, had to be offered special conditions in order to be convinced to undertake the long and difficult journey into a no man's land under the control of an alien language and culture. Furthermore, the German who could afford such a trip had to be wealthy enough to sell valuable possessions to make the whole venture possible.

Despite these hindrances to a major migration from Germany to Russia, the conditions were favorable enough: within only a few decades more than 3500 German towns had been established in middle Russia. The German settlers had been guaranteed freedom of religion and language, freedom from taxes and military service. And, most important, they were given the right to own the lands they cultivated, which gave them a position far superior to that of the Russian serfs. They came from many different areas of Germany, which in the eighteenth century was characterized by hundreds of small principalities and no central government. Their strenuous journey usually involved foot, boat, wagon, and barge travel. It almost always involved arriving in an uncultivated wilderness, where the first concern was to build lodging, particularly if the bitter winter was looming in the near future. In short, it meant the kind of pioneer settling that would happen once again to far more German settlers on the prairies of Canada and the United States in the nineteenth century. The Volga was the 'Wild East' of the eighteenth century for the Germans; it represented a final eastern bastion for the German language, which would hold fast for about two hundred years, while it scarcely survived a generation in the 'Wild West' of North America.

In the first five years after the settlement proclamation (1763–7), the population of Germans in Russia increased by 30,000 on the Volga alone. When that area became cultivated, more German settlers moved into areas around the Black Sea, which became the southeastern outpost of the German language. In general the Germans, like the Jews of Russia, maintained their Germanic language, resulting in a census count of 1,100,000 native German speakers among 1,900,000 ethnic Germans in the USSR as late as 1979, virtually all of whom were by then living in Soviet Asian exile.[16] It should immediately be added that these statistics should not lead to the conclusion that the German language is alive and well in the Soviet Union today. As with Yiddish, the actual state of the German language in the USSR today is difficult to assess. But members of both linguistic groups claim that there exists a great prejudice against their languages, which results in basic problems in education, business, and religion for any native speaker of German or Yiddish in the Soviet Union today. This surely helps explain why Germans (100,000) and Jews (65,000) emigrated from the Soviet Union in record numbers in 1989.

The Volga Germans, most of whom moved eastward simply because the economic prospects of farming seemed more promising than they did in the fragmented political and economic German states, were not the only Germans to find a new home in Russia. Much as the Jews had migrated to the east in the late Middle Ages to escape the religious intolerance of the Germans, members of minority religions in eighteenth-century Germany – Protestants in Catholic principalities, and Catholics in Protestant principalities, as well as sects such as Huguenots, Hutterites, and particularly Mennonites – would also use the offer to settle new territories as an opportunity to find a land where they could practice their religion as they pleased. For the Mennonites, a substantial percentage of whom migrated from their northern German homelands to the southernmost regions of Ukraine, the original Russian settlements functioned as a base for the establishment of satellite colonies in a fertile land. They would successfully cultivate this land for a century and a half before being driven away completely.

From their easternmost centers north of the Caspian Sea, the 'Russlandsdeutschen' (Russo-Germans) established small German-speaking settlements even in Asian Russia. These, then, would be the final eastern colors on the German linguistic map, small spots outside of Europe that had spread from German settlements in European Russia and would briefly represent the only 'contiguous' German-speaking settlements outside Europe. The history of the withdrawal of the German language to the west would logically start with the loss of these most exposed eastern outposts, along the Baltic south of Leningrad, on the Volga southeast of Moscow, around the Black Sea, and among the Mennonites of Ukraine.

The final colonization, which must be mentioned to allow an overview of the position of German in Eastern Europe at the beginning of the twentieth century, involves the largest German power of the eighteenth century, the Austrian Empire. It was, like the Russian Empire, determined to settle unproductive but potentially fertile lands with German farmers. Thus, we have the migrations that would account for the presence of one of the most prominent German populations in East Central Europe, the so-called Donauschwaben (Danube-Swabians), who were convinced to settle the lands along the Danube basin from Budapest to Timisoara. Beginning as early as the 1720s, many thousand peasant farmers undertook the trek down the Danube and began the job of cultivating the eastern part of the Austrian Empire. The conditions of settling were less stringent than those awaiting the Volga Germans, but on the Danube, too, essentially pioneer farming had to be practiced before a stable community could be established. Unlike the lands along the Volga, the Danube basin was not left completely to one colonizing ethnic group, which then remained in cultural and linguistic isolation. Rather it was the pioneer goal of many different ethnic groups, among which, however, the Germans dominated, both in wealth and in population. Eventually the population pressure was heavy enough – in the course of a century the number of Donauschwaben had increased seven times – for a German presence to be evident throughout the general area of middle eastern Hungary, southwestern Romania, and contemporary northern Yugoslavia.

In addition, the Austrian-Russian frontier formed a kind of natural dam for German-language expansion and the underpopulated areas behind this dam were being filled in the nineteenth century with settlers who considered Austria their cultural homeland. This settlement led to the presence of substantial German-speaking populations in such areas as the Bukovyna. This easternmost section of the Austrian Empire, which had only 80,000 inhabitants in 1774, already had 650,000 by 1890. The German-speaking population of Bukovyna by then was 133,500, somewhat more than 20 percent of the population, a statistic that includes a Jewish population, which was becoming assimilated from Yiddish into German.[17] There is perhaps no better indication of what German culture has lost than the realization that Czernowitz – the easternmost urban outpost of that language and the capital city of Bukovyna – must have produced proportionally more major twentieth-century writers, whose native language was German, than any other city: Paul Celan, Rose Ausländer, Selma Meerbaum-Eisinger, Gregor von Rezzori, Aharon Appelfeld (who would end up writing in Hebrew), among others. They are all young enough to be alive today and they all come from a city and a culture that has become so alien to their background, although the architecture remains essentially intact, that they could not even remotely imagine returning to their home city to spend their final years. (Meerbaum-Eisinger died in a Romanian slave-labor camp in 1942, Celan committed suicide in Paris in 1970, Ausländer, after decades in the United States, died in West Germany in 1987, von Rezzori lives in Italy and Appelfeld in Israel.) The authors from Czernowitz, scattered by the powerful quirks of twentieth-century history, leave behind them a city in which there are no Germans, no German-speaking Jews, and only a few old Yiddish speakers, whose language will die with them.[18] As such, the fate of the Jews and Germans of Czernowitz, and of the Yiddish and

German languages in that largely German-speaking city of only half a century ago, serves as something of a microcosm of what was about to happen throughout Eastern Europe, from the Baltic to the Black Sea and from the Volga River to Prague.

Before we look at the literature that describes this process of annihilation, it is worth taking one last summarizing look at the cold statistics, as far as we have them, of what was there as the old European world prepared to begin its first drastic period of change with the start of the First World War. If we consider Eastern Europe to have been sliced up to fit into the expansionary drives of the three major powers, Russia, Germany, and the Austro-Hungarian Empire, we come to the following statistical conclusions regarding the German presence in Eastern Europe at the turn of the century. In Russia, according to the census of 1897, there were 1,790,000 Germans, 1.4 percent of the total population, a number that exceeded the numbers of entire indigenous ethnic groups, such as the Lithuanians, Latvians, Estonians, and Georgians.

The majority of these Russo-Germans lived in the lands along the Volga, but almost one-quarter of them had settled eventually in the cities, particularly in St Petersburg and Odessa. The Baltic Germans – who became Russian subjects through a completely different historical process – numbered 165,000 and were made up almost entirely of landowners in the countryside or of aristocrats and merchants in such cities as Riga, Reval, and Dorpat. Of this total of nearly 2 million Russo-Germans, 400,000 lived, for the most part, as peasants in the Polish territories that had been given to Russia at the Congress of Vienna (1815). Thus, they were descendants of those settlers who had moved into Poland centuries before, during the flow of German settlers eastward from the Oder. A general trend towards participation of Germans in the industrialization of Poland can also be seen in the fact that the major Polish industrial city of Lodz had a substantial number of German-speakers by this time.

To the south, in the Austro-Hungarian Empire, the German population percentages were, of course, far greater. In the census of 1910, which gave a total population of 51 million for the empire, there were 12 million Germans (23.9 percent of the total population),

2 million more than for the next largest ethnic group, the Hungarians. In the Hungarian part of the empire, which included parts of what are now Poland, Romania, the USSR, and Yugoslavia (as well as Hungary), the Germans represented nearly 10 percent of the population; in the Austrian part, they were the largest national group with 35 percent of the total population. Germans made up 37 percent of the population of Bohemia, 28 percent of the population of Moravia, 44 percent of Silesia, and 21 percent of Bukovyna. These figures represent large German minorities in areas (western Czechoslovakia, southern Poland, western USSR) in which there are only remnant German populations today. In addition, Germans formed 5 percent of the population of Krain in northern Yugoslavia and Croatian-Slovenia, but only 1 percent of Galicia, where 800,000 Jews for the most part still spoke Yiddish.

Finally, in the German Empire in the north the demographic situation was determined by factors very different from those of Austro-Hungary, and to a somewhat lesser extent of czarist Russia. In the eastern part of the German Empire there were basically two languages and cultural groups, Polish and German, in competition for lands that had been given to the stronger group – the Germans – in 1815. The situation was by no means homogeneous, with Polish dominating in the old part of the Polish state (62 percent), German in West Prussia (65 percent) and East Prussia (90 percent), and Upper Silesia split more or less evenly.[19]

In many areas, plebiscites would be taken after the First World War to determine whether a geographical space would belong to the amputated German or to the rejuvenated Polish state. These plebiscites showed a great majority for Germany in non-contiguous East Prussia and a devastating split in Silesia, which effectively separated families and cultural entities in the interests of political settlements. Silesia was sliced up between Poland and Germany on the basis of close local votes, a process that caused much of the resentment leading to the violence and brutality of the Second World War in that area.

Were it not for the dramatic and devastating historical events surrounding the Second World War, these cold statistics might seem inconsequential. On a smaller and less dramatic scale, statistics could be brought forth to demonstrate the downfall of German and Yiddish in North America in the twentieth century as well. But in view of these historical events, these statistics underline the dangers in a situation that saw two Germanic languages established and thriving throughout areas that Slavic (or Hungarian or Baltic) majority groups felt belonged to them.

The three different empires produced three different kinds of irritations between the language groups. The German-ruled Poles felt oppressed and invaded and eventually would take advantage of the possibility of throwing out the German settlers. The Yiddish-speaking Jews were considered outsiders who did not belong to the Polish culture. Thus, Czeslaw Milosz's *The History of Polish Literature* (1969), for instance, does not have a single reference to I.B. Singer, his Polish-born Nobel Prize–winning colleague, whose first novel was written and published in Warsaw, although it does discuss works written in Lithuanian, Byelorussian, and Ukrainian.

In Austria-Hungary, the Germans had been forced to share political power with the other major language group – the Hungarians. But the Germanness of the bureaucracy and of the emperor (who was at the same time king of Hungary) was not lost on the other nationalities, who formed the large majority of the population in many parts of the empire, and who eventually helped bring about its end. For the Yiddish speakers in the eastern part of the empire, the process of assimilation into German, which had already eliminated Western Yiddish 150 years before, was under way. The German-speaking capital city of Vienna was the door to Europe and to Western civilization for the Yiddish-speaking rural population, and the switch to German was often the key. In Russia, German was an isolated minority language except in the Baltic. The First World War and the ensuing revolution of 1917 would unleash latent nationalistic tendencies, which included anti-German measures intended to bring the prosperous German settlements in Russia to their economic knees. The Yiddish-speaking population had been subject to frequent pogroms since the mid-nineteenth century and was used as the scapegoat for economic and political problems by both the czars and the revolutionaries. Both Germanic language groups would survive the revolution with heavy wounds; both were given autonomous Soviet republics for brief periods between the wars; but neither seems to have really survived the Second World War as a viable linguistic and cultural entity. Both were first decimated and then scattered, a process that in a broader sense can be said to have happened to Germanic language speakers throughout Eastern Europe in the twentieth century. The statistics here verge on the unbelievable: 3.5 million Polish Jews before the war (most of them Yiddish speakers), 5000–6000 today; more than 1 million native German speakers in the European part of the Soviet Union in 1935, almost none by 1950. The statistics crassly tell the tale of the end of two worlds. We will now look at this process in its subtle literary form, through artistic attempts to portray cultural annihilation.

The presence of these strong Eastern bastions of German language and culture offered a cultural and linguistic pattern that would eventually serve well the simplistic version of history that the Nazi government presented to the European powers in the 1930s. What the Nazis chose to see was a map of Eastern Europe that displayed a German linguistic and cultural presence stretching all the way from the eastern borders of the contiguous German Empire through to the Volga River. In between, according to this map, were millions of Germans, who had been settled there for centuries, waiting to be called 'Heim ins Reich.' Thus the final achievement of the eastern migrations was to have brought about the distribution of population which would eventually play such a large role in the justification for the beginning of the Second World War and the most consequential attempt of the Germans to make Eastern Europe truly German.

Chapter Two

The (relatively) Gentle Decline
Yiddish and the Modern World

Out of the darkness of superstition and prejudice, the rationalists wanted to lead the Jewish mass to the light of secular education: full of hope they looked to the state, national, and imperial capital of Vienna and, like Karl Emil Franzos, believed with all their heart in the blessings of progress and an improvement and refinement of the East European Jews through German culture.

Martin Pollack, *Nach Galizien* (To Galicia)

When the 'final solution' ('Die Endlösung') of the Nazis was put into operation for the Jews of Europe in the course of the Second World War, it came unexpectedly, violently, and overwhelmingly. Although it was designed to be applied to all European Jews, its most devastating blow was delivered to the Yiddish-speaking Jews of German-occupied Eastern Europe and resulted in the virtual annihilation of their centuries-old culture and language. But the beginning of the decline of the traditional way of life of East European Jewry was already becoming evident by the turn of the twentieth century through relatively subtle changes in the social structure caused by intrusions from the outside world. For the younger generation, in particular, the technological advances of a more modern Europe were becoming a tantalizing and seductive possibility, which often demanded a compromise with the old pattern of village life, and not infrequently with the old language as well.

In its broadest sense, the history of the European Jews has been characterized by the gradual movement of an economically limited, inward-looking Yiddish-speaking population, which functioned as far as possible as a self-sufficient community, towards an economically varied, outward-directed, non-Yiddish speaking population, which attempted to find a niche within the majority language and culture of the state in which it resided. In Western Europe this transition had already taken place to a large extent by the turn of the twentieth century. The native-born Jews of England, France, the Netherlands, Belgium, Scandinavia, and Germany had abandoned any peculiarities of language (except in the sense that Hebrew played a similar liturgical role for practicing Jews to Latin for Roman Catholics), and for the most part no longer lived strictly according to the orthodox religious traditions that still largely determined the rhythm of life among the East European Jews. The situation in East Central Europe and Russia was, however, much less uniform. Any attempt to treat as a whole Jewish communities as radically different as those of Franz Kafka's German Prague, Paul Celan's German/Yiddish Czernowitz, and Sholom Aleichem's Yiddish Anatevka is doomed to failure because of the differing rates of linguistic and cultural change that these populations were undergoing in the course of the late nineteenth and early twentieth centuries.

In the decades before 1918, almost all the Yiddish-speaking Jews of Europe were subjects of either the Russian czar or the Austrian emperor, with populations in the millions in Austrian Galicia, Russian Congress Poland, and the Pale of Settlement. The relatively few native Yiddish speakers in the German Empire were largely restricted to the formerly Polish eastern territories. In the areas of Yiddish concentration, such rapidly growing cities as Warsaw, Lemberg, Lublin, Kiev, and Czernowitz acted as catalysts for linguistic assimilation into the language of the majority, be it Russian (in the Pale of Settlement), Polish (in Russian-ruled Congress Poland and Austro-Hungarian

Galicia), or German (in the rest of the Austro-Hungarian Empire). For all Yiddish speakers seeking linguistic access to a major European culture, however, German provided the easiest route because of its close relationship to their native language.

After the dismembering of the Austro-Hungarian Empire at the end of the First World War and the establishment of a Polish state with lands taken from the eastern German, northern Austro-Hungarian, and western Russian empires, the Yiddish population was settled into new political constellations that would to a large extent determine its fate during the Second World War. In Galicia and Congress Poland, the new Polish state inherited the Jewish 10 percent of its population (over 3 million according to the census of 1931) that would be the easiest prey for the occupying Nazis when the 'final solution' went into effect and the trains started rolling, first to ghettos in cities like Warsaw and Lodz, and then to the killing centers at places like Majdanek and Auschwitz. In this census of 1931, 80 percent of this population indicated Yiddish to be its native language.[1] Across the border in the newly formed Soviet Union was the majority of remaining Yiddish speakers, whose remnants – those lucky enough to escape Nazi killing squads during the brief invasion of the Soviet Union – now constitute the last sizable Yiddish population. Smaller numbers of Yiddish speakers found themselves in Romania, the Slovakian part of the new state of Czechoslovakia, and Hungary, all of which would become allies of the Nazis, or in the Baltic States, which were soon to be annexed by the Soviet Union and shortly thereafter conquered by the Germans.

Since the 1860s Yiddish had gained a new public function; it had become a vehicle for imaginative writing, no longer just a written language for borrowed stories, but one that could deal with the contemporary world of the shtetl and make main characters out of the familiar figures of shtetl life. With the publication of the first Yiddish fiction of Mendele Mocher Sforim (pseudonym of Sholom Abramovitch) in the 1860s and with the great public success of the stories and plays of Sholom Aleichem (pseudonym for Sholom Rabinovitch) beginning in 1882, major changes in the rigid structure of the orthodox Jewish world had become apparent. For the first time, the secular world of everyday life had become an object worthy of description and discussion. The transformation of a spoken language into a literary language made possible the creation of a powerful image of a readily identifiable poverty-stricken small-town world peopled by familiar characters struggling to survive, and automatically also suggested that something must be done to better the miserable situation. Yiddish literature had little more than half a century to describe its world before that world ended. When the first two major Yiddish writers, Mendele Mocher Sforim (1836–1917) and Sholom Aleichem (1859–1916), died within a year of each other during the First World War, the probable last and internationally most prominent Yiddish writer, Isaac Bashevis Singer (1904–), was just about to go to Warsaw to begin his career as a journalist and writer. Thus, within the two lifetimes that it has been in existence, Yiddish literature was able to describe both the richness and poverty of its world and also its catastrophic end.

For postwar Western Europe and North America, the small-town Yiddish-speakers of Poland and the Pale of Settlement have become the most familiar representatives of this sunken world. This is to some extent because of the evocative power of such Singer novels as *The Magician of Lublin* (1960), in which the assimilating Polish-speaking title figure clashes with the orthodox Yiddish world of his youth and his family, but even more so because of the great success of *Fiddler on the Roof,* the Joseph Stein/Sheldon Harnick/Jerry Bock musical and film based on carefully selected tales of Sholom Aleichem's milkman, Tevye. The extremely popular film version features an artistically shoddy village of Anatevka, and a well-fed Tevye, and draws much of its power from a feeling of sentimentality about a lost homeland. Martin Pollack's recent imaginative re-creation of a turn-of-the-century journey through the world of the shtetl offers a fascinating opportunity to test the picturesque poverty of *Fiddler on the Roof* with the miserable squalor of the world in which the real Teyves lived, and from which millions were emigrating. The nostalgia, which infiltrates the stage and film version of Anatevka (in German they even use the town name as the title of the musical, which has become one of the most popular of the postwar German stage), is as absent from Pollack's description of a typical Galician town as it is from Sholom Aleichem's portrayal of Anatevka:

Many Jews lived by buying and selling, especially grains and other agricultural products, as little middlemen, peddlers, whose weekly 'sales' were often no more than a bunch of eggs and a couple of chickens; as handworkers, tailors, shoemakers, bakers, tallis weavers; as leasers of the liquor shacks, which belonged to the Polish landowners, who had at least one representative in each village; as hired hands. According to an unofficial statistic from 1900, of the 810,000 Jews in Galicia 150,000 ran the liquor shacks, 100,000 had no determinable occupation – which is to say they were peddlers – 400,000 'dealers,' and 10,000 handworkers and hired hands. The Polish bureaucracy made sure that they did not find their way into government jobs; the growing union movement drove them out of village business and out of the liquor shacks. The life of the Galician Jews was indescribably miserable.[2]

In the stories of Sholom Aleichem we find both this economic, social, and political misery, and the evidence of the growing revolt in the younger generation against the conditions that allowed it to continue. In this context we also find the gradual breakdown of an apparently stable, long-standing community in the face of outside influences and inside pressures that could not fit the given rigid pattern. In effect, any outside intrusion of the modern world into the shtetl was bound to bring with it the potential for disruption. Such developments as railroad lines, newspapers, political publications, and increased educational opportunities outside the Jewish community (Sholom Aleichem himself went to a Russian high school and spoke Russian with his family) were bound to suggest different opportunities to a younger generation. Thus, the transformation of Yiddish into a literary language and the sudden availability of a critical body of literature by popular writers also plays a key role. In addition there were the many disciples of the Haskaleh, the Jewish Enlightenment, which had already changed Jewish life in Western Europe. Spurred on by the anti-Semitic pogroms of the 1870s and 1880s in Russia, many Jews were more than ready to hear the seductive messages of both Zionism and Communism.

All these potentially disruptive influences are at work in the narrations of Sholom Aleichem.[3] The somewhat ironic point of a story like 'Dreyfus in Kasrilevke' about the reaction to the Dreyfus case among the inhabitants of the shtetl may well be that the Russian Jews were living in naive and ultimately dangerous ignorance of the strength of anti-Semitism, even in the supposedly tolerant societies of Western Europe. But there is also a telling point made by the very fact that new methods of communication have made such information about a court case in France available deep in provincial Ukraine. On the day when the newspaper with the latest news from Paris arrives in Kasrilevke, the entire town gathers at the post office to hear the latest reports read out. Events in Western Europe suddenly become part of shtetl life, and even if its inhabitants are not yet ready to believe the message of the newspaper reports (when the guilty verdict is announced, the people vent their anger at the Yiddish newspaper and the subscriber for spreading such an obvious lie), the medium of fast news communication has already made its irreversible impact. In his memoirs about his childhood in the Jewish community of Bulgaria, Elias Canetti also records the sacred moment when the (Viennese) newspaper arrived and the father could not be disturbed (*The Tongue Set Free*, 1979, 26). The study of the news from the outside world had become part of the daily ritual.

In Sholom Aleichem's eight stories told by Tevye the milkman (published between 1894 and 1916), we find a compendium of the pressures for change in the old way of shtetl life that convince most of the daughters of the milkman to leave the village even before the remaining family and all the other Jews are forcibly expelled. In Tevye's pre-First World War Anatevka, this disintegration of the family is as great a threat to the stability of the community as is the historical pressure from the periodic pogroms set loose by the czar. The familial disruptions caused by only three of these daughters are included in *Fiddler on the Roof*, giving a simplified and misleading version of Sholom Aleichem's account of the problems facing the orthodox Jewish settlements at the turn of the century. On the stage and in the film, responsibility from within the Jewish community for the breakdown is centered almost exclusively on the almost endearing inability of the patriarchal father to understand and accept the desire of these three daughters for changes in the rules of marriage. *Fiddler on the Roof* limits itself to the problems caused by the marriage plans of Tseidel, Hodel, and Chava. The proposed grooms are increasingly unacceptable, the first because he is poor and the marriage has not been approved by Tevye, the second because he is a cultural outsider and a revolutionary, and the third because he is not Jewish. In both the Sholom Aleichem stories and *Fiddler on the Roof*, Tevye slowly adjusts to the idea of the poor tailor, manages to bring himself to accompany Hodel to the train that will take her off to join her revolutionary in Siberian exile, but expels Chava from the family. Teyve is thus capable of reluctantly accepting a change in deeply established custom and even more reluctantly he gives in to the idea of a Jewish intellectual revolutionary, who challenges the given social and political order, but he refuses to acknowledge Chava's existence when she stops him on the road, for the presence of *her* husband automatically would mean the abandonment of the foundations of his entire world. In *Fiddler on the Roof*, there is the suggestion at the end of a possible reunion of the entire family, including Chava and her husband, in the America that is given as their goal. In the tales, however, where it is unclear where they might be going after being driven from the shtetl, there is no such potential happy end, and Tevye can only puzzle over his proper response to the uninvited returnee Chava, who seems to have abandoned her husband and wishes to return to the faith. Sholom Aleichem, in his First World War New York exile, had no answers for Tevye, but all possibilities suggest the shattering of the old family order, as most of Tevye's children had abandoned the world into which they were born, not being willing to play out the roles that had been assigned to them at birth.

There are, however, other forces present in Sholom Aleichem's Anatevka, and absent in *Fiddler on the Roof*, that come from within the Jewish community and illustrate the deep rift between the world of Tevye, who follows the strictly prescribed rules of an economically weak but spiritually strong system, and that of the rich city Jews, who pursue powerful economic positions, if necessary at the expense of spiritual ones. Sholom Aleichem had lived in Kiev for awhile and sent Tevye there to learn about the seductive lure and destructive power of money and secular status. Tevye's various adventures with moneyed urban Jews are always misguided and potentially precarious, but there is a relatively comic harmlessness to the first of these stories, in which Tevye suddenly strikes it rich (so the title) as payment for emergency taxi service rendered to rich Jews summering in the country – only to blow the small fortune (so the second title) in the hands of a remote relative who claims to have a sure way to win more money on the stock exchange. These stories are still within an understood milieu of poverty, familial relations, good fortune, and misplaced trust in the life of one of those eternal dreamers who wandered the Yiddish-speaking world in search of financial betterment, only to lose a potential windfall through unwise speculation. It is here in this milieu that the world of Sholom Aleichem comes closest to that of I.B. Singer.

Tevye's disastrous relationship to money and to some of his relatives is part of the tale's black comic undertone, which also characterizes the irony that dominates his discussions with God and the world. Tevye may act unwisely with his money, but the reader understands his behavior to be within an ethical framework, ruled over by an all-determining God. A cantankerous individual like Tevye may argue with this God about the justice of his position in life, and may even make a fool of himself in an attempt to improve his situation within the framework without in any way shaking the religious pillars of the society. But in these stories there is also a community of prosperous Jews from the city who look down upon their shtetl brethren as backcountry embarrassments whom one would rather not recognize. These wealthy urban Russian-Jews, therefore, understand their social position and their relationship to their Yiddish-speaking brethren in much the same way that the bourgeois German Jews did. And then there is the stock exchange itself, which Tevye visits in his attempt to find out what happened to his enterprising second cousin and his money. There, amidst the chaos of the money exchange, Tevye comes across a frenzied ritualistic worshipping of the God of money. This money worship helps explain the tragic circumstances surrounding the marriages of two of his other daughters, whose stories were left out of the film and the musical. Those marriage problems did not arise because of Tevye's stubborn defense of the old way of life but because of the prosperous suitors' imposition of an ethical framework based on economics as the standard for a new way of life.

These urban financiers have their descendants in such new-world characters as the protagonist of Mordecai Richler's 1959 novel set among the second-generation Jewish immigrants of Montreal, *The Apprenticeship of Duddy Kravitz*. Duddy spends his apprenticeship learning the ways of money and eventually tries to win back his disgusted Yiddish-speaking grandfather by presenting him with the piece of land he had wished for since the exodus from the old country. When the grandfather discovers that Duddy had betrayed his friends while fraudulently accumulating his resources to buy the subdivision on which the land sits, he refuses to accept it and leaves his grandson alone in his prosperous but sterile world.

Duddy's grandfather and Tevye have the same problem: they have relatives who have put the pursuit of money before the demands of the established understood ethical system. Tevye's daughter Shprintze, whose story follows that of Chava by ten years, has a tragic love affair with just such a Duddy Kravitz from the wealthy urban Jewish class. The vacationing Jews who endow Tevye with his fortune in the first of the Tevye stories now present him with a proposed family member whose conduct breaks all codes of shtetl behavior. For Ahronchik, the spoiled son of a rich widow, brings with him into the framework of Tevye's family – and thus into the world of the shtetl – all those false gods that Tevye had seen being worshipped at the stock exchange. Ahronchik is urban and he is rich and he claims to be in love with Shprintze. Tevye correctly understands the problems of such a marriage between rich and poor, but nevertheless can't help but imagine the benefits of finally having a wealthy son-in-law. Tevye interprets his dilemma from within the given code of conduct of the orthodox Jewish world; the problem is that he is too poor to offer the proper financial endowment to his daughter in her marriage to such a wealthy suitor. This may be one of the weaker Tevye stories for the modern reader because of the predictability of the outcome – Ahronchik disappears one fine day, never to be seen again, and leaves the problem of Tevye and Shprintze to his family – and the melodramatic response of Shprintze – she drowns herself. But it also contains disturbing information about the internal sources of danger to the Yiddish community that are completely absent from *Fiddler on the Roof.*

Tevye is given the news of the cancellation of the marriage proposal by an uncle of Ahronchik he had not met previously, and who understands such problems and their solutions within the framework of economic relations. He proposes a financial solution to what Tevye understands to be a moral and religious problem. His offer of a bribe to Tevye to break off the embarrassing engagement of his nephew to the daughter of a poor milkman results in a response not at all typical of the argumentative milkman. In the face of the caprices of fate Tevye has ironic queries for God, and in the face of a hesitant mob ordered to destroy his house, he has sarcastic and bitter questions. But in the face of such a blatant betrayal of an understood Jewish code of conduct, he is simply speechless. In Duddy Kravitz's failed attempt to buy back morality by presenting his grandfather with the piece of land, there is a new-world equivalent of this unbreachable gap between the old religious world and the new secular one.

In the tale of the fifth daughter, Beilke, Sholom Aleichem takes his cynicism for the nouveau riche urban Jewish society one step further. This time the marriage does take place between a Tevye daughter and a wealthy young urban Jew. The scandal that surrounds the suicide of Schprintze thus is avoided, but a new relationship comes about in which Tevye, the patriarchal head of an ancient family order, suddenly discovers that he is merely the embarrassing poor father-in-law in a rich family. Podhotzur, the husband, who is a contractor involved in the industrialization of the new Russia, has a solution to the problem of Tevye, and it is the in-family equivalent of the bribe. Podhotzur will cover the costs so that Tevye can go to spend his final days in the promised land, be it America or Palestine. Podhotzur is so desperate to get rid of the old man, whom he identifies to his society as his millionaire father-in-law, that he also proposes to pay the bribes to get Hodel and her husband Pertchik out of Siberia, if only they will all remove themselves from the part of the world where they could embarrass him by being identified as part of his family.

By putting in opposition a rich urban Jewish class searching for financial gain and a poor Jewish class living within long-established religious practices, Sholom Aleichem set the fictional precedent for much of the Jewish literature of emigration in the new world. The successful adjustment to life in the new world demanded a switch in language, which would have turned Tevye into a sad Yiddish-speaking recluse in the lower East Side of New York if he had gone to America. His family would have had little choice, if they wished to pull themselves out of the same isolation, but to abandon Tevye's language and way of life, a process we often see under way in the new-world stories of Singer. Even in the old world of Tevye, however, the end of a whole communal order is foreshadowed. In the course of the stories and the quarter-century in which they were written, Tevye loses one daughter after another to outside forces, which include technological progress: the train takes Hodel and Pertchik to Siberia; new political ideas: Pertchik has studied the works of Marx; generational change: each one of his daughters argues that she has the right to choose her own husband; demographic movement: only one of the daughters remains in the shtetl; historical developments: the abortive uprisings of 1905, in which Pertchik is involved, lead to anti-Semitic pogroms; commercial expansion: Podhotzur has business in Japan and all over the world; religious rejection: Chava marries a Christian; and economic dislocation: Schprintze and Beilke choose rich husbands who attempt to employ their financial power to remove Tevye from his previously uncontested standing as patriarch of a small but completely stable world. In the last of the eight Tevye stories, 'Lekh-Lekho' ('Get Thee Out'), he even loses his house and his land (his ironic question to the commissioner who comes to read the decree is whether the commissioner realizes which of them has been longer in this part of the world), and is given the traditional meager belongings of the wandering Jew to seek a refuge elsewhere.[4]

Tevye, the old patriarch, is driven away like a dog, but millions of others were voluntarily leaving to seek a better life elsewhere; and for the Yiddish speakers of the Austrian Empire that 'elsewhere' would be most frequently found in the great German-speaking cities to the west: Vienna and Berlin. German-language writers of the period, however, showed no inclination to make use of this major historical movement for fictional purposes. With few exceptions, the image of the Jew in nineteenth-century German literature is limited to potentially anti-Semitic stock caricatures set in western Germany or Austria by writers such as Gustaf Freytag (1816–95) and Wilhelm Raabe (1831–1910). Attempts by German-Jewish authors to describe the exotic world of the East European shtetl from which the great new masses of Berlin and Vienna came were fatally falsified by the desire to make these shtetl fit into the contemporary German image of the small town as a place of idyllic security following the disruptions of mid century. This attempt to make something bourgeois and German out of the miserable shtetl – Jost Hermand points to the stories of Aaron Bernstein (1812–84) and Leopold Kompert (1822–86) as typical examples of this genre[5] – provides a dramatic contrast to the short stories and single novel that Karl-Emil Franzos (1848–1904) wrote in German about 'Halbasien' ('Halfasia') as he called his homeland of East Galicia. In the works of Franzos, a native German speaker born into a Yiddish world, we have the first indication that German literature could offer an alternative to Yiddish literature in its ability to portray the difficult life of the Jews of Eastern Europe. In the twentieth century this alternative would be chosen even by writers like Joseph Roth, Alexander Granach, or Manes Sperber who came from Yiddish-speaking families and whose subject matter, at least on occasion, involved the people of the Yiddish-speaking world.

Bernstein's or Kompert's sentimentalized portrayals of an East European idyll that find their contemporary equivalents in such American versions of this world as *Fiddler on the Roof* and Barbra Streisand's *Yentl* visualize a world that never was. These portrayals are related to the most popular contemporary German depictions of the lost paradise of places like East Prussia, the Sudetenland, or Silesia in many so-called 'Heimatromane' ('novels of the homeland'). But Franzos's *Der Pojaz* (The Clown) depicts a world of poverty and filth, of starvation and cold and child-death, all of which recall descriptions like those used by Martin Pollack, or by Manes Sperber in his recollection of his shtetl birthplace, Zablotow, which was next door to Franzos's home town Chortkov (Czortkow). 'Zablotow – its very name is unpleasant; it refers to the clayey soil, the unpaved streets, into which one could easily sink whenever they were softened by the endless autumn rains.'[6] Sperber, writing in the 1970s, can still remember a Zablotow of his childhood that easily recalls Sholom Aleichem's Anatevka or Franzos's Barnow (as he renamed Chortkov in his fiction), but does not seem remotely related to the towns of Bernstein or Kompert.

Franzos, who is probably still best known for his discovery of Georg Büchner's *Woyzeck* manuscript and the publication of the first complete edition of Büchner's works, was born directly on the

Austrian/Russian border, in the year 1848, when historical watersheds were being created. In his foreword to *Der Pojaz* (written in the 1880s, but posthumously published in 1905) Franzos underlines the peculiar position of the westernized Jew in Austrian Galicia on the Russian frontier as the disturbances break out that continued on as elements of the First World War. Caught between linguistic and religious prejudices from all sides, Franzos's father, a German-speaking Jewish doctor in the Austrian bureaucracy on its formerly Polish eastern frontier, would have to send his pregnant wife across the border into czarist territories in order to escape the wrath of the Poles against the Austrians. For the time being, his Jewishness was secondary to his Germanness as a reason for attack, but a different time would come soon enough. Despite his double-outsider status (as German and Jew), the father sticks to his post, and as a result the leading German-Jewish writer of the latter half of the nineteenth century was born in Russia:

> For late autumn 1848 was a bad time in East Galicia; the Poles rebelled and took it upon themselves to do the same things to the individual Germans who were scattered about the country as their countrymen in Posen had done to the Prussians half a year before, or at least had tried to do. My father was among those who were threatened, first of all because of his role as a provincial doctor of the Austrian Empire and second because he had always been a defender of all things German. Every day he was bombarded with threatening letters; out in the country-side the rebellion had already been openly declared; an attack on the town was expected at any time. They advised my father to flee but he was not a man to leave his post. So he just sent my mother, pregnant with me, and my older siblings across the border ... So you see the reason that I was born in Russia was that my father felt himself to be a German and acted accordingly. (*Der Pojaz*, 1–2)

In view of twentieth-century history, the irony of this description need hardly be underlined, but there is one aspect of the situation that plays a key role in all the novels we will look at dealing with the end of German and Yiddish in Eastern Europe. Franzos's father, as a representative of a minority group, in his case German, is threatened by the majority, in this case Polish, for religious, linguistic, and cultural reasons. Crossing a border – the event that Franzos first experienced inside his mother's womb – had become a matter of life and death for the ethnic, religious, and/or linguistic minority. How insecure and uncertain the supposed sanctuaries would be is well demonstrated by a situation in which a German-Jewish father sends his family eastward to seek refuge in Russia, a journey that would be reversed in the decades surrounding the First World War, when Jews fled in droves westward from Russia into the apparent security of Austria and Germany, only to have the process reversed again during the Second World War.

Franzos's brief autobiography also focuses on the disturbed relationship between the German- and Yiddish-speaking Jews in Eastern Europe. In his description of the complete social and linguistic gap between the educated German-speaking, Western-oriented doctor and the mass of the Jewish population of Chortkov, we can detect a foreshadowing of the self-delusion of the German Jews half a century later: they thought that Nazi anti-Semitism was not really aimed at them because there was a clear distinction between German- and Yiddish-speaking Jews:

> I went to the only school in town, which was taught in the Dominican cloister; there I learned Polish and Latin. My father taught me German by himself. I had a special tutor for Hebrew. This man was the only Jew in Chortkov with whom I had any real contact during those ten years. My schoolmates, my playmates, were all Christians. I seldom went into a Jewish home, never into a synagogue. Neither religious rituals nor kosher cooking were practiced in my home. I grew up on an island. Belief and language made me different from my schoolmates, and exactly the same things made me different from the Jewish kids. I was a Jew, but a different kind from them and their language was not completely comprehensible to me ... I was separate from all the others, someone different from them. But I knew exactly what I was, my father had taken care of that. I was a German and a Jew at the same time ... That's the way things were in my childhood in Chortkov. I was very enthusiastic about Jewish matters, but had hardly any understanding about the real life of the Jews living around me. (Ibid., 2–3)

After the death of his father, Franzos's high-school years were spent in Czernowitz. For the fictional hero of *Der Pojaz*, Sender Glatteis, this journey from the misery of small-town Galicia to the easternmost German cultural center of Czernowitz becomes the central aim of his short life. The frontier city of the Austro-Hungarian Empire, with its German university and assimilating German-Jewish cultural life, that seems so near on the map of East Central Europe proves to be almost impossibly far away for Sender, in both a geographical and cultural sense, from the world of his orthodox Jewish birthplace.

Franzos chose his hero's name carefully: Sender, Yiddish for Alexander, which Franzos identifies as a proud name 'that the Jews in a triumphant historical moment had taken over from the Greeks and that lived on during their miserable period of servitude in East Europe,' and Glatteis, treacherous ice, 'which some kind of coincidence or the mood of some bureaucrat had given his grandfather' (p. 8). The name thus contains the dangerous combination of bravery and slippery footing that would be the companion of any Yiddish-speaking East European Jew trying to make his way out of the confines of his preordained orthodox life into the world of a different culture. The instruments of this transformation – books, language, outward appearance, eating habits, working routine, in short everything that would define the life of a Westernized German Jew – would have to be illegally obtained. Over this effort hung the threat that the discovery of such forbidden actions would lead to the immediate and permanent expulsion from the community of the shtetl, while certainly not guaranteeing acceptance by the outside world.

The attempt to undergo this transformation is the basis of the story of *Der Pojaz*. Sender Glatteis is sent out on the slippery path of attempted assimilation into the Western world and suffers the double tragedy of expulsion by the inside world and nonacceptance by the outside, becoming in the process a tragic failure in both worlds. For the Yiddish-speaking Sender, the world opens up not to the north or east towards Poland or Russia, but to the west and south towards Austria. Franzos sends his hero from the shtetl of Barnow out in search of a tentative foothold in the German theater in Czernowitz. The attempted journey of Sender Glatteis from the medieval orthodoxy of mid-nineteenth-century Galicia to modern enlightenment within German cultural space is, as we know from other writings of Franzos, also his proposal for East European Jewry in general. Franzos was an assimilated German Jew brought up in Tevye's world without the religious foundation. From his perspective there was only one way out into a more acceptable life for his poverty-stricken brethren and it was the way of the assimilated Jews of Western Europe.

What Franzos fictionalizes in his novel is therefore to some extent the story of the first part of his own geographical journey from Chortkov to the German-speaking west where he became a quite successful literary and journalistic personality. What he does not do, however, is romanticize the journey or pretend that a Yiddish-speaking Jew with no background in Western European cultures or languages will make this trip as readily as he himself did. From the beginning, Sender Glatteis has been a complete failure in the shtetl without having gained any of the skills needed in the outside world. He excels only as a clown and storyteller, and by the age of thirteen has shown every indication of becoming a good-for-nothing 'schnor-rer' like his father, fated to wander from town to town in Galicia in search of the charity of others. Placed in the service of a carter at this point, Sender is sent off on business to Czernowitz, where he meets the dangerous and seductive world of a Western European culture at the German-Jewish theater. This chance occurrence alters the fate of Sender from that of a hopeless wanderer through the economic misery of Galicia to that of a desperate struggler, determined to make every possible attempt to gain entrance to that other world he has been confronted with in Czernowitz.

In a farcical scene, Franzos portrays his hero as a great fool from the most backward province as he confronts for the first time the German language and its theater, which are both involved in the intensity of his first reaction to theatrical illusion in place of interpreted authority. Here in Czernowitz, where his traveling companion does not wish to go because 'the Jews speak High German and eat pork' (p. 55), Sender finally meets the new world in the second floor of a small Jewish inn, which serves as the theater for the German-Jewish theater troupe. Immediately he demonstrates the enormous informational gap between Eastern and Western Jewry. His first admission to a waiter – that he is looking for the theater because he wants to become a comedian ('Komödiant') – is met with derisive laughter and a tug at his (for orthodox Jews) obligatory earlocks, and the suggestion that he better do something about them before the director sees him. Of course, Sender has other more serious problems than earlocks, the most difficult of which is his language. When Sender meets 'the German' ('der Deutsche') – as Nadel, the assimilated Jewish director of the theater is called – the waiter is delighted at the opportunity of directing a scene of high comedy: the Yiddish-speaking rube with the earlocks wants to become an actor. As the waiter continues to laugh hysterically, the director asks to hear some of the stories for which Sender had gotten the name 'Pojaz.' 'The man looks at the woman, the woman at the man, they don't laugh like my listeners usually do, but still I think they like it. "Enough," the man finally says and begins to talk with the woman. But it was High German and incredibly fast, so I didn't understand too much' (p. 55).

Sender's first physical confrontation with the inside of the theater is equally alienating. His companion, Schmule, breaks into loud wailing when Sender suggests they go together to the theater; for Schmule it is an unpardonable sin. Once inside – by himself – Sender once again can only interpret the physical evidence around him in terms of his own past. Thus the theater space becomes for Sender a hall, familiar from the prayer room, with 'benches for the men below, and two galleries for the women above, and with a big curtain up front, like the "Schul" has in front of the Thora. But the word "Osten" [East] was not stitched into it but rather naked kids were painted on it, who were rolling on top of each other' (p. 56). His next surprise is that the people coming in were 'all Germans [by which he means German-speaking Jews] and that some men went up to the women's gallery and women were sitting in the men's rows' (p. 56). Finally he interrupts the performance by loudly identifying the set as a street and one of the actors as the director, to the amusement of the other patrons and annoyance of the company. Sender has arrived in the world of the theater missing all of the prerequisites demanded of aspiring thespians, except one, talent and acting ability, although it's in the slightly wrong language.

From this point on, Sender's life is dedicated to the assignment that is then given to him by Nadel: before he can become a member of the troupe he must learn the basics of its performing style. As has become apparent in Sender's retelling of the play, he has not understood more than the main outline of the German-delivered plot and this he has interpreted in a comically realistic way; he must, therefore, learn to speak and read German rather than the Yiddish with which he addresses the director. The director is bilingual in Yiddish and German, and his troupe performs only in German even though they may speak Yiddish to their patrons and among themselves in the inn downstairs after the performance.

Sender Glatteis's assignment for the next two years is thus to return to the shtetl and there to break all the rules of that given communal order to transform himself into a German-speaking actor. Every step along his apprenticeship route is a potential cause for expulsion from the community, where even the presence of a German-language book is considered to be an indication of a serious disorder. Appropriately enough, it is the revolution of 1848 that leads Sender to such a book, through the hands of a revolutionary soldier, who has been banished to the frontier. This book of revolutionary poems by the Jewish writer Moritz Hartmann is the open sesame to a complete break with the rules of the orthodox community. The transformation of a futureless poverty-stricken Yiddish-speaking good-for-nothing into a potential German-speaking actor is no easy task for Sender. For even Moritz Hartmann's poems are not decipherable. His first confrontation with the written German language leads to the conclusion that the book had been published backwards and that his tutor has been cheated because there is so much blank space on each page. His first great sin against the community – far more serious than his theater visit – is to take illegal reading lessons from the soldier in the evening by the ruins outside the shtetl. It is the beginning of a conspiracy between Sender and Western cultural informational sources that will eventually inevitably drive him out of the community.

Sender learns the essentials of the written language and within a short time is able to make sense of the German text, which is the only book to which he has access. The suggestion that he buy himself a German primer to facilitate the tutoring process is rejected because the bookdealer would immediately want to know why he wants it, as the community would certainly not be in agreement with his search for outside knowledge. Sender is willing to take on almost any risks, however, as becomes apparent from the next station on his road to education: the unused library of the half-abandoned Dominican cloister – a reminder that shtetls such as Barnow-Chortkov were by no means exclusively Jewish, although in Galicia most had majority Jewish populations that were Yiddish-speaking. The dusty books on the shelves of the unheated ice-cold rooms (to which he gains illegal access by bribing the custodian) become his university. Eventually he will pay for this study with a fatal dose of tuberculosis. Every entrance into this library, where he spends his winter evenings as often as possible, carries with it the threat of expulsion from the community if the crime is discovered. Every book he picks off the shelves is an attack against the entire authority inside the shtetl, for every book carries information that opens up other channels of authority than the only one accepted within the shtetl. In all ironic innocence, Tevye can ask Chava – when she claims her Russian fellow is a second Gorky – who the first Gorky might be. But Sender Glatteis's evenings, spent gathering information about the outside world, can only lead to a confrontation with this society in which all authority has been established in an unchangeable pattern.

Franzos chooses the books carefully for his student. The very first book he picks from the shelves in his first evening foray is from the classical language shelves and the second is from the Polish shelves; they are both, of course, unreadable. The third is from the German shelves, but is badly written – something that Sender can hardly believe. But the fourth, from the theater shelves, is Lessing's *Nathan der Weise*. Sender thus begins his journey into Western culture with the most famous drama of the German Enlightenment, which he has difficulty reading ('it was hard work, first of all because many words were new to him'). He has just as much trouble comprehending it, because the ideas of tolerance between peoples or the equality of all religions expressed in it are as strange to him as are the occasional words he does not understand. Soon he moves on to the political plays of Schiller and finally to the *Merchant of Venice*, which presents him with Shylock, the role (he thinks) of his life.

Thus the journey into assimilation for Franzos's shtetl child demands both a linguistic and a philosophical transformation. The theater that opens up before Sender's amazed eyes in the freezing Dominican library inescapably carries with it the idea of a complete change in communal orientation and of a process in which the individual has not only the right, but the obligation, to act like a free person, drawing independent conclusions. There is no doubt about the position of the author with regard to this process. He is obviously on the side of those proposing assimilation into a majority culture and against the stubborn conservatism of Tevye or the village rabbi. Franzos may not have been alone in attempting to portray fictionally this route out of the poverty-stricken environment of Galicia, but no other German writer of the period approached his success in avoiding the pitfalls of sentimentality, preaching, and romantic optimism that lurk as stylistic traps all along the route.

Franzos's hero, after his period of intense work at westernization, does indeed get his chance to return to the theater in Czernowitz. However, far from romantically portraying Sender's debut as a great success, Franzos concentrates on the outer reality that made such an adventure a dangerous risk for anyone determined to abandon his entire past. On his way to Czernowitz, Sender does exactly this. Casting off his caftan, the traditional coat of the orthodox Jews, he dons Western clothes and cuts off his earlocks, symbolically erasing his background. However, nature, which plays such a devastating role in so many works from this part of the world, intervenes; the bridge across the Dniester is wiped away by an ice flow in front of his eyes and Sender never makes it to Czernowitz, which is the only place where he can survive after abandoning Barnow. The sole performance of his life with one of the many wandering theater groups of Galicia is announced for an unimaginably squalid inn-theater, a performance he agrees to in order to have something to eat. But even this event never occurs. Tracked down by his mother, and plagued by his tubercular coughs, Sender never does make it onto a stage and dies not long after, back in Barnow.

Der Pojaz is the story of a failed artist for whom, through no fault of his own other than the miserable conditions of his birth and his background, the doors to the world of German culture do not open. As we follow his desperate struggle, though, we are also following the manipulated argument of his creator that the Jews of Galicia, with whom he lived but did not communicate, were, to some extent, the masters of their own misery, and that the only road to improvement was a dangerous one that ran through Czernowitz on its way west. That this inevitably meant the abandonment of the orthodox Jewish culture and the private Jewish language, Yiddish, did not bother Franzos in the slightest. Quite the contrary, such a development was a precondition for the changes proposed by Franzos.

Sender Glatteis never even comes close to making the journey out of East Central Europe. In his role of prospective westernized Jew he never even makes it from Galicia across the Dniester to Czernowitz. But millions of his brethren from Eastern Europe did make it, and their stories have also provided literature with the stuff from which epic novels are made.

Joseph Roth's *Hiob* (*Job*, 1931) takes up the world of *Der Pojaz* and traces the disintegration of the shtetl Yiddish family by following the biographies of the children of the central figure, Mendel Singer, who eventually immigrates to New York. Like Tevye, he sees an apparently solid and proved communal structure collapse around him, even though he plays out his role in the approved traditional fashion. *Job* was published only a quarter-century after *Der Pojaz,* but the certainty of the disintegration of the world of the shtetl is a crucial factor in the creation of the major plot developments. Thus, the assimilation proposed by Franzos takes place with the children of Mendel Singer, but the conclusions drawn by Roth are not at all necessarily positive. Like Franzos, Roth sends his apprentices out into the world to test their expanded knowledge, but they confront a new environment that demands enormous cultural and linguistic sacrifices from its new citizens. This world leaves the aging Mendel Singer abandoned in a completely alien environment, and it does not necessarily lead to the happiness and success of his children.

Like Tevye, Mendel loses his offspring one by one, each to a disruptive new historical power against which Mendel's spiritual strength is impotent. Miriam, the only daughter, prefers the company of Cossacks to that of Jewish men and is expelled from the community when caught. A sexual rebel in the shtetl, Miriam fails to find security elsewhere and eventually ends up in a New York mental institution.

Schemarjah might be seen as a distant relative of the stock-exchange urban Jews of Kiev who so alientate Tevye, but the whole new element of the immigrant world of New York has been attached to his story. After illegally fleeing from Russia to America in order to escape impressment into the czarist armies of the First World War, Schemarjah becomes Sam, a figure out of Singer's world, although Roth's New York remains a cardboard caricature of Singer's. Sam's career among the Yankees is successful enough so that he can finance the immigration of Mendel to New York. Unlike Tevye, Mendel does undertake the trip but it is at the expense of all the ritualistic and cultural values that determined his life in the old world. Along the way Sam has abandoned language (Sam does his wheeling and dealing in English, while Mendel eventually ends up talking Yiddish only to a few old cronies), name (Schemarjah becomes Sam), religion and ritual (deals are made on the Sabbath), and to some extent morality in financial matters. Sam is not yet a Duddy Kravitz, but he has learned to compromise. Nevertheless, Sam does remain faithful to his family, and he ultimately gives the impression of a character not so much morally corrupt as forced to adapt to new-world codes in order to survive.

Jonas, the second brother, follows a different call, one that we will also find among the sons in Siegfried von Vegesack's *Die Baltische Tragödie* (The Baltic Tragedy, first published in 1935), the lure of soldierdom, camaraderie, booze, and uniforms. He is only all too happy to sacrifice himself to the army of the czar and let his brother go to America. Before Mendel's disbelieving eyes, Jonas turns into an enthusiastic reveling member of the military forces. Eventually he disappears on the battlefields of the First World War, and although his ultimate fate remains uncertain, it is absolutely certain that the Russian-speaking soldier will never be part of his old community again. This Russification of Jonas combines with the Americanization of Sam to remove two of the sons from the spiritual world of the father. Thus the pillars of the next generation of the communal structure are simply gone. One has completely lost all traces of his Jewish cultural background; the other carries on in the North American manner so often skewered by Singer. One follows the call of war, the other of real estate.

The fourth child, Menuchim, whose story serves as the linchpin of the plot of *Job*, is the artistic son, and thus the one whose situation most closely resembles that of Sender Glatteis. Unlike Franzos, Roth allows miracles to occur around Menuchim, who is abandoned during the immigration to America against the advice of the rabbi, who predicts a brilliant future for the apparently mute child. Eventually he will show up in New York as a conductor and carry out the wish of the lost Mendel to return to Europe. But Menuchim does not talk about returning to the shtetl, where, of course, there is no place for him, a Russianized musician who has been trained in St Petersburg.

While Roth (1894–1939) chose to describe the decline and fall of a Russian-Jewish family under historical and linguistic pressures peculiar to Russia at the time of the First World War and the Russian Revolution, his own biography is a good example of the path of German assimilation espoused by Franzos in *Der Pojaz*. Born in the largely Yiddish-speaking Austrian/Russian frontier city of Brody, through which a substantial percentage of the 2 million Jews fleeing Russia after 1881 passed on their way west, Roth preferred to suggest in his biographical statements that he came from the neighboring German colonial town of Schwaby. His family, the first of its line to switch from Yiddish to German, included brothers with such German names as Fritz and Max. Joseph himself attended the last German gymnasium in Brody before it was Polonized and essentially received the Western education that Sender Glatteis sought. At the first opportunity he made the journey Sender only dreamed of and moved west beyond Czernowitz to Vienna. Roth's success there as a journalist and novelist is reminiscent of Franzos's career. His alcoholic death in Parisian exile in the 1930s suggests the tragic fate of twentieth-century German-Jewish literature.

While Roth was drinking himself to death in Paris, Alexander Granach (1891–1945) was in Moscow on his long flight from the Nazis that would end in New York, where he would write an autobiographical novel, *Da geht ein Mensch: Roman eines Lebens* (Now There's a Real Person: The Novel of a Life, originally published in 1945). Granach continues the story of the proposed assimilation, begun by Franzos in a mood of optimism and carried on with doubt by Roth, to the overwhelmingly pessimistic moment when the Nazis assemble their forces to bring about the destruction of assimilated and non-assimilated Jews alike in the fire of racism. Granach's work is a unique mixture of carefully chosen episodes of his own life,[7] the imaginative interpretations of historical events by a tale-telling actor, and the ongoing story of Sender Glatteis, whose story Sasha Granach reads as a youth and determines to carry on to a successful conclusion. Granach narrates the adventures of a twentieth-century Pojaz on his picaresque journey from a Yiddish shtetl in Galicia to Berlin, the metropolis of the Weimar Republic. Granach was born shortly before the turn of the century in one of the endless poverty-stricken villages strung out along the railroad lines of East Galicia. His branch ran from Franzos's birthplace, Chortkov, to Granach's birthplace, a mainly Ukrainian settlement so small it made Chortkov or Brody seem like an urban centre. Thus, the child is born at a railway stop on a line of forgotten dreary settlements that lead only to a forgotten dreary city: 'The village of my birth is called Wierzbowce in Polish, Werbowitz in Yiddish, and Werbiwizi in Ukrainian. It is situated next to Seroka. Seroka is next to Czerniatyn. Czerniatyn is next to Horodenka. Horodenka is next to Gwozdziez. Gwozdziez is next to Kolomea. Kolomea is next to Stanislau. Stanislau is next to Lemberg, which has become world famous through the Hollywood film *Hotel City of Lemberg*.'[8]

The story of Granach's process of assimilation bears a remarkable similarity to those of the protagonists of the Sholom Aleichem, Franzos, and Roth novels, which portray the breakdown of a culture by focusing on a family in the process of disintegration. In each novel, members of a younger generation refuse to play the roles that have been preordained for them. These rebellions against a way of life find their outlet in solutions ranging from the military (Jonas) to the political (Pertchik), from the economic (Sam) to the sexual (Chava and Miriam), from the cultural (Sender Glatteis and Menuchim) to the linguistic (Sender, Sam, Jonas, Alexander, Menuchim, and presumably many others).

In Granach's family, the stories are perhaps less dramatic, but they still result in a disintegrating family structure by the time the ten-year-old Alexander moves with his parents, who plan to open a bakery, to the regional capital of Stanislau. Only the oldest brother,

Schachne Eber, stays behind in the shtetl. The second oldest, Abrum, 'went one day with travelers to Lemberg and stayed there' (*Da geht ein Mensch,* 102). Eventually he marries and impresses the father with stories of life in the big city. Jankel, the third brother, packs his bags one day and announces that he is going off in response to the request of a rich Hungarian to have Jankel make him laugh before he dies. Like Sam on his way to America, Jankel promises to return with his fortune and save the family from its endless poverty: 'And he took his bag and said he would be right back to say good by and disappeared. And he never came back and we never heard from him again, and if anyone asked about him we always said: "Oh Jankel he's very happy, he inherited millions in Hungary and he sits there dressed in silk and satin and counts the rooms full of gold, and when he's through with that, he'll come home and take all of us with him to make him happy." We waited our whole lives for Jankel; he never wrote and we never heard from him again' (pp. 101–2).

The fourth brother, Schmiel, 'had two passions: he loved to lie and he loved horses' (ibid., 28). One Friday after the horse market and an argument with his older brother about horses, as the family sits down to Sabbath supper, everyone realizes simultaneously that Shmiel's place is empty and that no one has seen him since market time. Schmiel's exit from the family is placed within the context of an insulting break with the traditions of the family and its religious context. Also, like Chava and Miriam, Granach's sister Rachel leaves home because of the scandal of her relationship to the gentile Ivan.

Thus by the time of the move from the village, 'the four oldest brothers were all gone: first Schmiel, Schachne Eber, the oldest, stayed in the village, Jankel went off to count his millions, and Abrum was married in Lemberg' (p. 102). Rachel comes back briefly, only to leave for good because of the incompatibility of her sexual preferences with family traditions. The oldest remaining brother, sixteen-year-old Leipzi, then also disappears one day without explanation to the father. 'He said to me he couldn't stand it at home any more, all the grown-up boys were leaving and he was leaving too ... When father came to work that night and noticed that Leipzi was gone, he just said, "My beloved children are like birds, as soon as they get feathers they fly away without saying a word to the father – maybe that's the way it has to be" ' (pp. 105–6). Only Schmiel returns briefly to the nest. At twenty-one he must report to the military authorities and shows up 'very elegantly dressed in a fine fur coat with Persian collar and with riding pants and brown boots like a cavalry officer' (p. 108). The most striking characteristic of his new personality is, however, that he claims no longer to be able to speak Yiddish, preferring instead what is clearly a broken German, and that he carries with him a thick wad of bills, which Rachel discovers to consist of play money good only for a glass of beer at an inn in Bohemian Mislowitz. Eventually, it is mentioned in a whimsical aside, Schmiel ends up in America, changes his name to Sam, raises very American children, and becomes a rich man. Thus the Sams of Roth and Granach cross paths in the money centers of New York.

Alexander, like Menuchim and Sender, takes the route of escape through the arts. Within that framework, his path is not that of the printed word or the concert hall, in which East European Jewish artists made and continue to make what is probably their most prominent contribution to Western culture, but like Sender through the much more difficult path of acting in the Western theater. For Granach, who is affected by his first theater visit (in Lemberg) in the same way as Sender was (in Czernowitz), the decision to pursue a career as an actor immediately confronts him with the linguistic problem with which Sender struggled for two years in the cloister library. The relatively small but absolutely crucial difference in pronunciation between his native Yiddish and the stage German he would be required to speak would have to be eliminated if he wished to become anything more than a member of one of the many wandering Yiddish theater groups.

Granach's arrival in Berlin as a seventeen-year-old baker's apprentice brings all these threads together. Fascinated by the theater he joins an amateur stage group and is 'discovered,' but is immediately advised that he must forget his Yiddish and spend his time learning to speak German. 'But you as an actor are too limited with Yiddish. Learn German and become a German actor. With that the man said something which had long been my secret wish' (p. 217).

Jessaya (as he is still identified in the program, the Germanized Alexander comes later) stumbles on a copy of *Der Pojaz*, and sees in the fictional life of Sender Glatteis his own real life. 'He had the same worries, the same plans, the same hopes, the same difficulties' (pp. 220–1). He also discovers through *Der Pojaz* the figure of Shylock and realizes that his Yiddish accent would probably turn this potentially tragic figure into an anti-Semitic parody. Granach finds a patron, who remains for Sender Glatteis unreachable across the Dniester. He is sent to a language teacher whose main job is to save an acting talent from the comedy of his accent, not to teach voice control or articulation:

> Without any ceremony I started in reciting my roles: Shylock, Franz Moor, Belsazar – I was all worked up and went full steam ahead. He looked at me, smiled at first – then he put his arm around me and gave me some encouragement, something about temperament-organ-feeling, and then he began to laugh like mad. I was hurt – he saw this, controlled himself, and explained I was a great talent, but the poor German language, and once again broke out in loud laughter, as if he had told a great joke. Then he wiped away his tears and said seriously: 'You see, a language you can learn, but the other things which you have, those you can't learn.' (Pp. 224–5)

Granach's two-year apprenticeship, like Sender's, is then devoted exclusively to changing him from a Yiddish comedian to a German actor. 'He forbade me to see countrymen, I was only allowed to speak German, and soon I began to think and dream in my new language' (p. 226). Even after his successful linguistic metamorphosis and his acceptance into the foremost German theater ensemble of Max Reinhardt, Granach cannot escape the cultural and linguistic prejudices of those who were not willing to grant any assimilatory rights to an East Galician Jew. Ironically it is one of his Jewish teachers at the Reinhardt school who particularly resents his attempt to become a German actor. In his description of this teacher, Granach calls to mind the story of his supposedly Germanized brother Schmiel upon his forced return to Galicia and characterizes the grotesque phenomenom of anti-Semitism in an East European Jew who parades his assimilation and is determined to keep other Jews from his background out of the German world:

Herr Held was from Hungary, certainly from somewhere near my Galician birthplace. He probably didn't feel exactly at home in his position. He dressed like a provincial gentleman who thinks they dress that way in Paris. Most of the time he wore a cutaway with white spats, glittering gloves, and a monocle attached to a string. He only wore this monocle when he was rehearsing minor actors for role changes or when he was teaching us. When he wanted to explain something, he always used himself as an example. He always spoke about himself to us. But when Reinhardt was there, he never wore his monocle and hardly ever his white spats, and he smiled subserviently at everything and looked like a whipped dog. He particularly had it in for me. And he imitated me, made fun of me. If he hadn't been a Jew himself, I would have assumed he was an anti-Semite. In fact he was a Jewish anti-Semite. They are the worst, for in their subconscious they transfer their own personal inadequacies onto their folk, try to desert through lackey assimilation, and get stuck somewhere in the middle and so hate themselves in their race. (Pp. 238–9)

Granach's novel of a life does not take its hero into the world of catastrophe. It allows him to complete the process dreamed about by his hero, Sender Glatteis, and to become a highly successful actor on the leading German stages of the Weimar Republic. In the novel there is no indication of the fate that would overwhelm the entire world of the assimilated Jews during the period of Nazi rule in Europe and put an end, not only to the world of Granach's birth, but to the illusion that there was a place for him in the culture of Germany as well. Granach thus is content to describe his voluntary abandonment of his native culture and language and his difficult struggle to gain acceptance in the German world. He prefers not to write about what had happened to both the German and Yiddish Jews by the time he sat down to write.

When Jessaya Granach was growing up in the center of Jewish Eastern Europe, the signs of the breakdown were everywhere. Children were refusing to live in the old way, families were immigrating to the new world, the political stability of the entire region was changing unalterably, and intellectuals were learning German. When Granach went back to East Galicia in 1915 as an Austrian soldier, he found his brother still carrying on in the original family hovel, raising children in the same way as if the world had not changed. The rest of the family was gone, except for the mother, who had remarried after the death of her husband. Granach's homeland had become a battleground fought over by the Russians and the Austrians, and the vagaries of victory and defeat were turning a poverty-stricken land into a wasteland. The Russians hanged the Jews in the shtetl as Austrian spies, he notes, and then the Austrians hanged the Ukrainians in the villages as Russian spies (p. 242).

When he returned to his home in 1918 at the end of the war, the old order was gone and he was given the choice of joining the army of the new and short-lived Ukrainian state or leaving for Germany. The relatively gentle transformation of the Yiddish world of Eastern Europe was evaporating and the violent conclusion was rapidly coalescing. When it had completed its process of fermentation and exploded into an orgy of violence in the next quarter-century, Alexander Granach was living out his last years in New York exile. He would not get the chance to see the results of the Second World War on his homeland, or to experience the fact that his brother and his mother and all the Tevyes who had made Eastern Europe their home for hundreds of years would find that they no longer had the luxury of refusing to adapt to the modern world. Nor would he be able to witness in the year of his death, 1945, the panic-stricken end of all things German in East Central Europe, and the virtual elimination of a language there that so few years before had seemed to offer the hope of entry into a modern culture.

In his book, the final chapter, however, is devoted to Shylock, whose life Granach joins to the story of the eternal wandering Jew, carrying his Star of David with him on the escape by boat to Holland, itself full of émigrés from the Spanish Inquisition, and then on eastward through Hungary, Romania, and finally East Galicia where the ancient patriarch begins a new family:

> The children grew up there on the black liquid soil and cultivated it, and they sowed and reaped and saw four seasons come and go and no longer heard the light, seductive music under the eternally blue southern skies. The slow, melancholy Slavic song became mixed with the Hebrew melo-

dies and the children grew up broad-shouldered, hard-working, and curious. Many, many generations came then, and in some of the descendants the desire for the west sometimes arose, and they once again began to wander further. (Pp. 417–18)

Granach's eternally wandering, eternally marked Shylock is not taken on the last journey of the East Galician Jews to the gas chambers of Auschwitz and Majdanek, nor does Granach wish to leave him in the city of exile in the new world where Granach wrote his book and where he died.

When Granach set down the finale of his tale of Shylock, he was avoiding the reality of the situation of the East European Jews, whose unjust burden his character was meant to carry with at least a portion of hope for the future. 'He was not yet the way I wanted him, but with the years it will get better' – the final sentence of *Da geht ein Mensch* suggests an optimistic future that, in fact, was being annihilated both in his East Galician birthplace and in Berlin at the moment he wrote it. At the same time, in the same exile city of New York, I.B. Singer was breaking out of the silence that had marked his first decade in the new world and was continuing his career as a Yiddish writer that had begun in Warsaw. Singer has found room for great sweeping epic novels such as *The Manor*, *The Slave*, or *The Family Moskat*, all set among East European Jews on their home turf. But through his masterful short stories of the Yiddish-speaking exiles in New York, Miami Beach, or Buenos Aires a fragmented claustrophobic world of isolated lost individuals gradually has grown into a unified whole. Hundreds of characters from scores of stories merge and form a summarizing overview of the fate of the lost old-world refugees in the new-world environment. For the most part, Singer has let his North American native English-speaking counterparts – Malamud, Bellow, Richler, Roth – continue the story into the next generation of English-speaking children and grandchildren. His is the story of the breakdown of the old culture as reflected in the fates of the emigrants.

In his best short stories, Singer is capable of suggesting within a very limited space the tragic and unbelievable fall of the East European Jews from a culture numbering in the many millions to a few pitiful remnants wandering the corridors of apartment hotels in alien cities. Their children usually have abandoned the old language, religion, and way of life and their grandchildren sometimes have disappeared from the face of their cultural and religious map. In a story such as 'Old Love,' which can stand for many others, all this takes place within the close confines of an apartment house in Miami Beach, the place of exile for the hero, Harry Bendiner, who has successfully escaped from the ravages of history in Eastern Europe only to spend his last years alone and friendless with nothing else to do but go to the bank every day to check his financial progress. Abandoned by his children and forgotten by his grandchildren, who have moved on to another country, Canada, and do not come back to find him (as do the children of Tevye and Mendel Singer), his fate suggests the final dissolution of the cultural and religious background of his youth.

The sudden mysterious reappearance of lost hopes in the form of a new female neighbor, who speaks his Yiddish dialect and suggests the possibility of marriage, can only end in catastrophe; she is transformed before his eyes into a death-like figure and later commits suicide. In the end, Singer's hero has an extraordinary thought, a last desperate idea for a quest that runs against the grain of his life. The second generation has completely failed: the abandonment of religion at the prospect of financial gain, which Tevye sees in the stock market of Kiev and which Duddy Kravitz epitomizes in the real estate market of Montreal, becomes the nightmare reality of New York and Miami. The fathers are abandoned by their children to a fate of inner exile. Harry Bendiner's last thought, however, skips this generation and leaps to the unknown daughter of his neighbor living in a tent in an unknown place and to the question of why she had 'run away so far' and whether she was 'endeavoring to find herself, or God.' In the final sentence of the story, Singer has Harry consider whether it would not be appropriate for him to find this out for himself and 'fly to British Columbia, find the young woman in the wilderness, comfort her, be a father to her, and perhaps try to meditate together with her on why a man is born and why he must die.'[9]

The journey from Tevye's shack in Ukraine to the wilderness tent of the girl in an unimaginably foreign land is at the same time the journey from the center of a culture that, for all its shortcomings in the financial sense, was a spiritual certainty to a mountainous empty world that is notable for its natural splendor but not for its community of orthodox Jews. For Harry Bendiner, it, too, will remain as much a dream as the return to the marriage canopy did. For the emigrant East European Jew, there can be neither Anatevka nor British Columbia, but only the sterile corridors of apartments behind whose doors the last Yiddish speakers spend their remaining empty days.

Others, of course, concentrated in their writings on the violence that accompanied the end of Yiddish and German in Eastern Europe. It is a different story, one that is seldom filled with the melancholic sadness that defines Granach's relationship to his past or with the irony of Singer; and it no longer displays the desire to fit into German culture so evident in the works of Granach, Franzos, Roth, and many other German-Jewish writers. It is to this story we now turn, first to look at the fate of the Germans in the Russian Revolution, then of the Jews in the Second World War and the Germans at the end of it. These stories add up to the most catastrophic loss of territory and influence in the history of Germanic languages and the virtually complete destruction of two vast Germanic-speaking worlds that, at the turn of the twentieth century, must have seemed solid and secure.

Chapter Three
Germans in a Russian War

The tears, which flowed at that time, are as uncountable as water drops after a storm. And the flood of world history poured over the German islands until there was nothing left of them.

Is.P. Klassen, *Die Insel Chortitza* (The Island of Chortitza)

When Alexander Granach returned to his homeland at the end of the First World War, he was confronted with a political change that would ultimately play a major role in determining the fate of both the German and Yiddish populations of Eastern Europe within a quarter-century. He was no longer within the boundaries of an empire with a sympathetic ruler in Vienna, but in a short-lived Ukrainian state that would quickly be swallowed up by the newly created Soviet Union. For Granach, the founders of the new Ukrainian Republic represented the polar opposites of the father-figure Emperor Franz Josef. 'He [the Ukrainian commander, a former regimental comrade of Granach] spoke about the Ukrainian government and the liberation of his people, about Hetman Petljura and General Wrangel. These names were symbols for both of us. He considered them the saviors of his people and I considered them the murderers of mine' (*Da geht ein Mensch:* 401). The establishment of comparatively small nationalistic states in East Central Europe brought home to the formerly Austrian Jews in this area that they had become even more exposed to the whims of the ruling majority; the imperial power in Vienna no longer could offer even its admittedly tentative protective hand. In the ensuing chaos in Ukraine, which was fought over by the Reds, the Whites, the Poles, the Ukrainian nationalists, and roving bands of anarchists, there was one uniting factor: the Jews were available for punishment. 'The Galician Jews, who had previously lived in peace, now realized that they had lost the war along with Austria. For both armies [Polish and Ukrainian in the described incident] had the same solution: By Zyda! Beat up the Jews!' (p. 404).

For the most part, the Germans of Eastern Europe did not share the 'indescribably miserable' life of the Jews, and thus they were not the most obvious and easily available target during the period of turmoil. The millions of Germans sharing the geographic space with the Yiddish speakers were by no means living the hand-to-mouth existence of Tevye, Mendel Singer, Sender Glatteis, or Alexander Granach. It was not only along the eastern Baltic, where the German population consisted mainly of landowners and aristocracy, that there were well-established, financially secure German settlements. From the Mennonite colonies near the Sea of Azov through the agricultural settlements along the Danube and on the Volga and in Poland, German communities usually provided a dramatic economic contrast to the Jewish shtetl.

In his tour of Galicia, Martin Pollack also came across the German settlements and his description is of a world that shares little of the uncertainties of the shtetl:

The villages were the backbone of Galician Germanness, which disappeared much more quickly in the assimilating cities. In the towns, which were usually isolated, it remained. The German colonists were farmers and hand workers, and they were industrious, sober, and pious. Life in the towns, well-organized and uncomplicated, revolved around three things: work, church, and inn. In exceptional cases the order might be reversed. The towns did not all look the same, but all were clean: straight swept streets, whitewashed houses, usually made of stone or brick, with flower gardens in front, next to the church on the square the linden tree and the inn.[1]

The description is of a settlement in Galicia, but it could just as well be of a Mennonite town in southeast Ukraine or a village on the Volga. Despite the security and tranquillity of such a scene, the events of the war and the Russian Revolution were about to make absolute chaos out of order and terror out of peacefulness. Within a matter of months, the German speakers from Latvia through the Volga River to the Sea of Azov would find themselves in much the same precarious position vis-à-vis their majority-group neighbors as did the Yiddish speakers.

In the case of the Germans, the reasons for this antagonism were surely more economic, social, and political than religious (although such discrimination may have played a part in the case of certain Protestant sects), but the results were much the same. One decade after the end of the war, the Germans could recognize themselves as pariahs in the Soviet Union and in the new Baltic States, and had begun to draw the consequences. By 1929, approximately one-quarter of the Mennonite population of Russia had left for the Americas, and one-half of the Baltic Germans for Germany or the new world.

Unlike the Jews, the Germans found this hostility to be, for the most part, a new experience. It swept across a naively secure population during the First World War, when the German cultural and linguistic homeland became the enemy of the Russian political homeland. Thus, the fate of the Russo-Germans in the First World War may be seen as establishing a pattern that would be repeated for all Germans outside the German-language states at the end of the Second World War. In a military sense, much the same situation was in effect in 1918 for the Russo-Germans as would be in 1942 for virtually all 'Volksdeutsche.' German or Austrian troops occupied such areas as Latvia and Ukraine and gave the ethnic Germans the opportunity to welcome them as rescuers from anti-German outbreaks. Within a very short time, the German or Austrian troops were forced to retreat, thus leaving the resident Germans to try to deal with a majority population that considered them to be traitors.

The chaos accompanying the transfer of power from a czarist regime, which had already begun to threaten the sources of livelihood and power of its German citizens, to a Bolshevik regime, which considered wealthy German farmers and landowners to be class enemies, placed the German population in situations where it could not help but antagonize various warring forces. These forces drew at least a substantial amount of their power from nationalist energies that made Yiddish or German ethnic or linguistic input problematic at best. Already in the late nineteenth century, czarist Russia had begun to erode seriously the rights and privileges of its German population. At the onset of the First World War, government decree forbade the public use of German; and shortly thereafter 'land liquidation laws' were declared, aimed at dispossessing 'alien' Germans of prosperous lands. For such groups as the agriculturally based Mennonites of southern Ukraine, these declarations should have been reason enough to reconsider their future in a land into which they had been invited a century and a half before. But wartime was chaotic and neither law was ever enforced on a large scale.

For historians and for creative writers, the fate of German and Yiddish speakers of Eastern Europe in the First World War has been completely overshadowed by the extraordinary events involving these populations as a result of the Second World War. For the most part, until the end of the nineteenth century, the German populations of Russia had prospered within the framework of German language and culture for hundreds of years without any overwhelming conflicts with the czarist regime with regard to ethnic disputes. Despite outward signs of great potential political disrupture, particularly during the abortive uprising of 1905, they were completely unprepared for a situation that pushed them to the edge of cultural and personal destruction by 1919.

As we have seen, the Baltic Germans were urban merchants or rural aristocratic landowners who had gathered their lands in the wake of the conquests of the Teutonic Order on the Baltic coast north of Lithuania in the Middle Ages. Thus, in the Baltic states, with relatively small Russian populations, the Germans were at the top of the social order, and the Latvians and Estonians, who often worked as peasants on German land, were at the bottom. In these areas, the Germans filled a role similar to that of the Russian aristocracy in the rest of czarist Russia, and it should be no great surprise that they found themselves treated in a similar manner when the Bolshevik Revolution arrived. However, their position was particularly exposed because of their German cultural and linguistic background, which made them an easily identified minority. Perhaps it is also no surprise that the person who would write the most imposing epic work about the Germans in Russia during the Russian Revolution was a Baltic-German product of a society with a long-established school system and university and with relatively close ties to a cultural fatherland that was only a short boat ride away.

Siegfried von Vegesack's *Die Baltische Tragödie* (The Baltic Tragedy, 1935) was first published just after the rise to power of the Nazis and tells a story of the 'tragic' destruction of a long-established German culture in Eastern Europe that could easily fit into the simplified version of Eastern European history preferred by the Nazis. However, it differs fundamentally from the usual fictional accounts of German/East European relations from this period by presenting a tragedy in which guilt and innocence are not easily assigned and are certainly not simply drawn along ethnic and cultural lines. While related to the 'Heimatromane,' which attempt to conjure up the idyllic view of a lost homeland, von Vegesack's novel also in many ways represents an early example of what Horst Bienek would call 'kritischer Heimatroman' ('critical novel of the homeland')[2] in describing his fictional account of the destruction of German Silesia during the Second World War.

Die Baltische Tragödie covers the last thirty years in the life of one of the landholding baronial German families in czarist Latvia and depicts its utter destruction during the Russian Revolution. Because it covers the same historical period as the Tevye stories, *Job*, and *Da geht ein Mensch*, it offers an interesting comparison to the better-known accounts of the difficulties of the Yiddish speakers in Russia during these times. Like the authors of these other tales, von Vegesack forms his novel of decline and fall around the fates of children, who move quickly from a world of apparent stability to one of great turmoil and who witness in the process the splintering of the family and the home. Like Granach, von Vegesack allows this world to unfold gradually through the eyes of a surprised child who grows into a man at the same time that his idyllic childhood world is coming to a violent historical end. The strength of such a narrative approach is underlined in all these novels precisely because the psychological exit of the child from a world of security into a world of anxiety is mirrored by a surrounding historical period in which the environment of the child has drastically shifted from safety to danger. The inner development of the child thus finds a companion in the outer world and the converging narrative lines join and support each other.

In *Blumbergshof*, the first of the three books making up the Baltic saga and at the same time the name of the family manor, Aurel, the central figure of the novel, opens his eyes to view a slumbering world of tranquillity. 'In the beginning was a great, soft darkness, a comfortable warmth and absolute security.'[3] Aurel's childhood perspective is maintained until flashes of disorder threaten his understanding of the world as a place of sanctuary. At the same time, von Vegesack portrays a developing personality who is open to many influences, capable of both being amazed by the limitless power of his father and confused by the occasional misuse of that power on the Latvian peasants, who serve as Aurel's protectors and friends. Thus, his apparently unendingly secure world begins to crumble when his personal nurse, Mila, his angel against the terrors of the night, disappears one day without explanation. Years later, in the midst of the anarchy of the war, he will meet her again, old and broken, and realize without surprise that she had been sent away by his all-powerful father because of an unwanted love affair. Between these two events, which provide the framework for total cultural dissolution, the child Aurel turns into the confused youth and the stunned young man who finds the reasons for the tragedy on all sides, including those of the Germans and his own family.

Aurel's journey into the world is also the journey out of Blumbergshof, his elegant home in the forest close to the Estonian frontier. By concentrating the reader's attention on the child's growing awareness of the world around him, the author also succeeds in relating the long history that leads to the building of Blumbergshof and other German estates, like his uncle's 'Altschwanensee,' where Aurel experiences first love and first death. Through the child's eyes we witness both the vestiges of power still remaining to the Baltic Germans at the turn of the twentieth century and its misuse. Through the youth's eyes we experience the scenes that led him to conclude that the Germans were on a sinking ship (the metaphor Aurel himself uses in the final pages as he sails off to Germany) and that the period of baronial rule was coming to an end, even in this easternmost outpost of Western Europe, even in the prosperous German community and the apparently solid religious and educational system in Riga and Dorpat. As he looks back, Aurel realizes that he is losing a deep spiritual bond to a landscape that is both magnificent and threatening, containing not only large animals and wild forest-rimmed lakes, but also wolfmen and icy death traps.

This spiritual relationship between the individual and the surrounding environment, a quintessentially German Romantic relationship, is missing from Yiddish works. In the shtetls of Galicia and Ukraine there was little time in the daily struggle for survival for contemplating the wonders of nature, nor was there a literary or cultural tradition that suggested it. But it is one of the essential elements of the German novels of Eastern Europe, particularly if they are read today in the confines of small national states in which the woods are dying and the lakes are surrounded by holiday apartments. The world in which Aurel grows up (or, to use another example, Zygmunt Rogalla in Siegfried Lenz's *Heimatmuseum* [translated as *The Heritage*]) still contains the myth of a romanticized nature, alive and embracing, that contemporary Germans have had removed from their lives, but continue to long to have conjured up for them. In the hunter brothers of Aurel, who spend their youth in search of legendary stags, we find perhaps the last German fictional characters who can still function in the same way as the Romantic figures who dominate the German forests of the nineteenth century. Their closest relatives in the contemporary world of German creative arts are more likely to be found wandering the open spaces of the Americas than any German forest of postwar Europe.

Aurel himself develops into an observer rather than a participant in the old world of his brothers, his father, and his uncles. *Die Baltische Tragödie* is much more than just a sentimental conjuring up of a lost world precisely because it is through the questioning of Aurel – and not through his brothers, who accept their given roles and play them to the end – that we experience the world. Eventually we will come to follow the fates of these brothers, just as we did the children of the shtetl, and in the process we also witness the shattering of a family-structured culture. But we always see through the eyes of Aurel, the one figure who responds to the cross-currents of social change, even when they begin to move against his own culture.

For the Baltic Germans, the route to disintegration was determined more substantially by historical developments than by the inner pressures that destroy Tevye's family. Nevertheless, Aurel, too, observes a family that is to some extent in the process of abandoning the tight structure that had dominated the conservative community of the Baltic Germans for centuries. One of his older brothers, Reinhard, is like Alexander Granach's older brother, interested only in improving the agriculture of the homestead; the second, Balthasar, moves on to take a leading role in the urban community; and the third, Christof, like Mendel Singer's son Jonas, is interested only in the military, earning the George's Cross fighting for the Russian czar and then the Iron Cross fighting for the German army during its 1919 counterattack against the Bolsheviks. In the war between the Russians and the Germans, in which the minority Baltic German community is eventually squeezed into submission, he is certain of his loyalties – first, to the czar, to whom he has sworn an oath of allegiance, and then, upon the downfall of the czar in the revolution of 1917, to the Germans, to whom he owes his cultural and linguistic inheritance.

The entrance of the child Aurel into the world of confusion and instability occurs, however, not so much as a result of the splintering of the family, but because of the political events of Russia between the turn of the century and 1920. These events make it impossible for the minority Germans, despite their money and power, to maintain their long-established positions in the face of growing pressures from both the majority Latvian population and the Russian political rulers. What Granach determines to be the only common cause of the enemy troops ('Beat up the Jews') can also be said to be the shared goal of the marauding armies that tried to gain control of the Baltic in the course of the First World War ('Beat up the Germans'). The brief excursion of the German army led to the temporary security of the German populations, but the retaliation that followed the withdrawal of those German troops brought about the short-term decimation, and eventually permanent elimination, of the German population.

For the Baltic Germans of the countryside, apparently secure in their wealth and power, the attempted revolution of 1905, which Aurel experiences as a schoolboy, involves an outbreak of anarchy, which they had never considered remotely possible. It is followed not by an attempt to come to grips with a shifting social order, but by an illusory withdrawal into the old way of life. For Aurel, the violent confusion of adolescence and first love are thus played out against a background of historical disorder that settles down into a nervous order.

Aurel experiences at first hand the precarious and ultimately paradoxical position of the Baltic Germans during the general strike of 1905 in Riga, where he has been sent to the German school. The building is surrounded by Latvian students, who threaten any German attempting to enter. With a mixture of relief and shame Aurel, who has been disciplined for refusing to speak Russian, sees that czarist troops with drawn bayonets are protecting the German students. Upon the director's announcement that he has promised the revolutionaries that he will close the school, the German students spontaneously sing the czarist Russian anthem as a sign of protest. For the moment, the Latvians are the more imminent threat to the security of the Germans, but in the course of the next ten years, Aurel will experience pressure from all sides.

Torn between Russian, Latvian, and German demands, Aurel understands the justice of each of the arguments and wants nothing to do with the position of some members of his own family, who consider a German ruling class to be a given right. Unlike his brother Christof, who has sworn an oath to the Russian czar determining his course of action, Aurel wavers between loyalty to Latvians, whom he recognizes to be an unjustly repressed underclass, to Russians, who initially represent the only protective force for the Germans against Latvian revolutionaries, and to his own culture, family, and language, which he recognizes to be incapable of changing. Ultimately his struggle to maintain a fair position and to try to help set up a governing system that has room for all native cultures runs into the same impossible obstacles that changed the world of the East European Jews – the rejection by the majority of the minority on purely ethnic grounds. Eventually he realizes the futility of his struggle as it becomes impossible to distinguish whether it is the Whites, the Reds, the Latvian nationalists, or anarchists who are burning and looting the German holdings. Like the Jews of Ukraine and Galicia, the Germans of the Baltic would eventually become moving targets for the entire surrounding community.

In the short term the revolution of 1905 was unsuccessful, but in the long term it helped to mold a militant nationalist movement that would eventually make the majority Latvian population rulers of an independent state that would last barely twenty years. For the rich German landowners in the countryside, the ripples of the mainly urban uprisings were far-reaching enough that, for the first time, the social system of German landowners and Latvian peasants was rocked by scattered outbreaks of class warfare. In the course of the revolutionary activities of 1905 in the Baltic provinces, 184 German estate houses were burned down and 88 Germans killed.[4] Blumbergshof remains unscathed, although Aurel's second home at Altschwanensee, as well as those of neighbors, comes under violent attack.

Von Vegesack's trilogy has three stations on the road to destruction. They also mark the three main landmarks on Aurel's journey into a maturity that he will have to experience somewhere else. *Blumbergshof* depicts the magical illusion of security in the midst of a peaceful and magnificent nature and corresponds to the child's naive view of the world. The second section, *Heer ohne Herren* (Army without Leaders), focuses on the first major threat to this apparent stability in 1905 and is witnessed by Aurel in the midst of adolescence. Afterwards Aurel learns to distinguish between armed conflict in an urban revolution and anarchic terrorism in his rural idyll where the landholders band together in self-defense groups in the attempt to protect each other against marauding mobs in an area where the Russian military does not have the troops to offer stability.

The third book, *Totentanz in Livland* (The Baltic Dance of Death), which describes Aurel's experience during the successful Russian Revolution a decade later, is the major link between this novel and those describing the end of the Germans and Jews in the rest of Eastern Europe as a result of the Second World War. During the years after 1905, Aurel remains in the splendid isolation that had been afforded Blumbergshof and the Baltic German community. Although tempted by arguments from all sides on where to experience his first adult years, he chooses the traditional path of the Baltic German aristocracy and spends his last potentially constructive years in his homeland, desperately (and ultimately successfully) trying to gain entrance into Livlonia, the German fraternity at Dorpat. Upon completing his schooling, he does not take the advice of Uncle Jegor and go to St Petersburg for advanced study, but to a German university, where he never feels quite at home.

In the decade before the First World War, attempts were actually finally being made by the Baltic Germans to rectify some of the most basic injustices that had always determined the fate of the Latvians. These injustices had been aggravated by the force by which the czarist troops had eventually put down the uprisings of 1905 with the execution of over 900 Balts and the deportation to Siberia of thousands more, as well as by the burning of far more homesteads than had been accomplished by the revolutionaries.[5] Baltic-German attempts to effect some kind of Latvian and Estonian input into regional government affairs were refused by Russian authorities. In any case, it was too late to abort the growth of Baltic nationalism, which had been given a great burst of energy by the events of 1905. Nationalism would eventually find its easiest target among the native Baltic Germans, as there were few Russians actually living in the Baltic states. In the second book of von Vegesack's novel, Balthasar, who hires a national German administrator because he thinks that 'all Latvians are crooks' (p. 253), finds an announcement nailed to a tree during the 1905 uprising. 'We have two enemies, against whom we must fight: the Russian government and the German landowners' (p. 255), it proclaims. When the Russian government finally did fall, only the Germans were left to be enemies.

The Baltic dance of death puts an end to Aurel's illusory careless student years. It forces him into the world as an active participant in the apocalypse that surrounded the entire population of the Baltic states in the framework of the First World War and the Russian

Revolution. In its broadest sense, the Bolshevik Revolution has a certain familiarity for Westerners because of Russian expressionist films (particularly those by Sergei Eisenstein) and some of the major works of Russian literature; but this revolution has not played a large role in the histories of Western literature. For the Germans caught up in it, however, it was the event after which nothing would or could be the same.

For the Germans of Czechoslovakia, Poland, Hungary, and Yugoslavia, the cataclysm would come at the end of the Second World War, first through the violence of military engagement, and then through expulsion. For the Germans of Russia, however, the apocalypse began in 1918 and 1919. In von Vegesack's novel, the fates of the four brothers in regard to the events surrounding the establishment of the independent state of Latvia at the end of the war represent a death knell for the world in which young Aurel has grown up: death on the battlefield (Christof), execution by the Bolsheviks (Balthasar), continued cultivation of the land in a shack on a tiny portion of the former holdings (Reinhard), and exile (Aurel). History had thus removed the possibility of a continuing, if reduced, place for the Germans in the new Latvia. Von Vegesack allows this idea to be placed before Aurel. It comes through the mouth of the old Latvian servant, Janz, who had helped save the family by smuggling food to them during the days of starvation following the withdrawal of German forces. Janz gives his lesson to Aurel in a physical setting that excludes outsiders and strips away formal differences, in the traditional Baltic steam bath:

> Laughing Janz started talking about the time that a couple of German soldiers came into the steam bath – but they just collapsed on the floor moaning and got out as fast as they could. 'Yes, the Germans can do everything and make everything,' Janz went on thinking out loud ... 'Airships, wagons without horses, and lamps without oil. They say they even invented the ape! But a steam bath? With a real steam bath we could get rid of them all!' Janz broke into a loud laugh and showed his white teeth. 'And do you want them to leave so that the Russians can come back?' Aurel asked. Janz hesitated. Then he said softly, almost to himself: 'Who needs Russians? Who needs Germans? Everyone should

stay where he's at home. God gave him a home to live in, and that's where he should stay. Who needs wars? Who needs marching? If I had stayed home, I'd still have my leg. Now it's rotting away in some strange land.' Janz raised the red stump of his leg and tapped on it nervously. 'And me?' Aurel asked after a while, 'I also happen to be German – should I leave too?' 'No,' Janz looked up and shook his head. 'You were born here, and this is your home' ... And there they lay, two naked people. Not German, not Latvian, not master and servant – two people, as God had once made them. In the smoky narrow bathhouse the glass wall had finally disappeared. (*Die Baltische Tragödie*, 442)

In this scene, von Vegesack both recognizes the existence of the invisible wall between the Germans and the Latvians and limits its successful removal to the confines of the steam bath. The utopian vision of an egalitarian future for all native groups remains a chimera in the face of history. The ultimate strength of this novel lies in von Vegesack's presentation of a Baltic homeland populated by heroic Latvians and bigoted Germans, and vice-versa, with Russian- and German-oriented uncles, with brutal Russians, Latvians, and Germans. In short, he has created a panoramic epic of the downfall and eradication of his culture by focusing on a wide range of people who all eventually become helpless pawns of overwhelming historical forces. Under such conditions, it makes little difference how the individual acts. What matters is only that he belongs to a minority group, and that that minority group will be eliminated as a whole.

For the Baltic Germans, the antagonistic relationship to the majority Latvians before the First World War represented only a foretaste of the events to follow. In Aurel's family, it makes, in the final analysis, absolutely no difference what position the individual took vis-à-vis the surrounding cultures. All that matters is that the individual is considered to be a German. Thus, the ultra-nationalistic German Balthasar (one is tempted to suggest proto-Nazi) is executed in the same process that eliminates the Russophile Uncle Jegor. Reinhard, who takes no interest and plays no role in the politics and history unfolding around him, is economically destroyed by the land-reallocation program of the new Latvian government: his formerly prosperous holdings are ruined by new owners inexperienced and uninterested in the workings of a modern farm. His forest is chopped down before it is harvestable; his land, reclaimed in endless toil from an apparently unreclaimable moor, is allowed to return to its original unproductive condition. Reinhard, who had always refused to accept Balthasar's demand that he hire German managers and import German colonists (another example of Balthasar functioning as a precursor of Nazi land policies in Eastern Europe), is almost as hated by the new rulers as is Balthasar. Although he is not executed, he is condemned to the poverty that was left to many of the Germans who did not leave the Baltic with Aurel after 1919. With the Stalin-Hitler non-aggression pact of 1939, which included a provision for the forced evacuation of the Baltic Germans into the German Empire, this number was reduced to close to zero. Thus Latvia and Estonia became the first states of Eastern Europe to have their German populations expelled and would be identified only a short time later as the first Nazi provinces to be 'judenrein' ('free of Jews'). For the rest of the Germans in the European Soviet Union, this expulsion (to Central Asia and Siberia) would occur almost immediately thereafter, when the Nazis invaded the Soviet Union.

Von Vegesack's Baltic tragedy, like Granach's Galician one, stops with the establishment of the new independent state, in this case Latvia, which twenty years later would be swallowed up by the Soviet Union. Except for Reinhard, who faces a very insecure future on his tiny plot of land, Aurel's immediate family has been eradicated. Aurel, on the bow of a boat heading out from the Latvian Republic on its way to the Weimar Republic, faces the uncertainties that have been the rule rather than the exception for those Germans of Eastern Europe who have been forced to seek refuge in the west, where a different culture speaks the same language:

> A piece of earth, not much, just a little piece. A crazy wish. As crazy as this whole trip – without a goal, a plan, a direction. Nobody knows you, no one is expecting you. The few people you briefly knew before the war are all either dead or God knows where ... You could just as easily immigrate to Brazil or Africa: this land that lies there before your eyes now will be just as foreign to you. A thin strip on the horizon appears, a blue strip of woods, a golden strip of sand. (P. 509)

Although it is true that *Die Baltische Tragödie* ends with an absolutely uncharacteristic outburst of German nationalistic patriotism on the part of Aurel ('It seemed to Aurel that he was returning home after centuries of wandering, as if, strong and hard, the arms of a mother embraced him' [p. 510]), it is certainly not the sentiment that dominates this novel. (One is tempted to speculate that the final page might have been added to increase the chances of publication in Nazi Germany.) For there is a great deal in this novel that certainly would not have pleased the Nazis: the martyrdom of Janz, who is eventually murdered because he helped his German masters; the injustice done to the servant Mila, who receives an apology from the mother in the last scene in Latvia for having had her life destroyed twenty years before at the whim of the master; the distrust of Reinhard, who wants nothing to do with the foreign Germans, who come to run farms more efficiently and at the same time destroy the basis of trust with the native Balts; the musings of Uncle Jegor, who sees the future in St Petersburg and whose daughter takes part in the Bolshevik Revolution (she is incapable of saving him from execution); and, finally, the conclusions of Aurel himself, who only chooses to join the German side when it is no longer possible for the various ethnic groups to live on the same piece of land without the outside influences that ultimately allow only one group to rule. (The contemporary independence movements in the three Soviet Baltic republics make it quite clear that by the 1990s the Russians, once a very small minority in this area and now the majority population of Riga, have replaced the Germans as the target of ethnic resentment in the Baltic peoples.) Before the violent destruction of his family, his home, and his culture, Aurel resists arguments suggesting that the Germans should fight with the Russian nobility to maintain their given role as rulers vis-à-vis the majority population:

Erhard laughed and blew smoke rings in the air ... 'And Russia will swallow us up some day. Just look at the map: we are not even the little finger on this big fist – and even on this finger we're only the fingernail, the thin upper layer, all the meat underneath is Latvian and Estonian. It's not against the Russians, but against the masses underneath us that we must fight, maintain our position as masters together with the Russian nobility. These Latvians are nothing but a pack, like every other mass!' Aurel didn't know what to answer, but darkly he felt there was a contradiction: were Janz, Mickel, Indrik, and old Marz Andris, Jekab, and Karel, were all the Latvian peasants that he knew really a pack? And the only Russian whom he loved, Herr Bjelinski, precisely that Russian was fighting against the czar for the people. Should one really be fighting instead with the czar against the people? (P. 185)

After 1917, the question Aurel asks himself is superfluous. The position of the individual becomes completely inconsequential in a society in the midst of class and ethnic warfare. In both cases, the Baltic Germans were on the wrong side of the flow of history. They ultimately were left with no chance to become part of a new society, which could be run along the lines of Janz's suggestion: Latvia as a homeland for all its natives, whatever their ethnic background might be. It was precisely this idea that was being eliminated throughout East Central Europe as a result of the Treaty of Versailles. The aristocratic empires, which had a certain tolerance for their minority cultures, even if it was not enough tolerance to prevent uprisings, were replaced by a series of smaller national states in which the majority language and culture was the dominating concern for the drawers of boundaries. As a result, all across East Central Europe, large minority cultures, languages, and religions were left stranded in nationalistically inclined political states that basically had little interest in the rights of their minorities.

For the Germans in Russia and the formerly Russian-ruled Baltic states, the new political situation also brought with it a revolutionary change in the economic and class structure that made them outsiders both ethnically and socially.[6] Those who chose to stay would pay the economic and often personal consequences of that decision for a quarter-century before the dynamics of the Second World War forced them west into the German Empire (in the case of the Baltic Germans) or drove them far to the east into the heart of the Asian Soviet Union (in the case of the Volga Germans). The dramatic and catastrophic fall of the Russo-Germans has not provided the historical backdrop for major works of German-language fiction, as has the fall of the Baltic-Germans or of the Russian Yiddish-speaking Jews. However, in Dietrich Neufeld's secret journal, *Ein Tagebuch aus dem Reiche des Totentanzes* (Emden, 1921), translated as *A Russian Dance of Death*, describing the fate of the Mennonite communities of Ukraine, there is an intensity and immediacy in the face of total chaos and violence which forge a powerful link to *Totentanz in Livland*.

Like von Vegesack, Neufeld chooses the image of the dance of death as a title, because for the ethnic Germans of Russia the years of revolution brought a succession of military forces, each of which found them to be an easily exploitable prey. The marauders changed, but the once-flourishing Mennonite villages provided them all with foodstuffs until the bounty had disappeared, and often with victims as well for violent acts of exploitation and repression. Neufeld's dance of death takes place in the same Ukraine that Sasha Granach left forever at the end of the war because as a Jew and an Austrian he could sense that he had no future in an independent Ukraine. Granach himself did not linger to watch the carnage as that state was forcibly annexed by the Soviet Union.

Like the Baltic Germans and the Volga Germans, the Mennonites had been citizens of Russia for many generations while remaining culturally and linguistically German. By the beginning of the twentieth century the Mennonites had colonized successfully large areas of southern Ukraine. They had become prosperous enough to establish daughter colonies in an ever-widening geographical area. For them, the first two decades of the twentieth century brought about the swift and stunning move from idyll to calamity. For the mother colony of Molotschna as for Blumbergshof, the violent catastrophe of the First World War and the Russian Revolution can be seen, in retrospect, to not have been quite as surprising as the inhabitants experienced it.

Czarist Russia, in its search for scapegoats in the wake of the political upheavals of 1905, had already made the situation for the Germans, as well as for the Jews, far more precarious than they assessed it to be. Thus, both Tevye's and Aurel's families are dumbfounded when the violence of the uprisings aims so carefully at them even though general political developments over the previous half-century had already convinced millions of Jews to immigrate to the new world, and had removed many of the privileges that the Baltic Germans had enjoyed for centuries. For the Molotschna Mennonites the shock seems to have been even deeper. Far more economically secure than the Jews, and far more isolated than the Baltic Germans, the Mennonites entered the period of the First World War confident and prosperous. After over a century of hard work and gained experience they had turned the fertile but uncultivated lands of southern Ukraine into bountiful farming country. That had been their goal, and it had finally been achieved. Nothing could have been further from their mind than the idea that, within five years, this entire work would be almost completely destroyed, nor that, within thirty years, there would hardly be a trace of the Mennonite colonies left in the European Soviet Union, and that the surviving population would be scattered throughout the world. In his introduction to *The Russian Dance of Death*, Al Reimer describes the naïveté of the community as the First World War broke out:

> Living in the rich heartland of Ukraine, the Mennonites were among the first to feel the daggers of revolution and counter-revolution. Yet who could have foreseen, in the golden decades before 1914, that these devout, hardworking, and self-sufficient colonists would suffer such a horrendous fate? Certainly they themselves had no inkling and they remained blissfully unresponsive to the danger signals around them. Complacent, self-centered, and politically uninvolved, they were not unduly alarmed when World War I broke out. They believed that their village world was too solid and remote to be disturbed.[7]

In their land-settlement documents, the pacifist Mennonites had been granted freedom from military service, but nevertheless loyally served the czar in the First World War in noncombatant roles. Unaccustomed to the violence (which had often accompanied Jewish life in Russia), they were completely unprepared for military defense (the creation of defense corps in some of the Mennonite villages remains a thorny issue for the pacifist Mennonites to the present day). Unlike the Baltic Germans, who eventually managed to raise a small but surprisingly effective army that in 1919 actually counterattacked into Russia, they were sitting ducks for the bands of Reds and Whites, as well as for the anarchists and Ukrainian nationalists who roamed the area in the years following the revolution.

Part of the naïveté of the Mennonites was shown in their inability to react consequentially to the growing evidence of the precarious position of the Germans in Russia at the outbreak of the war. Dietrich Neufeld's family encounters the same proofs of anti-German sentiment as does Aurel's. The legal attack on the use of German, which leads Aurel into a confrontation with his schoolteachers, also brings the Mennonite mill owner John Berg and his miller two and a half years in Siberia (*A Russian Dance of Death*, 78–9). The land-liquidation laws of December 1915, which required all property owners of German ethnic background to sell their holdings within eight months or be sent to Siberia, were met by a Mennonite attempt to establish a Dutch rather than a German ethnic ancestry. These lands were not lost because by 1917 the czarist government had more pressing problems at hand. In view of the events that immediately followed, the attempt by prosperous German-speaking farmers to escape a Draconian punishment by claiming Dutch ancestry takes on almost a macabre tone. When armed marauders finally entered the Mennonite colonies in late 1919, there would not be the slightest interest in their potential Dutch ethnic background.

As in the Baltic, the long-term implications of the revolution of 1917 for the German colonists were not immediately clear. Certain aspects of the revolution, such as the abolition of the land-liquidation acts, were clearly favorable to the Germans. The arrival of the Bolsheviks in the Mennonite communities brought with it a serious upheaval of the old ordered way of life, as well as a regular 'requisitioning' of supplies that seriously affected the economic stability of the colony, but it did not yet bring the dance of death. Before that arrived – Dietrich Neufeld's journal begins on 19 September 1919 – events had happened that would ultimately seal the fate of the Germans in Russia.

In the spring of 1918, as a result of the treaty of Brest-Litovsk, the German army occupied Ukraine. The reaction of the German Mennonite population was predictable, and exactly the same as in the Baltic. The German troops were the rescuers of the German populations from the Bolsheviks, and with their own welcome of the invading German army, the Mennonites had ensured themselves of the enmity of all their non-German neighbors. By the fall, the German army, having helped to establish a friendly Ukrainian government, withdrew, and the Mennonite settlers who had welcomed them were then open to the various armies and governments that fought over Ukraine for the next several years, before the Red Army finally gained control.

Dietrich Neufeld's dance of death thus begins in the year when the true terror began and moves, like Aurel's, from serenity to catastrophe. The immediacy of the diary form gives Neufeld's version more eruptive power than the Baltic dance of death, where the violence gradually infiltrates an intact world of long-familiar characters and landscape. Aurel's world comes to an end as carefully established environments are overwhelmed and annihilated by political and historical developments, whose seeds Aurel had vaguely recognized since his childhood. In *Die Baltische Tragödie* a horrified Aurel sees just how terrifying the revenge would be when the majority was finally in a position to assert its power over the minority, formerly privileged, class. The resonance of far-off violence is noted in Blumbergshof, but the approach of destruction is presented as only gradually comprehensible. A secure world slowly grasps its insecurity as neighbors and relatives meet fates that become more and more brutal, until the dance of death begins. It is a long journey, although short in years, that Aurel makes from the first meeting with a poacher in the family forest, through the encounters with drunken mobs controlling the roads and threatening Blumbergshof, to the mass execution of the leaders of the German community in Riga.

Dietrich Neufeld's diary does not have room for such unfolding. As a student in Germany, the Ukrainian-born Neufeld had been caught by the war and interred as an enemy alien. In a situation still surprisingly familiar, an East European German found that he was unwanted in Western Europe because of his East European roots and in Eastern Europe because of his West European roots. Returning to Ukraine at the end of the war in September 1919, Dietrich Neufeld took up his new position as a schoolteacher in Chortitza on the Dnieper River somewhat north of the main Molotschna Mennonite settlement near the Sea of Azov. He had only a few days to savor his new location. In the very first diary entry he allowed himself the luxury of viewing the kind of idyll that also characterizes Aurel's childhood years at Blumbergshof:

September 15, 1919 I have lived here on the banks of the Dnieper for five days now. From our beautiful, sunny house high up on a slope I look down over the peaceful settlement. It lies below me as if it had been deposited there by the calm Dnieper water, which flows down from the northwestern plains beyond which lie the distant Germanic lands from whence these settlers came to Russia. The spiritual ties with those ancestral lands remain unbroken, although the physical separation took place many years ago ... As I look along the valley below I can see, in addition to the fine farmsteads, half-a-dozen steam flourmills, several farm implement factories, and a brickyard topped by tall chimneys. There are also banks, shops, schools, and hospitals in the community ... Today, however, as I view the charming landscape through the branches of our big pear tree, everything looks so pleasant that I can still believe in the serenity and peace that surrounds me. (*The Russian Dance of Death*, 7–9)

By the fall of 1919, of course, the serenity, as Neufeld suggests with his 'however,' is more than a little deceptive. His opening entry is accompanied by a brief aside, which throws a shadow over the idyll, but which scarcely prepares the reader for the events to come:

I sit here by the window and gaze out over the houses at the distant steppe. All around is the great Russian plain where thousands of villages and towns lie dreaming under a high blue sky. Dreaming, do I say? No, the dream is over. The villages have been awakened. But the apathetic muzhik (peasant) is as yet only half aware and has not fully found himself. He attacks blindly: is not held back by any inner restraints. He will no longer allow our people to stand aside as non-participating spectators. With increasing frequency, we are forced to realize that the Russian peasant is not kindly disposed towards our Mennonite settlers. (P. 9)

Like the Baltic Germans, the Mennonites would soon discover just how unkindly disposed the peasants really were. For the Mennonites, the first leaders of the dance of death would be the troops of the peasant anarchist leader Nestor Machno, who roamed southern Ukraine in the chaos following the revolution. Fighting against the

Bolsheviks and the White Army of General Denikin, the Makhnovites entered the defenseless Mennonite villages at will and by the end of the winter of 1919/20, had reduced the prosperous communities to depopulated ruins. In the space of half a year, Neufeld's journal brings the still flourishing community of 15 September 1919 to its knees with isolated flashes of daily destruction, accentuated by the arrival of Russian winter and the outbreak of typhus, which accompanied the impoverishment of the community. A few days later, on 21 September, he is confronted with the desperate situation that a peaceful unarmed community faces when invaded by armed troops who feel they have the right to take any revenge they please on a prosperous minority. The time of security had passed:

> September 21. They're here. Who they are and under what political banner they are fighting nobody knows. We see nothing but brutal madness, looting, and killing ... We realize only too well that these intruders don't value our lives any more than a Sunday hunter values the life of a rabbit. There is no 'closed' season for us, as there is for people living in law-abiding countries. Who cares when and how we forfeit our lives? ... Was it actually today that Henry and I enjoyed the grandeur of the steppe sunset? And was it only today that I stood before my students at the Teacher's Seminary reciting lyric poems to them, with all of us in a serene and happy mood? (Pp. 12–14)

Neufeld's journal covers only the period of violence and destruction. Like von Vegesack, he does not deal with the historical consequences of these acts, but with the impact of the realization that an apparently secure world has been transformed into a hunting ground. While *Die Baltische Tragödie* eventually finds the heart of its plot in the description of the violent deaths of familiar people, Neufeld's *Russian Dance of Death* acquires its shocking force by focusing on characters we meet only briefly, perhaps long enough to get a glimpse of their tidy house and solid families, who are then wiped away by forces that do not pick and choose but simply eliminate. 'Today one of my students, a girl of eighteen, confirmed with silent nods the rumor of her father's tragic fate, a prominent citizen who did a great deal for the settlement; he was taken away as a hostage. His body now lies on the far side of the Dnieper Bridge. When his sons tried to recover the body they were driven off with savage insults' (p. 28).

For Dietrich Neufeld, like Aurel, the narration ends when the unalterable decision is made to abandon the homeland. For Neufeld, it, too, comes only after the elimination by violent death of virtually his entire family. As befits the style of a diary, where the unexpected is presented unrefined, the death of the family appears suddenly and brutally in the form of a list. His immediate family members had not played a prominent role in Neufeld's diary because they were in his home village of Zagradovka, 100 miles to the southwest. In his last diary entry of 5 March, Neufeld responds to the news from Zagradovka:

Today I held the list of murder victims in my hands. I still can't comprehend what I saw. I scanned the column of names – they swam before my eyes. Two hundred and fourteen people – I knew them all. My father. My brothers. Murdered. I want to howl to make the earth tremble! Henry, my brother, if only I'd been able to die in your place. You had a wife and seven little ones. A tireless fighter for truth and ideals. Does crime have no limits then? Is there no end to atrocity? (P. 64)

Neufeld's *Russian Dance of Death* makes a fitting companion to Vegesack's *Die Baltische Tragödie*. Although written in secret diary form, with none of the subtleties of plot development and stylistic nuance that characterize von Vegesack's novel, Neufeld's work nevertheless also effectively portrays the violent destruction of a false paradise. South of the Mennonites was the Black Sea and north of the Baltic Germans was the Baltic Sea. For most of the large population of ethnic Germans who lived on Russian territory between these extremes, the events of 1917 to 1920 meant the end of a way of life that had existed there for centuries. A world of apparent security and relative prosperity had been replaced by a new social order in which security and prosperity were reason enough to be considered part of the enemy class.

Thus, the speakers of the two Germanic language groups of Russia found themselves after the revolution in a similar situation: outsiders on the basis of ethnic background, language, and religion. As a result, the German and Yiddish speakers of Russia deserted their birthplaces en masse. In his second-to-last entry, before the discovery of the list of his dead family, Dietrich Neufeld speculates on the position of the Mennonites in Russia in March 1920:

> We Mennonites are aliens in this land. If we didn't realize that fact before the War we have had it forced upon us during and after the War. Our Russian neighbors look upon us as the damned Nyemsty (Germans) who have risen to great prosperity in their land ... Most of our colonists are seriously considering the possibility of finding a home in another land. And with good reason, considering what they have been forced to bear. During the war they were regarded as stepchildren and treated like enemies because no other state would have them ... This is no longer our homeland. We want to leave! The magic word 'emigration' travels like a 'buran' (winter wind) from place to place. Whenever two or three colonists get together the conversation is sure to be about emigrating. It is the one idea which keeps us going, our one hope. But how? Where? With what means? (P. 63)

Basically these are also the questions asked by Tevye, Mendel Singer, Aurel, and Sasha Granach in the Russia of the revolution. The answers might be different in details, but are the same in general. We are ultimately not sure what happens to Tevye after he is forced out. Perhaps it is appropriate that, like so many East European Jews, he simply disappears after he is driven from his home. The others definitely leave their Russian homeland; somehow they find the means and move westward. Mendel Singer takes the classic route for the East European Jews to New York and joins the largest Yiddish urban group in the world. Aurel, like the majority of the emigrating Baltic German community, which by the 1930s had reached 50 percent of the original population, takes the relatively short boat ride to Germany. Dietrich Neufeld drew the consequences of his second-last diary entry and escaped to the Weimar Republic of 1920, which he considered 'not only bearable but actually splendid' (p. 126). In 1923 he continued his emigration westward and joined the Mennonite colonies on the Canadian prairies.

By 1929, 25 percent of the war-depleted Mennonite Russian population (approximately 20,000 people) had immigrated to Canada and South America, where they had been guaranteed rights for their pacifist beliefs (Neufeld, 121). The Mennonites and Volga Germans who stayed behind in an attempt to reestablish their former position within the context of the new order of the Soviet Union would feel the full fury of Russian hatred of their remaining German settlers after the Nazi offensive into Russia in 1941. Those who could not escape west ended up in Siberia and Central Asia, and now, almost fifty years later, are arriving in large numbers at the resettlement camps in West Germany.

Today it is estimated that there are approximately as many ethnic Germans as Jews in the Soviet Union. Together they continue to make up unwanted and virtually outcast minorities, insofar as they don't assimilate. The Mennonites and the Volga Germans, who had a Soviet Republic of their own from 1918 until two months after the Nazi attack on the Soviet Union, have been scattered among provinces in central Asia. Recent attempts to gain the right to return to the regions from which they had been deported have failed because of the antagonism of the current inhabitants. Despite the fact that German is still being passed on through families, there is no sign that any official effort will be made to save German as a minority language of the Soviet Union. Yiddish speakers are no better off; in practice they are subjected to the same cultural and linguistic pressures as are the Germans. In reality, most of the Tevyes, Aurels, and Dietrichs of Russia have either left the Soviet Union or are preparing to leave. The liberalized emigration policy instituted in 1989 by the Soviet Union has led to record numbers of ethnic German and Jewish emigrants (100,000 and 65,000 respectively in 1989); the future of both the Germanic languages of the Soviet Union seems to be anything but bright.

Alexander Granach had no problems leaving Ukraine in 1918, for of all these characters he was the only one who had come to accept a new homeland even before his old homeland was taken away from him. Sasha Granach had transformed himself from a poverty-stricken, Yiddish-speaking Galician baker's apprentice into a German-speaking actor on the best stage of Berlin. By the mid 1920s, he was the only one of these figures who could claim that he had established himself in a foreign country in which he felt at home. We now turn to the unpredictable and apocalyptic events that destroyed Sasha Granach's vision of a new homeland and made him very lucky to be able to die in 1945 in New York exile. For in 1925 nobody could have predicted that of all these desperate emigrants, Sasha Granach in Berlin would soon be the most threatened of all.

Chapter Four
Whatever Happened to Tevye?

But the tragedy of the Jews is also the tragedy of Europe in the sense that the Jews more than anyone else embodied both the reality and the promise that there could be movement and communication across borders.

Richard Swartz, 'Det låsta rummet' ('The Locked Room')

The events should be taking on the patina of settled recorded history. Yet today, almost sixty years after Hitler became the democratically elected chancellor of Germany, and more than forty-five after the victorious Red Army opened the doors of Auschwitz and Majdanek and the other extermination centers of East Central Europe to discover the pitiful remains of European Jewry, there is abundant evidence of how wrong it would be to interpret the events of that decade as having been purged by the passing of time. The fortieth anniversary of the end of the war in May 1985 served as a catalyst to bring together elements to test the state of remembrance with respect to the contemporary Germans and the atrocities committed in their name by the Nazis two generations ago. The results have been sobering for anyone assuming that the time has come when the moral and ethical devastations of the Nazi period can be set aside as a deviation and that the economic and democratic triumphs of the postwar period can be understood to have become representative for an evaluation of twentieth-century German history.

From absolutely predictable (but also from apparently unexpected) sources the proofs came in, as Germany marked that fortieth anniversary, that the events occurring between 30 January 1933 and 8 May 1945 have not been forgotten, and that Germany will have to pay the price for its actions during that decade for decades to come. To investigate the consequences of those years, both Austrian and German television sent off crews in search of the remains of Jewish culture and the Yiddish language in formerly Nazi-occupied Eastern Europe. Neither group was allowed to film in the Soviet Union, where there are Yiddish speakers; the Austrians were also not allowed into Czechoslovakia. In Poland, both crews found only neglected cemeteries, abandoned synagogues, and virtually no one who could still speak the language that only half a century ago was the native tongue of 10 percent of the population.

In Vienna, a month-long symposium was held on the theme of the sunken world of the East European Jews. The major documents were Roman Vishniac's powerful and moving photographs of the Polish-Jewish community on the edge of its destruction and a film festival with the theme 'Judentum und Film' ('The Jewish Culture and Film'), which screened four films a day for two weeks.[1] Alongside more than fifteen postwar U.S. films, there were only two West German entries: Peter Lilienthal's *David* and Theodor Kotulla's *Aus einem deutschen Leben* (From a German Life). Both are attempts at realistic quasi-documentary versions of lives of individuals on opposite ends of the experience of the Holocaust: the Jewish victim, David, and the Nazi criminal, Rudolf Höss, the commandant of Auschwitz. By definition, they aim at clear and easy targets, and can evoke no other normal emotional response from the viewer than sympathy for the innocent victim, which easily leads to melodrama and pathos, and abhorrence of the criminal, which easily leads to cliché. German film, like German literature, has found it very difficult to deal with the events of the Second World War involving Germans and Jews other than through the attempted realistic depiction of these extremes. It has recognized an extremely sensitive area here that strongly resists any German approach using such weapons as irony and satire, changing perspective, or self-commentary. Elsewhere these elements have become familiar as main characteristics of literary descriptions of other aspects of the war and of the modern world in general. Thus, Volker Schlöndorff's film version of Günter Grass's *Die Blechtrommel* (*The Tin Drum*, 1978), for instance, employs a wide variety of narrative and cinematic approaches to the portrayal of the rise of the Nazis and the destruction of Danzig, except where the one Jewish character figures prominently, at which point pathos takes over. Similarly, what are probably the two best (and most popular) German films of the 1980s, Wolfgang Petersen's *Das Boot* (*The Boat*, 1981) and Edgar Reiss's *Heimat* (Homeland, 1984), are set either entirely or prominently in the war. But Petersen's powerful adventure film about life on a German submarine involves no Jews, and Reiss's magnificent re-creation of life in a small town through most of the century includes Jews only in rather minor and peripheral scenes. It is certainly not the case that any of these artists is trying to deny the centrality of German-Jewish relations to twentieth-century German history. But the presentation of that story has a tendency to overwhelm any other areas of modern German life these artists might want to explore.

It is therefore no surprise that in a society where a major playwright and filmmaker, Rainer Werner Fassbinder, could be accused of having written an anti-Semitic play, *Der Müll, die Stadt und der Tod* (Garbage, the City and Death, 1985), because of the prominence in it of a shady Jewish real-estate dealer, there is no film remotely resembling an American film like Mel Brooks's *The Producers* (1967). The plot of this film involves the attempt by two Jewish producers to avoid prosecution for a money-raising scam by producing a Broadway flop, which they are sure they will achieve with a musical comedy about Hitler. In the script, which also has something to say about the theater of the absurd, the musical becomes a great hit because of the comic incongruity of a hippie Hitler surrounded by chorus lines singing 'Springtime for Hitler and Germany, winter for Warsaw and Prague.' This film, which has been met with revulsion by most German film critics, enters a taboo area in Germany where Nazis, Jews, and comedy do not meet. In America it won the Oscar for best screenplay.

While the symposium on the sunken world of the East European Jews was under way, West German (but not Austrian) television debuted a three-evening film about the trial of the wardens of the Majdanek killing center. Eberhard Fechner's *Der Prozess* (The Trial, 1985) spends 450 minutes exploring the longest court case in the history of West Germany. It inevitably invites comparisons with Peter Weiss's *Die Ermittlung* (*The Investigation*, 1966), in which the documentary evidence of the Frankfurt Auschwitz trials is put on stage in oratorical dramatic form. The cold, pitiless, and artificial language of destruction used in Weiss's attempt to portray the journey from the sorting platforms to the gas chambers of Auschwitz contrasts dramatically with the live, self-pitying, almost friendly defenses and explanations of the wardens in the film. These often engaging and chatty Germans and Austrians, who did the accompanying and the watching, are contrasted with the identifiably native Polish and Yiddish speakers, who represent the small minority who survived.

Already it seems fair to say that Fechner's trial, filmed more than fifteen years after Weiss's numbing investigation, will gain a position as one of the most convincing and extraordinary works about the ordinariness of terror, to use Hannah Arendt's term, about the banality of evil. The witnesses in Fechner's trial present evidence for deliberation on a theme ultimately more terrifying than that brought center stage by Peter Weiss's investigation. Instead of focusing on the designers and organizers of plans for mass murder, Fechner gives us the often almost randomly chosen guardians of its final holding place. This trial is, for the most part, about the 'normal' person next door and what he or she did when 'abnormal' men came to power and gave them license to do evil. In addition, it is about how 'normal' they again became after the license expired. It also demonstrates convincingly the gray areas. We meet wardens who were chosen for no particular reason and carried out their duties without adding to the misery, and who themselves have never recovered from the nightmare. We hear about the prisoners who went to any length to survive, including betrayal of their fellow victims.

The interviews that make up virtually the entire fabric of the film present, for probably the last time, a Yiddish- and Polish-accented German chorus describing what these apparently jocular native

German-speaking men and women did at Majdanek. Finally, a composed, relatively unemotional (given the circumstances), and objective presentation of crushing memories is strung together, through a masterpiece of cutting and editing, to form an unbreachable barrier of evidence through which denials cannot pass. The result is an extraordinarily live and convincing presentation of a world gone out of kilter, in which the unbelievable behavior of apparently otherwise normal men and women goes right to the edge of black humor as a momentarily absurd but deadly world is described from both sides.

In Fechner's film we are confronted not by the diabolical fanatics, but with average Joes, full of anecdotes and hazy memories, who made the system work. But even Fechner's film is an oral documentary, a presentation of remembered incidents by those who were there, and not a fictional account. His film describes the end, takes a trip through forty years of memory to the few years of shame that Germany has not yet begun to overcome. But for the small percentage of European Jews, who, by luck or exile, survived the Second World War, the nightmare did not begin with the gas chambers of Auschwitz and Majdanek, but a decade earlier. It began initially with somewhat unspectacular acts of discrimination, which increased in such a steady relatively undramatic manner that millions of Western European Jews did not recognize the deadliness of the threat to them until it was too late. Perhaps it should be added as well that no Western government seems to have been able to conclude at the time that these measures were the first steps on the road to genocide.

Tevye, if he had survived the revolution and stayed in Russia, would have had more than enough to worry about in the aftermath of that revolution to have taken much notice of turbulence in far-off Germany, which in 1933 brought an Austrian anti-Semite to power in Berlin. Alexander Granach, having advanced to the major theaters of Berlin, was confronted with the anti-Semitism of the Nazis as they began their rise to power in the late 1920s; as an East European Jew he must have found it both familiar and threatening. He drew the consequences and escaped to Moscow and finally to New York before the trap closed. After the naming of Adolf Hitler as chancellor of Germany in 1933, the German Jews were confronted at first with such relatively small matters as the forced removal of Jewish civil servants from their positions, or the delisting of Jewish pharmacists and doctors from government insurance lists. In 1934 they were declared ineligible to serve in the armed forces; in 1935 their children were removed from classrooms where Aryan children sat; in late 1935 the Nürnberg laws of race determination came into effect; and shortly thereafter, voting and other civil rights were eliminated. By 1938, the 'aryanization' of Jewish property began; all Jewish residences had to be registered; the first deportation of East European Jews took place; all Jews had to take on the name of Sarah or Israel and carry a J in their passports; and in early November almost all synagogues and many Jewish businesses were burned to the ground. After the outbreak of the war in September 1939, Jews were not allowed to walk on the street at night or use public transport, and were forbidden to have phones or radios, or, eventually, even pets. In short, by then German Jews had been caught in a trap which few managed to escape before it shut finally with the prohibition of Jewish emigration in 1941. Immigrant East European Jews like Granach were marked men for deportation by 1938, and if he had not already become a star on the Moscow stage, his chances of escaping the concentration camps would have been minimal.

For those not wise or lucky enough to escape before 1939, the historical moment had come that in recent times has been identified in the major Western languages by one word: Holocaust. For the survivors and their descendants, wherever they might be now, this word has a fearful meaning and indelibly stamps the catastrophic attempt by the apparently civilized Germans, under elected barbaric control, to eliminate the Jews of Europe. But for the mass audience of Germany it was not a major novel, an exemplary historical analysis, an overwhelming film, or a stunning theatrical performance that first brought this monumental event in their history to the center of their imagination, but an English-language melodrama: the U.S. television series 'Holocaust.' It was telecast on German television in January 1979, thirty-four years after the end of the war, and seen, at least in part, by an extraordinary 48 percent of the adult population, although it was shown only on the educational channel. This percentage has been described by Uwe Magnus, director of media information for the West German Broadcasting Service in Cologne, as 'astonishing and encouraging, also in comparison with other series with a similar number of serials reaching an even higher percent of the viewers – such as "Roots" with over 60 percent.'[2] The comparison with the U.S. TV melodrama about slavery, 'Roots' raises serious questions, not only about the Americanization of German culture, but also about the implications inherent in the borrowing by German media of a foreign, and aesthetically and historically suspect, version of the most catastrophic event in German history. Also related is the question of why that 'borrowing' was so successful for an audience that was apparently more ready to view an entertaining story about the Holocaust than any of the versions that had been put forward by major artists in its own language. Whole books have been assembled just to attempt to interpret the message of the media event of 'Holocaust' within a German context. Already in March 1979, Fischer Verlag had available a 330-page book about the showing of the series, the historical situation that led to the Holocaust, and the media and viewer response.[3]

German and Jewish reactions to this American television serial ranged from outrage at the melodramatic soap-opera version of mass murder to jubilation at its success in informing an audience, and in particular an otherwise seriously underinformed German youth, about the most horrifying events of the Nazi period. But one thing had become very clear. With their stunned and stunning response to 'Holocaust,' the German audiences gave notice of the fact that in the thirty-four years since the end of the war, they had not been told in a lasting and successful artistic manner of this projected genocide. It had not been imprinted imaginatively on their understanding of history in a manner remotely comparable to other aspects of the war.

Despite the fact that a surprising number of major Jewish writers continued, and continue, to write in German after the war – Paul Celan, Wolfgang Hildesheimer, Elias Canetti, Manes Sperber, Erich Fried, Peter Weiss, Friedrich Torberg, Stefan Heym, Georg Kreisler, Nelly Sachs, Rose Ausländer, and others – they had failed to find a successful imaginative way to inform the German public of the dimension of the catastrophe for both the German and Jewish cultures. Of course, here we must make a distinction between 'serious' literature and a 'popular' television entertainment. These are two different kinds of media and they are aimed, at least to some extent, at different audiences. However, in the case of the fictional presentation of the historical event of the Holocaust, the reaction of the television audience underlined the fact that this extremely dramatic story of genocide had simply not been brought across to the broad German audience in the same way as had, for instance, the dramatic story of the German military catastrophe at Stalingrad, widely known from both films and literature.

The extraordinary success of the artistically suspect 'Holocaust' which was made for crass commercial reasons (on U.S. television, it was even interrupted with ads for detergents), and the relative popular failure of works by such vastly superior artists as Sperber, Canetti, Sachs, and Weiss, who can only describe the events from a standpoint of personal commitment, moral outrage, and familial catastrophe, lead to speculation about the relationship between author and the process of aesthetic description in this context. The question arises as to whether a passionate involvement in the contemporary horror of the Holocaust, which is then reflected onto words on a paper or images on a screen, may not clash with the imaginative presentation of that reality to an audience of non-victims. It is possible that the victims have been so stunned by the enormity of the historical crime that they have been incapable of employing effective literary weapons, such as shifting narrative perspective, irony, sarcasm, melodrama, and even black humor.

In the case of Yiddish literature, the renunciation of literary weapons is particularly apparent. In the short period of its existence, it had described the often vicious caprices of fate in the land of the East European Jews with a certain melancholic self-irony. Even at the moment of his expulsion from his home, Tevye defends himself with a sarcastic question. It is the kind of hopeless linguistic defense that would no longer have a place when the Nazis began rounding up their Jews. The sometimes black humor of Sholom Aleichem about the difficulties of being a Jew found its emigrant heirs in the sarcasm of the Marx Brothers, who disguised themselves as Italians, Wasps, mutes, or quacks, but never played Jews, and in the irony of I.B. Singer, who maintains a sometimes not-so-benevolent distance from the emigrant Jewish society. But it is not found in the works of the describers of the Holocaust. There are no Yiddish works about the destruction of the European Jews that are comparable to Sholom Aleichem's tragicomic stories of the Russian pogroms. For in the case of the Yiddish language and culture, the Holocaust was more than just another episode in a centuries-old tale of discrimination and harassment; this time it was the story of the end of a language, a culture, and the great majority of the people who lived within it. This time there was no place for the ironic asides and theological questioning of Tevye. There could only be the attempt to describe a white exterminating heat that was so intense that it could not be approached except with shielded eyes. Aharon Appelfeld describes the process as follows: 'I would say that artistically, it is impossible to deal with it directly. It's like the sun. You cannot look at the sun; the temperature is too high. The Holocaust is a kind of temperature you cannot speak, you cannot utter, you cannot feel. You have to degradate it to an extent in order to speak of it' (Lewis, 16).

Of course, there have, in fact, been many attempts, in all the languages involved, to describe in words the actual horrors involved with life in the concentration camps and the extermination centers.[4] Appelfeld's point is that such memoirs and reminiscences cannot possibly convey this ultimate heart of darkness, that automatically, through the process of word and sentence formation, not to mention visual formation, there is an aesthetic distancing that nullifies the possibility of accurate reproduction of this event. In the novels and short stories of I.B. Singer – still writing in Yiddish after more than fifty years of New York exile (although it hardly seems like exile anymore, as the homeland no longer exists), and probably the most prominent author in the entire history of Yiddish literature (and very much likely to remain so) – we find the most striking example of the unwillingness to attempt to confront the Holocaust directly, to use Appelfeld's metaphor, to look at the sun. Although Singer's fate and the fate of virtually all his original-language readers were largely determined by the Holocaust, he approaches it only with shielded eyes, through mirrors that reflect the impact of the destruction of the known world of the survivors, mourning, but also carrying on in a new world far away. In his closest approach to the sun, in *The Family Moskat* or in *Shosha*, we sense the disaster coming over the doomed

Jewish community of Warsaw. We even experience the arrival of the exterminating troops in a world that would cease to exist within half a dozen years. But we are not led to the loading platforms of Auschwitz. Certainly we feel the almost numbing pain in the reactions of relatives and friends in the Americas in numerous masterful short stories, but his characters and his readers are shielded from the unimaginable reality by the buffer of memory.

In this context we can look again at the story, 'Old Love,' which we have used to trace the dissolution of a Yiddish ancestral line in the wilderness of Canada. In 'Old Love,' Singer creates one of those epics in miniature that many critics feel to be his supreme accomplishment as a storyteller. Here, he is apparently not writing about the Holocaust, but, as we have seen, about the sad old age of Harry Bendiner, who somehow escaped from Poland and made a fortune in America, only to find himself at eighty-two alone in the spiritual wasteland of his Miami Beach apartment. But sometimes Singer captures the staggering tale of the Holocaust in a sentence. He does it, not by describing the moment of destruction, but by writing about the Harry Bendiners of the new world, whose children have no interest in their parents' language, culture, and often even religion, and whose grandchildren have disappeared off the face of their known world. Singer then hits his target by not even aiming at it, as his characters talk about everything imaginable except what happened between 1940 and 1945.

There is only one reference to the Second World War in 'Old Love' and the manner of its introduction brings us to the kind of place where Singer's miniatures grow large. An almost casual comment, vouched for by the unidentified narrator, a source of inside knowledge, brings up the most serious threat to the spiritual strength of contemporary Jewry. Harry Bendiner, we are told, is not religious 'and often said that, after what happened to the Jews in Europe, one had to be a fool to believe in God' (p. 429). The narrator's remark is made from the same somewhat detached ironic perspective that is used to deal with Harry's sleeping habits or his diet. Our narrator knows everything about Harry Bendiner and undertakes no change of mood to tell us that he has received eleven thousand dollars in the morning mail, that he had a prostate operation, which has not been particularly successful, that he does not realize that his neighbor has been dead for six months, or that he feels that it is foolish to believe in God after the Holocaust. But the wind blows increasingly colder as the narration moves seamlessly from the personal to the universal, and finally the reader is led to understand that there is some connection between the spiritual ice age that has destroyed Harry Bendiner's homeland and the frozen isolation in which Harry is fated to spend his final days.

Singer's stories about Jewish survivors in America can still be linked through the melancholic self-irony of the narrator to the Tevye tales of Sholom Aleichem, but the monumental scale of the Holocaust itself defies the black humor with which Tevye could question the motives of Jehovah with his chosen people. What Ruth Wisse calls 'the classic expression of Yiddish irony' – 'Thou hast chosen us from among the nations, why did you have to pick on the Jews?' (Wisse, 47) – could no longer be asked ironically after the process of selection had been carried out by the designers of the Nürnberg race laws and the gas chambers of Auschwitz, Treblinka, and Majdanek.

It was a question that cannot be formulated with any trace of humor in connection with a selection process in which blood lines alone were the sole characteristic in determining the right to live or die. The potentially comic aspects of the request become immediately erased at the point where it became clear that the choosing would be carried out by bureaucrats and murderers, and that there would be no intervention by spiritual authority. Even in the few tales that have been written about historical figures who worked against the system from within, like Oskar Schindler (the main figure of Thomas Keneally's *Schindler's List*, 1982) and Raoul Wallenberg (the Swedish diplomat and title figure of yet another U.S. television serial version of the Second World War), the emphasis is on choice, on life lists that are used to counter death lists. The ironic question of Jehovah's motives is now reversed and put into secular form: 'How can I get Schindler to choose me for his list? How can I get Wallenberg to choose me for a Swedish passport?' The request is no longer to spare the Jews the harassments of centuries by choosing someone else, but to spare the individual Jew from near-certain extermination by being chosen by one of those few gentiles who had both the nerve and the power to get people off death trains, whether for bogus work in a Schindler factory or bogus citizenship in the far-off kingdom of Sweden. Here victimization is taken for granted; some other Jews will definitely be chosen for the trains. Tevye's salvation was no longer in the spiritual grip of a Yiddish-speaking Jehovah, who was expected to intervene long before the pogroms had turned into extermination camps, but in the precarious hands of German-speaking industrialists and Swedish-speaking diplomats. The understood world order of the East European Jews had been destroyed in a historical second.

Yiddish writers describing the Holocaust could scarcely have been expected to breach the perimeters transcribed by their drastically curtailed readership, almost all of whom had suffered from the Holocaust in one way or another. Theirs is a perimeter carefully guarded by the demands of respect for the victims, in both a personal and cultural sense. The best of those works within it, which attempt to use the Holocaust itself as a fictional device, may give some indications of the horror of it all, but run the serious risk of appealing only to the memories of the survivors, to use Jurek Becker's harsh terminology, to serve as 'a button. You push on it, and their eyes fill up with tears. But they are not normal spectators, they are not normal readers – they are not normal people, they are survivors' (Lewis, 100).

With the grand exception of I.B. Singer, postwar Yiddish writers have found themselves for the most part addressing only the survivors like Becker's father, who 'always wanted a book or a film to push that button, so he would experience the right feeling – sorrow or pity' (ibid., 101). German-language writers, in contrast, were using the language of the perpetrators, and for the Jewish writers who chose to write in this language, there was often a conscious decision to use it, despite or perhaps even because of the Nazis' abuse of that language. It is precisely here, among the immediately affected Jewish-German writers, that the communication of the story of the Holocaust tragedy to the postwar German generations, who were clearly interested enough to be greatly affected by the TV 'Holocaust,' has been so difficult.

Such grand old men of postwar German-language literature as Sperber and Canetti, like Singer forced to spend a creative lifetime in exile (the former in Paris, the latter in London) because of the events surrounding the Holocaust, confronted the results of that personal catastrophe for more than half a century. But although they have each written one of the major epic novels about Europe on the edge of the Holocaust (Canetti's *Die Blendung*, 1935 [*Auto da fé*, 1979] and Sperber's *Wie eine Träne im Ozean* [*Than a Tear in the Sea*, 1967]) neither chose to describe the ensuing Holocaust in fictional terms. Canetti abandoned his proposed continuation of the inner odyssey begun in *Auto da fé* and wrote instead one of the major sociohistorical works about mass power, *Masse und Macht* (*Crowds and Power*, 1960), a topic he had masterfully suggested in fictional form in his novel, before moving on to his autobiography. Sperber wrestled with the problem in numerous essays, a sample of which makes up the content of *Churban oder die unfassbare Gewissheit* (Churban or the Incomprehensible Certainty, 1979), in which for the first time he aims at his German public after thirty-four years of writing mainly in French, before he too turned to his autobiography. In this work, Sperber underlines the necessity for temporal distance before he could confront the Germans in their native language. 'With these remarks about my Jewishness I am in the main addressing German readers, thirty-four years after the end of the reign of Hitler and his innumerable accomplices, and the millions who stood at their side. Of course it would be logical to cut oneself off from the past and to follow the impossible but seductive advice "Let the dead bury the dead!" But my being, in particular my kind of Jewishness, can never forget.'[5] In Sperber's writings about the destruction of his culture, the essay form is balanced by the autobiography of a writer who was born in 'the filth and ugliness of the Jewish shtetl in which I spent the first ten years of my life. Zablotow was the name of this village, which was similar to hundreds of other tiny, crowded shtetls in which Jews lived until 1942 in Galicia, Russian Poland, Lithuania, White Russia and the Ukraine.'[6] As Sperber was a Communist who experienced the victory of the Nazis and the sowing of the seeds of the Holocaust in Berlin, his autobiography remains one of the most illuminating accounts of the rise of the Nazis and the fall of the European Jews. But his reminiscences and essayistic works about the Holocaust, unlike those involving the tragic fate of the idealistic Communists under Stalin, do not translate into fictional form. In his monumental 1000-page trilogy about the end of old Europe, *Wie eine Träne im Ozean* (*Than a Tear in the Sea*), he makes extensive use of his autobiography for his fictional account of the failure of Communism, but devotes only one short episode to the destruction of his homeland by the Nazis. In a novel whose very fabric is composed of scattered events throughout middle and southeastern Europe, the reader is taken only once to the shtetl, to the culture in which Sperber grew up and which he describes so effectively in *Die Wasserträger Gottes* (*God's Water Carriers*, 1987) in episodes from a childhood that occurs simultaneously with Tevye's expulsion from Anatevka. In that episode, the assimilated Viennese Jew, Edi, attempts rather futilely to organize the men of the last surviving East Galician shtetl into a defense corps in the face of the arriving transport trains, whose destination is no secret to him. We sense the approaching slaughter in those trains, but we are not taken aboard and nowhere is there a description of the death camps that would have made such an eloquent contribution to the ocean of tears. As is the case with Singer and Canetti, one senses that Sperber feels some unspoken taboo against attempting to express the deaths of 6 million in fictional terms, even in the context of the great sprawling form of the epic novel.

There have, of course, been notable attempts to describe the Holocaust in fictional terms in German, but until recently they have been limited to the approach characterized by such works as (to pick superior versions in three different genres) Friedrich Torberg's novella *Mein ist die Rache* (*Revenge Is Mine*, 1942), Peter Weiss's drama *Die Ermittlung* (*The Investigation*, 1966), or Egon Monk's television film *Ein Tag* (One Day, 1965). These works are most powerful and effective when most convincing in their presentation of bleakness, pitilessness, and despair. The horrible depressing grayness that dominates visually *Ein Tag* also dominates psychologically the documentation of *The Investigation* and the physical description of *Mein ist die Rache*. In each case the goal of the creator is to make the audience aware of the brutality imposed on the victims and in each case the method is the detailed description of that brutality in naturalistic terms. A suprarealistic approach is the linking element in the demonstration of the fate of the victims of that reality. Within that approach there may be room for a certain amount of idealized heroism or sentimentality to counter the bleakness, but there is little space for irony, satire, or humor, particularly not from the narrator, who is normally a survivor describing victims. Like the Yiddish-language authors, the German-language authors have, with only a few exceptions, chosen not to attempt to describe the Holocaust in the satiric, ironic, or fantastic terms that have been employed in other languages in such novels as Borowski's *This Way for the Gas, Ladies and Gentlemen* (Polish, 1967), Kosinski's *The Painted Bird* (English, 1965), Emil Knieza's *Jankel Tannenbaums Kompanie* (Slovak, 1975), Aharon Appelfeld's *Badenheim* (Hebrew, 1975), Josef Skvorecky's *The Bass Saxophone* (1977) or *The Cowards* (Czech, 1970), or in such films as Jiri Menzel's *Closely Watched Trains* (1966), Jan Kadar's *Shop on Main Street* (1964), and Mel Brooks' *The Producers* (1967).

The crucial obstacle to the presentation of the Holocaust in such terms in German may be found in the inability of the generation of victims, or for that matter of the perpetrators as well, to find an imaginative space in which the scale of the crime can be measured. Weiss tries by making the courtroom into a microcosm of the Holocaust itself, thus creating an abstract theatrical space in which it can play, but the brutal reality of the actual documentary material from the real trial in Frankfurt becomes the overwhelming literary factor. Torberg tries by creating a classical 'Rahmenerzählung' (story with an outside frame) with a New York exile frame, but the inside description of the concentration camp in the snow is all that remains. The New York setting seems nothing more than a disturbing literary device, used to set up a flashback, which then becomes completely the consuming interest. Monk tries by introducing a climactic plot development, but the vision that haunts us is of the work gangs in the snowblown ditch they are digging for their own grave. In each case the authors create their most effective scenes through the evocations of brutal realism; it breaks through even the stylized language of Weiss, because the existence of that reality changed not only the lives of these authors, but their understanding of the nature of man as well. Nevertheless, neither this elemental descriptive power nor the strength of the brilliant analytic essay reached the audience of the victimizing culture in an imaginative sense. When 'Holocaust' came to television they were still ready to be surprised and moved by a cliché-ridden story that had been told in far more authentic and honest terms many times before in the language of the audience sitting transfixed before a dubbed American soap opera.

We have suggested that a direct, contemporary, passionate involvement with the events of the Holocaust has been the major factor in determining the extreme realism dominating German literature about it, and that it has failed to reach a wide audience. The question is whether other narrative approaches are possible to this extremely sensitive area that might both fascinate an audience not directly involved (that majority of the German population born since the war) and at the same time accurately reflect a historical act that demands reflection. Certainly such an approach cannot come from the ranks of the perpetrators themselves. The fascination with evil in this case cannot be portrayed through the individual distorted vision of the exterminator, although, as Edgar Hilsenrath and Tadeusz Borowski have demonstrated (in *The Nazi and the Barber* [1971] and *This Way for the Gas, Ladies and Gentlemen* [1967]), the madness of this vision can be effectively communicated by an author who purports to be representing the views of the perpetrators and who is willing to run the risk of allowing them at times to seem to make an absurd kind of sense.

Until recently the very suggestion that an ironic black comic description of the Holocaust in the German language might be a way of presenting the material might have seemed impossible or at least tasteless. Those immediately affected felt compelled to document the horrible reality, while such horrified neutral observers as the Swiss could afford the luxury of aesthetic games but hardly the luxury of humor. Thus we have plays by Max Frisch, interpreted by many critics to be parables about the rise of the Nazis (*Biedermann und die Brandstifter* [1958], [*The Firebugs*]) and the extermination of the Jews (*Andorra* [1961]), neither of which has any Jewish characters. But we have no black comedies from Dürrenmatt on the topic. These events are now two generations old, and the distance of time and history may well have brought the possibility of artistic distance as well. Authors who were children during the war are already late middle-aged and have had the time to consider how they can most effectively describe the events surrounding the extermination of the Jews while carefully considering narrative strategies. Thus, Jurek Becker, objecting to the suggestion that he is 'a Holocaust writer,' argues that he had no intention of setting a heroic monument for the victim-hero of his novel *Jakob der Lügner* (1969), translated as *Jacob the Liar* (1975), even though that was what was expected of him by his father and other readers of stories from the ghetto:

> My father said that the man was a great hero, and that I should write about him. Probably he thought the man needed a monument. I thought that the man had enough monuments in Holocaust literature and I felt no longing to write about him. Years later I thought again about this story, [the story of a ghetto dweller, who at the risk of his life, maintains a radio] with one change: that man behaved the same way, but he did not have a radio. The other people in the ghetto just thought he had one. Now that, I thought, was a good idea for a story. (Lewis, 103)

For Jurek Becker, the sacred area of his father, with the perimeters of sorrow and pity, has been extended to include the idea of a good story.

Becker goes on to suggest that it is perfectly normal that he wrote such a book, not because he wanted to memorialize the Holocaust, but because 'I had a story that was worth telling'; 'the comedy was very important because it was a great challenge to find out if there is something that cannot be written about as comedy' (ibid., p. 98). This linking of effective narrative techniques and the Holocaust leads straight to the heart of the situation with regard to German-language fiction about these events. Jurek Becker survived the Holocaust as a Jewish child in the ghetto of Lodz and the concentration camp of Sachsenhausen. Nobody can accuse him of having Nazi sympathies or of wishing to exploit a horrible historical situation in which he did not participate. No one can say that *Jacob the Liar* was written by someone who didn't know what he was talking about, and who violated sacred ground upon which he had never walked. On the contrary, Becker argues that he has accurate memories of the ghetto (in which *Jacob the Liar* takes place) but none at all of Sachsenhausen, because while Sachsenhausen was entirely gray and survival-oriented, 'the ghetto was alive – there was a community, family. I had friends. That's why I can remember so much more, even though I was so much younger' (Lewis, 102).

It is not only in Germany that Becker hits a raw nerve with the idea that even the Holocaust can provide an excellent source of stories for someone who feels that storytelling itself is something of value. In *Jacob the Liar*, Becker solves this problem ideally as Jacob the liar is also Jacob the storyteller and the bulwark of all sources of hope in the ghetto through his lying-storytelling.

But in Germany the suggestion that entertaining stories or even black comedy and the Holocaust can be compatable is an immediate guarantee for controversy on a most sensitive matter. The question is whether that compatability, even with good intentions by the best writers, theater directors, or performers, does not serve the cause of anti-Semitism in a land that cannot afford any more of it, and certainly should not display it. Thus, in recent years such theatrical productions as the 1980 Berliner Volksbühne version of Weiss's *The Investigation* in which the Auschwitz data were presented in macabre nightclub, talk-show style, or Peter Zadek's 1984 Hamburg production of the Israeli writer Joshua Sobol's *Ghetto* (translated from the Hebrew), in which the destruction of the Vilna ghetto is presented as a musical, have been great audience successes and caused great critical controversies. Peter Weiss himself approved of the Berlin *Investigation*, concurring that something different must be done with his oratorio of suffering if it were not to petrify, and Sobol's musical comes with at least the tacit approval of some of the victimized culture, because it had great public approval in Israel. In his defense of his work before a German press, which tended to represent the critical opinion that a musical about genocide was morally suspect, Joshua Sobol touches on the same points as Jurek Becker. Both argue that the demanded heroic or pathos-filled depiction of the victims is not an accurate description of life in the ghettos, as opposed to the concentration camps, and that the same demands for heroes and victims were being made in the contemporary cultures of both the former victims and perpetrators.

Both Israel and Germany would rather have the version of the ghetto that did not deal with the ordinary daily life that developed under these extraordinary conditions, in which scores of thousands of Jews were assembled and forced to try to survive in a space that was clearly too small and with living conditions that were clearly too minimal for the survival of all. 'I discovered that nobody from my generation had handled the problem of the pure desire to survive. Only one percent in the Vilna ghetto belonged to the resistance, while ninety-nine percent were only interested in somehow surviving. Survival was the most important factor.'[7]

Ultimately Sobol can reach back for one undeniable weapon to defend himself against morally outraged (non-Jewish) Germans; he is a Jew, even if an atheist, and that allows him a freedom in telling the tale of the Holocaust not available to Germans, especially not if they are old enough to have experienced the war. There is still a taboo line between Germans and Jews on this matter; it is only now being tested by young German writers who are attempting to get at the darkest moment in their culture's history with all literary weapons at their disposal. But the pioneering work here in the attempt to return Jews, both during and after the war, to the state of normal people who reacted to both catastrophe and prosperity in the same way as would anybody else had to come from Jewish insiders. They must themselves have been through the fire and become determined to describe the experience in the language of their tormentors and in the literary style they felt to be most effective in presenting their version of that fire.

More than a quarter-century after the end of the war, time enough to gain a certain distance from the Holocaust, these figures began to assemble on the periphery of German literature: Jakov Lind, Edgar Hilsenrath, Jurek Becker – authors who don't fit into any of the pigeonholes preferred by literary historians, wanderers with uncertain passports and domiciles, and with impossible national designations. With them emerged a powerful group of German-language writers who have chosen to represent the Holocaust in a manner other than through the supposedly realistic description of inexorable crushing despair.

As we have seen, Jurek Becker disputes the suggestion made in the English translation of his novel that he is even a Holocaust writer, claiming interest in handling this historical period only insofar as it provides him with an effective story. In telling the tale of Jacob Heym, Becker gives himself goals that specifically exclude the reawakening of memory, and he wants an audience of ghetto outsiders. 'What is the reason for meeting and remembering that fifty years ago the Nazis burned books? Just for remembrance? That's not good enough for me. I am not interested in these memories; they are not so great – I can imagine better memories' (Lewis, 99). Here Becker's ironic understatement of the quality of memories of the 1930s suggests the sad whimsy of Tevye or of Singer's lost souls of New York or Miami Beach. As Becker denies ever having read anything by Sholom Aleichem, while being familiar with *Fiddler on the Roof* (Lewis, 93), this is not a matter of literary influence, but of storytellers' common reaction to a desperate but not yet catastrophic situation.

As a writer, Becker demands of himself distance, intellectual coolness, an interest in the future rather than the past, and the professional author's desire to mold successful stories from apparently inappropriate materials (comedy from the story of the ghetto). In short, for Becker the experiences of the ghetto offer the challenging possibility of telling a good and entertaining story that has something to say to an audience of nonparticipants about life in general, and about the importance of the profession of storytelling (or lying?). In addition he hopes to convey something about the 'attitude [which] was behind that happening, and where do we find that attitude today?' (pp. 99–100). By including the last goal, Becker adds a moral and political purpose, which is never stated in the actual telling of the tale.

Jacob the Liar, Becker's first novel, makes its impact by apparently attempting to be nothing more than an anecdote which happens to take place in a Nazi-run ghetto scheduled for elimination. The storyteller is the only survivor of the ghetto, as we eventually discover, and allows himself the luxury of narrating his story of Jacob Heym in a consciously straightforward, almost childlike style. He enjoys playing the role of a tale-teller who pleads ignorance before a knowledgeable audience, thus drawing the desired response from readers with a reservoir of information that the narrator conceals. For this narrator is apparently not primarily concerned with the story of the tragic end of the European Jews – although this event nevertheless occurs within his tale – but rather with a tale of survival and false hopes.

Within that framework there is room for confrontations between Nazi captor and ghetto victim that in 'standard' works of the Holocaust must inevitably lead to degradation or physical harm, but that here end only with the verbal brutality of vicious irony. Jacob Heym is forced into the Nazi headquarters of the ghetto by a bored guard who has falsely accused him of breaking curfew. A dozing officer, awakened by Jacob's knocking, wants only to know what time it is. Having determined that Jacob is there solely because of the whimsy of a guard, the officer's potentially fatal superiority finds its outlet only in linguistic attack through comic understatement: ' "To what do I owe this pleasure?" Jacob is about to answer. He can't. His mouth is so dry. So that's what the officer on duty looks like. "No false modesty now," says the officer, "out with it. What's the hurry?" ... Jacob thinks too long. The officer is getting impatient and that's not good, for wrinkles are forming on his brow. "Don't you talk to Germans?" '[8]

Jacob is told to go home, but before he leaves he has heard information on the radio about the location of the Red Army, which puts him in a unique position in a community where possession of a radio is punishable by death. But like Sobol, Becker is not interested in stories of heroic behavior or conscious resistance. 'It is no story of resistance or even of the smallest attempt at revolution. Where I was there was no resistance' (Lewis, 93). It is rather a lie by Jacob about his own heroism that gets him into a situation where he very reluctantly must attempt to play the role of a hero. Jacob cannot keep quiet about his information and claims to his work partner Misha that he heard it on his own illegal radio. But promises of silence mean nothing in a community starved for news, and Misha has soon informed the community of Jacob's heroic deed. Jacob's fate is sealed; the lie must be continued and expanded.

In the beginning, Jacob's lie serves as a flash point for gossip; and the situations that develop suggest a tragicomic attempt by the ghetto inhabitants to cope with a miserable existence, which, however, is not understood to be without a future. For the most part, the problems that arise are exacerbated by the terrible living conditions of the ghetto; but they are also caused by the foibles of the inhabitants, which were undoubtedly evident outside the ghetto as well. The lie also brings about a true disaster, which the guarding authorities, who will eventually arrange the final catastrophe, do not have to organize at all. Misha's potential father-in-law, certain that the gossip with regard to the radio will eventually reach the gestapo and lead to a thorough search of the entire ghetto, feels obligated to completely destroy the only real radio in the ghetto, which he has kept hidden in his cellar and been afraid to listen to. Consequently, he cannot confirm Jacob's information about the nearness of the Soviets. And so it is that, as irony would have it, Jacob's lie about the radio leads to the destruction of the only radio that could indeed bring to the ghetto the information they could so desperately use about the progress of the war and the nearness of potential liberation.

Within the framework of such tragicomic irony, life goes on, as Sobol and Becker both say, as usual insofar as possible. Misha is concerned with nothing so much as receiving the permission of Herr Frankfurter for the hand of his daughter, Rosa. Frankfurter responds as Tevye did to his troublesome daughters' marriage plans, first with irony and then with an anecdote:

> We're in the ghetto, Misha. Do you know that? We can't do what we want, because they will do with us what they want. Should I ask you where you intend to live? Should I tell you what sort of dowry Rosa will receive from me? That will surely interest you. Or should I give you a few tips on achieving a happy marriage and then go to the rabbi and ask him when the chassene is most convenient for him? ... Now imagine that! His ship has sunk. He is stranded in the middle of the ocean. No one in sight to help him, and he is making up his mind whether he'd rather go to a concert or to an opera. (*Jacob the Liar*, 45)

Actually it is not the opera or concert hall Misha is thinking about for the night, but how to get Rosa to spend it with him. This problem, too, is ghetto-determined. He shares a room with Isaac Fajngold, and it is absolutely clear to him that he will have no success in getting Rosa into his bed as long as Isaac Fajngold is present. His attempts to overcome this obstacle – first with a visual barrier, which is not sufficient, and then with a tale of his own, namely that Fajngold is deaf and dumb – create an episode of bedroom farce that is familiar from French boudoir comedy, but not from German tales of the Holocaust. It is, in fact, just in this insistence that life went on as normally as it could, and that young men like Misha acted as far as possible as if they were not trapped in a ghetto, that Becker's tale gathers its power.

Jacob's radio gradually becomes a central support of the community, much to his consternation, as he is constantly called upon to provide more and more information. Acts of God, such as a week-long electrical failure, which eventually cost a group of Jewish electricians their lives, are met with great relief by Jacob, as he has a perfect excuse for his lack of news. His most promising attempt to solve the problem of the paucity of information coming from his new radio involves his occupation of the German outhouse after having noticed that the previous occupant had entered with a newspaper. At the risk of his life – and in this novel the execution of the Jewish electricians or the deportation of a couple caught without the Jewish star comes as a shocking surprise – Jacob takes possession of the newspaper, only to be trapped inside by the arrival of a German soldier suffering from diarrhea. Only an arranged accident at the loading platform saves Jacob's life and costs the arranger a beating. The ironic culmination of the entire action, however, lies in the discovery by Jacob in his room that evening of the news he will get from his paper radio:

> At the end of all his troubles what he has are two extremely fragmentary pages with tablecloth-colored holes, two pages that look as if a prudent censor had excised anything worth knowing and thereby insured that only insignificant material reached incompetent hands. The sports section, for example – just his luck! – is perfectly complete. How happy the Jews will be to find out that the air force boxing team beat a navy group ten to six. Or that the Berlin soccer team once again didn't have a chance against the Hamburg team, as so often in the past ... Not a word about Bezanike, which the Russians must surely have captured long ago! Not a single word about German difficulties! Instead, these dopes are playing soccer, having exhibits, and cultivating righteousness! (Ibid., 101–2)

Thus Jacob's dangerous attempt to gather authentic news for his spurious news announcements brings him the same kind of information that the narrator brings the reader: information about lamebrains playing soccer or trying to arrange sexual escapades. Jacob's newspaper has, by a grotesque piece of bad luck, apparently lost all its 'solid news,' all its stories having to do with decline and fall of empires, with prefabricated heroes and villains, with life and death on the battlefront – all of that, if it had really been there, has met the fate of newspapers in outhouses and Jacob is left with nothing more than the appropriately described world of the everyday Germans. Inside the outhouse he has left the only hard information about potential difficulties of the Nazi war effort, the pages of the newspaper filled with black outlined announcements of the deaths of soldiers. With the next visit to the outhouse these pages too will disappear and the only information left behind for Jacob to try to work into his radio announcements is that, somewhere outside the ghetto, many Germans are dying. Ultimately Jacob cannot know if that means anything at all other than death on some battlefield, but in the radio reports now demanded he uses at least that much information to bring the conquering Soviet troops ever closer to the ghetto.

Jacob is trapped. An attempt to have the radio stop working leads to the arrival of a radio repairman from the tool factory. Jacob's suddenly self-repaired radio becomes the only source of hope to a ghetto that has had its first breath of Auschwitz with the discovery of voices in one of the freight cars. The orthodox Jewish stationworker Herschel cannot stop himself from communicating with the voices. His message is Jacob's lie – that the Russians are coming. His reward is to be shot down by an anonymous figure in a far-off window, the responsible guard having been successfully avoided. This time the narrator, who often can tell his tale only through secondhand sources, is the only one to see it, and acts like a survivor rather than a hero:

And then I turn my head to the guardhouse. It has a small attic window, which is open. On the window sill is a rifle that is being aimed in utter tranquility. I can't make out the man behind it. It's too dark in the room. I see only two hands adjusting the direction of the barrel until they are satisfied, then stopping as if modeled for a painting. What should I have done, I, who have never been a hero, what should I have done? If I were one, at best, shout. But what good would that have done? I do not shout. I close my eyes. An eternity passes. Roman says to me: 'What are you closing your eyes for? Look, he'll make it, that crazy fellow!' (Ibid., 127)

Herschel, of course, does not make it. With his death and the stunned realization that the freight cars represent a proposed fate for all Jews, Jacob the liar is forced into the role of Jacob the reluctant hero. Becker's narrative fabric is built upon the clash between a desperate hope sustained by Jacob's radio and an ever-threatening reality. Jacob alone can nourish the hope with his spurious news. Character after character whom we have come to know in the context of the tricks of survival, everyday people with individual quirks that can make them endearing, comical, or annoying to others, become totally dependent on Jacob's daily dose of hope. Kowalski, Jacob's old friend and nemesis, who organized both the accident that saved Jacob from the outhouse and the radio repairman who came close to uncovering his lie, plans for the future, even after Herschel's death, because of Jacob's radio. His plans are endearing, comical, and annoying:

> 'I wanted to ask you something,' says Kowalski. 'I've been thinking that it's really about time to start thinking about other things, too.'
> 'For example?'
> 'About business, for example.'
> 'About business? About what business?' ...
> 'Now and then business reports are announced over the radio.'
> 'Yes.'
> 'Hasn't there been anything by which you could be guided? Any tip?'
> 'I'm not interested in such things.'
> 'You're not interested in such things!' says Kowalski.
> 'You've probably heard something.'
> 'What do you really want to know? I haven't understood a word up to now.'
> 'I simply want to know what line of business has the best prospects.'

'Sometimes you really get childish, Kowalski. Do you seriously think they announce over the radio: We recommend that you invest your money after the war in such and such a business?' (Ibid., 145–6)

Kowalski's interrogation of Jacob and his fate in the days that follow contains both the comedy and the tragedy, the heroism and the cowardice, the illusory nearness of life after the ghetto, and the sudden and shocking presence of death in the ghetto. Only then comes the certainty of death in the concentration camps. For Kowalski does not get the chance to consider further the most profitable disposition of his hidden gold after the freedom promised by Jacob's radio. He discovers beforehand that there won't be any such freedom, that Jacob's optimistic news reports are figments of his imagination, that Jacob is a liar, and that the radio doesn't exist. For Kowalski this is not only reason enough to stop worrying about his future business dealings. It is reason enough to stop living. By committing suicide, he brings home to Jacob both the consequences that will be drawn by an entire community in the absence of Jacob's lies and the crucial importance of his storytelling to the attempted rescue of the people in the ghetto.

In the long run, of course, Jacob fails, because storytelling alone cannot remove people from freight cars and in the end it is the narrator himself who takes over Jacob's storytelling role, and suggests two finales, one fantasy, the other true. In the fantasy the Red Army arrives just in time to save the ghetto from deportation, although not in time to save Jacob from a fatal escape attempt. While Jacob's motives for escape are complex in this fantasy, he has already succeeded in keeping alive the spirit of the community with his carefully arranged stories of the approach of the Russian troops. The orphan Lina has been placed in the protective custody of the happily united Misha and Rosa, and even Kowalski has reappeared to identify the victim of the escape attempt. It is the fairy-tale ending; the children are saved, the lovers live happily ever after, the dead return to life, the hero dies heroically, and the people we have gotten to know in the course of the novel do not end up on the death train.

In the second version we are given 'after the invented story, now at last the pale-cheeked and unpleasant one, the real and unimaginative ending whereby you are easily pushed to the silly question: What's the purpose of all that? Kowalski is irrevocably dead and, for the time being, Jacob lives on, giving no thought to fobbing Lina off on strangers, nor does he denude his jacket of the prescribed stars' (p. 156). For Jacob's ghetto, the end comes as unheroically, as bureaucratically, as it came for virtually all the ghettos of Poland except, in the end, Warsaw. There is no resistance, no heroes try to escape or to defend; orders are given to assemble, the entire population gathers in the square and everyone gets on the train. Becker's version of the Holocaust, however, does not end in Auschwitz or even at the loading platforms leading into its horror, but with the attempt of the new liar, the narrator himself, who will somehow survive the destination, to carry the orphan Lina through the journey in the dark cold of the freight car with stories. Jacob himself is finally speechless on the train, and incapable of continuing his fairy tale of the sick princess, who is rescued and cured. Now it is the narrator who protects the child with stories of clouds that are not made of bits of cotton, as Jacob had claimed, but of drops of water. In the end, therefore, there are true stories instead of lies in the cattle cars; these stories are not capable of saving Lina, but they do succeed in drawing a doomed group together on its final journey.

Outside the narrator sees a world passing by that he has only been able to imagine in his years in the ghetto. His story starts with trees and now it ends with them. They have been the setting for his first love affair, for the murder of his wife, and for the most memorable physical aspect of the ghetto, for there the trees were banned entirely. In the waiting-room of death, the potential symbols of life had been removed. In the end he sees them passing again through slits in the boxcar, villages, people, animals, grass, trees 'that I had almost forgotten, although I'm still a young man, enormous numbers of trees, beech and alder and birch and willow and pine. My God, all the trees I see. The trees never end!' (pp. 265–6).

In between is the story of the end of a community in which, even though the trees had been cut down and a spiritually based order replaced by an always menacing and unfathomable enemy, life goes on as best it can. There is one violent death we witness and we hear of one precarious birth. There is a scene of suicide and a scene of lovemaking; there is unwanted heroism and deliberate cowardly betrayal. There are even possibly sympathetic guards (the narrator is unsure if dropped cigarettes are an accident or an apology), and certainly annoying inmates. In this muted terror, the reader is lured by Becker into a world that he, like the inhabitants, may feel will survive, since the first accurate military report from the German radio is the only piece of information for him, too, with regard to the progress of the war and the potential for freedom.

Jurek Becker ends his novel with the train and its doomed passengers under way to an unknown destination ('We're headed wherever we're headed'), although both the narrator and the audience are sure that the sick princess of Jacob's fairy tale will not survive the place that has been prepared for their arrival. The story of that reception cannot be told with the controlled narration of a tale full of sadness and humor that characterizes Becker's version of the Polish ghetto, which did not serve as an extermination center, but as the holding center from which the extermination trains would gather their victims. For, finally, Becker's story is about the attempt to remain human at the edge of the precipice, not about the fall into the abyss from which very few could escape with their lives or their humanity.

Edgar Hilsenrath's first novel, *Nacht* (*Night*), begins beyond the destination of Becker's train, inside one of the hells which had been prepared for the Jews of Europe. But the journeys of Hilsenrath's characters had taken place even further east, and had transported them from Romanian Bukovyna, where the twelve-year-old Edgar had been sent from Germany in 1938, into the Romanian-occupied Ukraine. In the Bukovyna, not far from Czernowitz, Edgar enjoyed a short-lived idyll with his grandparents, briefly secure from Nazi anti-Semitism. Then in 1941, the assumed Romanian protectors turned into the Nazi allies. In the anti-Semitic actions that followed, Hisenrath joined the rest of the Bukovynian Jews on the trains and the final ferry to Transnistria, the land between the Dniester and Bug rivers. The conquering Nazis had ceded it to their Romanian allies after having destroyed its centers on their march towards Stalingrad, and the Romanians decided to use it as the setting of their own grotesque concentration camps.

After surviving the stunningly quixotic policies of Bucharest towards its Jews and later also towards the Nazis, Hilsenrath spent six years in Israel and twenty in New York. He returned to Germany in 1975 and has lived in Berlin ever since. His two New York novels, *Nacht* (*Night*, 1966) and *Der Nazi und der Friseur* (*The Nazi and the Barber*, 1971) represent, along with some of the short stories in Jakov Lind's *Eine Seele aus Holz* (*Soul of Wood* [1966]), the breakthrough in German-language literature of ironic, satiric, grotesque, even black comic descriptions of the annihilation of the European Jews. They form a counterweight to Günter Grass's use of similar literary weapons in his fantastic descriptions of the end of German Danzig. Hilsenrath attempts to avoid at all costs the sorrow and pity evoked by Becker's automatic 'button,' while fascinating the reader with an extraordinary narrative, so that the horror of the content becomes intermingled with the reader's horror at his fascination with the narrative process.

Like Becker, Hilsenrath is in the broadest sense describing the nightmare of his youth. As a Jew, he cannot be accused of sympathy with the perspective of the narrator of *The Nazi and the Barber* (which in a second English edition exists under the misleading title *The Nazi Who Lived as a Jew*), SS-man Max Schulz, and can allow his repugnant, but witty protagonist to discuss his crimes with mockery, satire, irony, and an often perverse double-edged humor that would hardly be acceptable if the author had a background like that of his fictional narrator. As a surviving victim, Hilsenrath can hardly be accused of being disrespectful to the 6 million who did not survive. As a child victim he could afford to let an entire generation pass before he even began to formulate his literary account of the nightmare of Transnistria. And, finally, he could let even more years pass before moving on from the somewhat autobiographical *Night* to the phantasmagoric *Nazi and the Barber*. He could wait still another decade before a small German publisher was willing to take a chance with *Der Nazi und der Friseur* as late as 1977, finally making one of the most important postwar German novels available in the original language, several years after its publication in English, French, and Italian translations.[9] In addition, in exile, Hilsenrath could make use not only of the distance of time, but of geographical space as well. As a New Yorker, he was open to the influences of a literature that could handle the relationship of victims and victimizers in the Second World War, as well as the fate of the survivors in new lands, with much greater irony than could the literature of Germany. Like Aharon Appelfeld, he had personal experience with life in Israel, which comes to the fore in the second half of *The Nazi and the Barber*, and he felt no obligation to treat the promised land of the survivors as a sacred cow. In New York he would also have been in the city of I.B. Singer with whom Hilsenrath shares certain biographical and artistic characteristics. Both are unorthodox Jewish refugees from the anti-Semitism of East Central Europe; both wrote major novels in their native Germanic languages in New York; and both treat their religious compatriots with the detached irony of the insider, although Hilsenrath clearly is capable of transforming irony into a brutal satire, which Singer would never attempt. Hilsenrath could have learned from such a masterful source, however, that he could describe the foibles of the Jews with ironic humor despite the catastrophe of the Holocaust. One cannot imagine a biting satirical account of the Holocaust from Singer, but the one insider's Yiddish anecdotal irony is related to the other insider's German satiric mockery.

Thus, it is perhaps no coincidence that Singer's tales of survival and Hilsenrath's novels of destruction were conceived and written in an exile that must have seemed worlds away from the events depicted. Singer's Nobel Prize was given on the basis of almost half a century of high-quality short stories and novels, many of which are still available only in Yiddish, while Hilsenrath's reputation rested for many years on one extraordinary work, *The Nazi and the Barber*. (His 1989 novel about the extermination of the Armenians, *Das Märchen vom letzten Gedanken* [The Story of the Last Thought], winner of the Döblin Prize, confirms his position as one of the most creative and daring writers of the postwar period.) By comparison, *Night* has received comparatively little attention, being classified (even in the advertisements of its German publishers) as a 'Ghettoroman' ('a novel about ghetto life'), which suggests a novel like many others purporting to give a realistic description of the hardship of life in the urban ghettos.

But unlike such ghetto novels (or *The Nazi and the Barber*), *Night* does not fall over the relatively familiar war landscape surrounding the Polish Jews in their final years of existence, but over the political and geographical no man's land of the Romanian-occupied Ukraine. If Sasha Granach had returned to Ukraine at the end of the Second World War instead of the First, he would have found not just an altered political situation, but a wasteland, where the small towns had been ravaged and the larger urban centers leveled to the ground. This science-fiction world of destruction provides a much different environment from the one that we usually understand under the term 'Ghettoroman.' It is different again from those novels that try to deal with the Nazi concentration camps and extermination centers. To an even greater extent than with the crimes perpetrated by the Nazis on the East European Jews in territories under their control, the Romanian extermination process has hardly been registered in the German consciousness. Thus the Deutsche Presse Agentur (German Press Agency), in a 1979 review of the Viennese performances of the Yiddish-speaking theater of Romania, could explain the paucity of a linguistic audience as follows: 'The approximately 40,000 Jews who still live in Romania (before the war it was a half a million, most of them emigrated after the war) live scattered throughout the land.'[10] This parenthetical historical explanation manages to ignore the Nazi-inspired, Romanian-executed concentration camps in the ruins of Transnistria, where most of the more than 250,000 Jews of Bukovyna and Bessarabia (territories gained by Romania after the First World War) failed to survive the war. Raul Hilberg, in his exhaustive study of the process of extermination, offers a different version of why there are so few Yiddish-speaking Romanian Jews today. 'In that territory, the Roumanians maintained true killing centers. Besides Germany itself, Roumania was thus the only country which implemented all the steps of the destruction process, from definitions to killings.'[11]

In Transnistria, the arriving deportees were confronted with a situation different from that of the Jews who were shipped into the Polish ghettos, where until the end there was a semblance of order in the attempt to carry on daily life. Instead of this attempted order, the Romanian inmates faced a grotesque survival test in the crumbling ruins of Ukrainian cities. The Romanian extermination relied on a kind of natural selection that allowed relative safety if a shelter could be found at night, and deportation and execution if it could not. Sobol's comments on the survival process of the ghettos become more immediate when survival could be defined as the ability to find a shelter for the night – a grotesque game of musical chairs in which the price of being caught without one of the chairs (which were always too few in number) was death. In addition, there were no regular food deliveries to the land between the rivers, and survival could only be maintained by those strong enough to live off the ruined land or the black market, clothing obtained only by those fast enough to rob the corpses first, health maintained only by those lucky enough and fit enough to withstand the typhoid plague. For the select few, a kind of normal life evolved in the ruins, with markets for bartering and coffee houses for entertaining; for the weaker, particularly for the women and the children, there was only increasing hunger and weakness with the easily imaginable 'death due to exhaustion.' Transnistria offered drastic possibilities for Sobol's proposition that all survivors have guilt feelings because all survivors betrayed someone at some time or another.

In Transnistria, the arbitrary disorder of survival or extinction allows an almost black comic description of the horror of the daily struggle for existence. That characteristic of Jewish, and particularly Yiddish, literature which allowed a certain melancholic self-ironic acceptance of even the most tragic and unfair whims of fate is in more familiar territory here, where the (dis)order was left to the caprices of the local commander, than it ever could be within the electrified fences of the ordered, bureaucratic, slave-work/extermination centers of Auschwitz or Majdanek. The very anarchy of the rules of the game of survival allows Transnistria to take on the image of an absurd berserk world rather than the form of a unique concentrated evil that arises from the descriptions of everyday life in the Nazi concentration camps. And this absurdity carries with it the possibility of the blackest comedy, a comedy describing the limitless lengths that men will go to in order to protect their chances of life for one more day, the distorted wail of those in the process of surviving. It is in this struggle between survival and an absurdly quixotic exterminator that Hilsenrath takes his first steps towards the full-blown grotesque satire of *The Nazi and the Barber*.

In *Night*, this exterminator is almost never present in the physical form of the captors. On the contrary, we rarely meet the captors and, when we do, it is almost always in the person of the Jewish police, who have found their own way to survival by serving the invisible creator of the deadly game. Ranek, the main figure of the novel who has turned down the chance to become part of the police force, occasionally receives tips from one of his old friends who has taken on this repugnant role, and thus he is actually more protected than threatened by the captors. Occasionally we are witness to the night-time roundups in which the victims without shelter are shipped off to an almost certain fate, but the characters we follow have become familiar enough with the absurd rules that they are almost never caught up in them. None of these characters actually meets his end through the process of roundups and executions. All who die, including eventually Ranek, are victims of exhaustion, starvation, or typhus, the disease whose introduction into the community adds one more potential fatal card to the stacked deck.

This shift of focus away from the uneven battle between captors and captives and to the daily struggle of the inmates for survival in an extremely threatening and alien world enables Hilsenrath to make use of these concentrations of desperate and dehumanized people in a new way in German literature. Hilsenrath's object is not only to display the horrifying fate of victims in a losing struggle between good and evil, or even to describe a horrible episode in the history of East Central Europe (which, of course, is present in any case), or to portray Becker's sadly doomed individuals, but also to present randomly chosen players in a world absurdly out of joint. We see this world largely through the eyes of the cynical Ranek, for whom there is, until the arrival of his sister-in-law Debora, only one law – the law of survival. Hilsenrath's victims are incapable of acting in an altruistic manner if they intend to survive, and the extremes they go to in their own interests is the heart of the darkness: 'Everything he had learned in the long, difficult months – what tricks you had to know and how you went about staying halfway alive.'[12]

The description of these 'tricks,' these methods of survival, lend the air of grotesque absurdity to the ruins of Prokow, the ghetto-city of *Night*. Ranek, always on the verge of starvation, always somehow finds food. In the apartment of the black-market dealer Dvorak, Ranek is momentarily left alone with the Dvorak baby and told to give him a pacifier:

> So that's the pacifier, Ranek thought. The kohlrabi had been whittled to a point; it just fitted into the tiny mouth ... The sight of the kohlrabi only made him more conscious of his hunger, and the empty feeling in his stomach became more and more acute. And because he could not bear it any longer he flipped open the rusty pocketknife he always carried with him, and cut off a piece of the kohlrabi ... He couldn't resist and cut off a second piece and stuck it greedily into his mouth. And then a third. The rest of the pacifier looked so unprepossessing now that he became afraid the child might choke on it. And so he picked up the remnant of the pacifier and ate it. (*Night*, 49)

In such scenes, and there are many in which the potential comic aspects are overwhelmed by the horror, there is little reminder that we are dealing here with an average person from provincial Romania who has been turned into a stalking animal by the whims of a fate beyond his control, or even beyond his ability to try to interpret. Here there is no place for the logic of Jacob's radio. Ranek accepts the absurdity of his condition and attempts to survive it. In *Night*, unlike in *The Nazi and the Barber*, there is, however, a temporary light in the darkness. It arrives in the form of the haunting and saintly Debora, who once stopped passersby in the streets of Litesti with the beauty of her Yiddish songs and who arrives in Prokow dragging her husband to his final confrontation with typhoid. In Ranek's response to her, and in her selflessness, we are reminded that these predators come from an almost unimaginable world just across the river where, when the wind is right, they can hear the church bells ringing. Like a beast of prey stunned for a moment by a half-familiar scent, Ranek in a hunger delirium has a vision of his homeland. 'He thought of Romania. He could see the broad corn fields again, which, at a great distance, touched the cloudless blue sky; he saw the squat huts with yellow thatched roofs in which the storks nested, and he thought of the gypsies roaming about the countryside who would play you a tune on their violins for a few pennies' (p. 39).

In such moments Ranek is the condemned cousin of Singer's Polish exiles in New York, or of Joseph Roth's Mendel Singer in *Job*, who from that same city imagines his return to his Russian shtetl. 'Before him lay the vast ocean. Once again he must cross it. The whole great sea waited for Mendel. All of Zuchnow and its surroundings waited for him: the barracks, the fir forest, the frogs in the swamp, and the crickets in the fields.'[13] But although this may be the dominant emotional relationship between the exiled Jews and their homelands, both in New York and in Transnistria, there is little time for it in Prokow during the endless struggle to outwit the Holocaust.

In *The Nazi and the Barber*, Hilsenrath concocts a plot so grotesque that its black humor even disturbs the victimized group to which the author belongs. For the hero(es) and villain(s) of this novel are one and the same – Mass Murderer Max Schulz, as he prefers to identify himself, and his victim Itzig Finkelstein, the Jew with whom Schulz had grown up and whose identity he takes over at the end of the war as a disguise, allowing him to abandon his true Nazi identity and flee from the concentration camp in Poland, where he has murdered not only Itzig but the whole Finkelstein family. With a bag of stolen gold teeth, he undertakes an epic journey through partisan-controlled Poland to Berlin and finally on to the forest of the 6 million victims in Israel. There the Yiddish-speaking Zionist Max Schulz finds a satisfying new life among the Jewish guerrillas of Palestine in their violent struggle against the British. Even such a brief sketch of the picaresque adventures of Mass Murderer Max Schulz indicates that Hilsenrath is entering taboo territory. As an outsider/insider in New York, Hilsenrath can tell his story in a manner scarcely available to the complete outsider or the complete insider.

This is, of course, not to suggest that the author's sympathies lie with his narrator, but that the distance between the author and his subject allows him to write from a viewpoint that takes in more than just the terrible plight of the Holocaust victims, some of whom themselves later find terrorist tactics appropriate in their own struggle and Schulz's military experience useful in this regard. Hilsenrath writes with the dark vision of the world as an absurd theater in which almost everyone, given the right conditions, can play a role permitting crimes whose awesome dimensions can be described effectively only with the weapons of total irony, cynicism, and sarcasm. Thus, through the narrative of Max Schulz, we not only hear the voice of the evil Nazi, who is capable of anything to gain power or to survive – and who resembles Ranek, who begins *Nacht* by stealing the shoes from a dying typhoid victim and then takes credit for having helped him in his final hours – but also the mocking voice of Hilsenrath as well. The author is suggesting throughout that the evil of the Nazis is the mass representation of the evil inherent in almost every character we meet. For example, the terrible anti-Semitism of Max Schulz has its milder equivalent in the barbershops of Tel Aviv, where Itzig Finkelstein-Schulz is told the meaning of the numbers on the customer's chairs:

> 'Yes, Mr. Finkelstein. Look: barber chair number one, the one by the window, the best chair in the salon, right by the window, you understand ... that one ... is reserved for German Jews!'
> 'Oh, I see! And what about barber chair number two?'
> 'That's for Jews from the other West European countries.'
> 'And number three?'
> 'For elite Eastern European Jews.'
> 'And who are they supposed to be, Mr. Spiegel?'
> 'The Russians and the Lithuanians.'
> 'And barber chair number four?'
> 'For Jews from the rest of Eastern European countries. Except Romania.'
> 'And where do the Romanian Jews sit?'
> 'On the last chair reserved for Jews from Eastern Europe. On chair number five.'
>
> ...
>
> Jizchak Spiegel explained to me next that barber chair number six was reserved for the elite of Oriental Jews: namely the Yemenites, after which came the others; on the last chair reserved for the oriental Jews sat the Moroccans.[14]

The basic situation in this tragicomic scene illustrates the reason why Hilsenrath opens new perspectives for approaching the Holocaust in German-language literature. Here there can be no talk of

Becker's memory-button; here we have a topsy-turvy version of the Holocaust, in which the perpetrator Schulz is given a lesson in anti-Semitism by the victim Spiegel, which shocks Schulz in his assumed role of a Jew in the promised land. But Max Schulz is, if anything, adaptable and he quickly realizes that he is once again in a privileged position, that barber chair number one has been reserved for him because of his native German background, and that he could end up as a respected member of the community. Indeed, Max Schulz eventually becomes the president of an animal protection society dedicated to the right of chickens to run about free. In his masochistic schizophrenic plea to Israeli authorities to check out the possible survival of his arch-enemy Mass Murderer Max Schulz, Finkelstein-Schulz finds only sympathy. His final drunken admission of his real identity in a mock trial before a German-Jewish judge leads only to the judicial confirmation of his own verdict, namely acquittal on the grounds that there is no conceivable punishment.

The final scene of Hilsenrath's novel shows to what extremes he is willing to go beyond the irony inherent in Singer's stories of the Holocaust survivors in exile. Singer's characters are burned forever by visions of the past, relived or escaped, but they have for the most part rediscovered that the Jews have been wandering for thousands of years, and have learned to cope with a hostile fate. Their role in the new world is to contest that ancient struggle once again, despite the overwhelming catastrophe of the recent past. The language in which this battle is waged is the language of parables, anecdotes, and ironically aggressive argumentation and questioning, the Yiddish language that had been the private language of the East European Jews for almost a thousand years. This Yiddish language, close enough to German so that the two languages are often mutually comprehensible, but far enough away so that it remains in its inflection untranslatable into German (Singer's works are usually translated from English rather than Yiddish into German, although that fact may, of course, be the result of a lack of qualified Yiddish-German translators), well serves the world of the ironic questioner of God and the fate of the Jews from Tevye to the cabalist of East Broadway. But this same literature cannot portray the injustice of the world by presenting a distorted view of that world through an absurdly misplaced narrator or through the reflections off a shattered mirror, employing instead an ironic observer as narrator.

In this final scene, Mass Murderer Max Schulz receives the transplanted heart of a rabbi, thus realizing in physical form the psychological metamorphosis he has undertaken as a method of survival. As such, he becomes the post-Holocaust heir of two other Central European Jewish writers, who came from recently assimilated Yiddish families, Franz Kafka and Bruno Schulz. In German and in Polish they created two of the most memorable figures of modern literature: one is a son who becomes an insect and the other is a father who becomes a bird, images of transformation that suggest the identity change demanded by assimilation. In these three cases, burlesque and demonic features of the 'first' phase find their metamorphosed form in a grotesque, but understandably connected, second version.

Franz Kafka and Bruno Schulz were describing the alienated situation of man in general and the European Jews in particular before the Holocaust (and Kafka has been assigned an almost magical prophetic power by writers such as Appelfeld, Wiesel, and George Steiner). Hilsenrath (in his first two novels, as well as partly in his fourth novel, *Bronskys Geständnis* [Bronsky's Confession]) is depicting the destruction of the European Jews during the Holocaust and the absurdity of the world into which its survivors dispersed. By attempting to write about the most catastrophic event in the history of Judaism and Germany in potentially comic terms (Kafka also considered his Gregor Samsa to be hilarious), Hilsenrath runs the risk that his satiric exaggerations might undermine the deadly seriousness of this theme and tip over into travesty, a genre that cannot be used to describe mass murder. But it is a misstep he never takes. We are never allowed to forget that Max Schulz's sarcastic version of the destruction of a culture is manipulated by the ironic voice of Edgar Hilsenrath, and we constantly feel that we are within the forest of the 6 million victims. This perspective allows the novel to stay on the razor's edge of black comedy.

With *Jacob the Liar*, Jurek Becker fulfills his own requirement that an author maintain the cool intellectual distance that protects a piece of writing from pathos and sentimentality. Edgar Hilsenrath's style is far more brutally satirical, which befits both the position of the narrator of *The Nazi and the Barber* and the physical conditions of the ghetto of *Night* as well. (In *Das Märchen vom letzten Gedanken*, Hilsenrath employs a similar technique to relate the fate of the Armenians in the First World War.) Both writers successfully use stories from the Holocaust to suggest that beyond the personal tragedies of characters, forced to demonstrate their willingness to compromise in order to survive, is the incomprehensible universal folly of a mad world in which unfathomable powers turn men into marionettes with invisible strings. Hilsenrath and Becker convincingly demonstrate that the German language is capable of describing the ghettos in which the Jews of Europe were prepared for the final solution in terms that defy criticism of sentimentality or pathos. But neither Hilsenrath nor Becker takes the next drastic step into the killing centers of Auschwitz, Treblinka, and Majdanek. For an attempt to describe the final circle of hell in such terms we can turn to Udo Steinke's 1982 novel *Horsky, Leo oder die Dankbarkeit der Mörder* (Horsky, Leo or the Thanks of the Murderers).

Like Hilsenrath and Becker, Steinke, who was born in 1942, employs a prose style characterized by a naive simplicity, which allows his narrative voice to express childlike astonishment at brutality and beauty, at humor and terror, at unbelievable murderers and incomprehensible forgivers. The unnamed narrator tells his story in the manner of Max Schulz, who finds it necessary to repeat names and descriptions of people many times as does a fairy-tale teller to children. He uses storytellers like the narrator of *Jacob the Liar*, who considers the advantages and disadvantages of different possible versions of the same event, and can admit that occasionally he must simply assume that what he reports might have been said. For all three authors, the centrality of storytelling is crucial; it is the factor that allows the readers to be drawn into a world so simply and naively described that one must be reminded that one is reading about the annihilation of the Jews of Europe. In *Horsky, Leo oder die Dankbarkeit der Mörder* Steinke attempts to take his fairy-tale innocence to the center of the inferno, to the gas chambers of Auschwitz, which is never named, but which looms silently and menacingly over the contemporary world.

The title figure has hanging on his wall a map of East Central Europe with a black flag pinned at Auschwitz:

> And if some people showed an interest in the map and the little flag and asked stupid questions and had no idea what to make of 'that place on the Upper Silesian plateau, right near the railroad junctions, steam mills and zinc refineries' then Horsky tapped with his ring and middle finger of his left hand on the little black flag. And quick as a flash, eyes and nose shot to the place with the needle in it, and although the point of the needle stuck right between the steep walls of the 'u', Horsky usually only heard the last syllable of the name of the place. He wanted to know how his patients hissed out this syllable. From that Horsky could determine the kind of interests they had about his place, he could judge how the patient lived with his disinterest, whether it gave him pleasure, tortured him, or if he had none at all, which he rarely encountered.[15]

Like Max Schulz, Leo Horsky has survived the killing centers only by means of an extraordinary quality. Mass Murderer Max Schulz looks Jewish and speaks fluent Yiddish, allowing his transformation at the end of the war; Leo Horsky possesses 'ten men,' whose talents become more and more indispensable to the guardians of the place at the railway junction. The ten men are the magical fingers of the masseur Leo Horsky, who one week before the scheduled start of his career as a medical student at a Polish university finds himself transported to the camp whose name he never mentions. Like Max Schulz, the only mass murderer to become a vocal Zionist in Israel, Leo Horsky is unique, the only person to have survived Auschwitz from the first day to the last. 'No person other than Horsky went through all the days of the fence age. Horsky's companions freighted in for opening day were soon sent on to the underworld' (p. 40).

Thus Udo Steinke builds his novel of genocide around the figure of the ultimate survivor, a fairy-tale figure whose ability to overcome the obstacles on his journey to Munich, where this novel begins and ends, ranges on the miraculous. Horsky's ten fingers gradually take on the status of all the heroic resistance figures, who for Horsky, like Jacob, existed only insofar as they managed the small acts that allowed life to go on for one more day. Unlike Jacob's tale, however, Horsky's is the tale of the last stop on the journey to the final solution, of the gas chambers and the ovens, where Leo Horsky also occasionally is sent to work. Like the story of Jacob Heym, this is a tale told by a not-further-identified, all-knowing, and occasionally intervening narrator. He steps in only from the contemporary world of Bavaria to add depth to the presentation of the two worlds of Auschwitz and Munich in which Leo Horsky plays out the same role. *Jacob the Liar* and *The Nazi and the Barber* are both told through the reminiscences of someone who was there and who can vouch for the authenticity of the report, even if he maintains a cynical perspective from the contemporary world. The distance that allows these two narrators to approach the Holocaust with humor, ranging from understated irony in Becker to brutal satire in Hilsenrath, is equally striking in the unidentified mocking narrator of Steinke, who vouches for nothing other than the depravity of the world around him. Becker's story ends on the train to Auschwitz, Hilsenrath's murderous satire moves on to Israel, while Steinke's tale is absolutely rooted in the society of West Germany.

Like Becker, Steinke was born in the industrial city of Lodz in Poland, which in 1942 contained not only one of the largest Jewish ghettos, but a significant German population as well. Forced west at the end of the war, when he was three, Steinke ended up eventually moving in 1968 from East to West Germany, where Becker also now lives. Thus Hilsenrath, Becker, and Steinke share biographical data, which suggest that a gradual distancing from the war, a gradual movement to the west, and a gradual realization of the eventual shortcomings of the new home in the west all foster a fictional look back at the wartime chaos in Eastern Europe. This perspective is buffered by the recognition that the contemporary states have a relationship to the events of the first half of the 1940s that builds a kind of macabre comparative base of black humor. Max Schulz becomes a welcome compatriot of Jewish guerrilla groups in Israel, as his Nazi-learned skills prove useful in their struggle against the British army. Leo Horsky continually runs into the former killers of Auschwitz, who in a macabre way have become highly respectable pillars of West German society. Macabre and almost comic, because the narrator's naive simplicity in describing these figures and their fates can suggest a kind of enthusiasm for their achievements in the first half of a sentence, before delivering them to an unexpected punishment in the second half.

For instance, one of the central stories of the novel, which is made up of a series of anecdotes shifting continually between contemporary West Germany and Auschwitz of the early 1940s, involves one of the sadistic medical experimenters of Auschwitz. He has Horsky's work partner, Jan, a former dancer in the Paris ballet, taken away so that his calf muscles, which have remained intact despite the total malnourishment of the rest of the body, can be added to his collection of medical wonders. The grotesque death of Jan, which comes to stand for the deaths of thousands at the hands of the Auschwitz medical experimenters, remains unpunished until the experimenter's apparent security in Horsky's new homeland allows him to forget his past. The good doctor, who 'had dissected a French artist on the altar of German science,' has been able to exploit this scientific obsession during three successful decades of doctoring in the Bundesrepublik: 'And the insanity of his obsession with his specialty ["Fachidiotenwahn"] drove him for the first two weeks of 1981 to an international symposium in Leipzig. There he gave a splendidly received lecture on the peculiarities of leg muscles, was arrested however one hour later just as he was catching his breath and nine months later executed' (p. 76).

The impact of this short episode is typical of the shock that Steinke creates with his combination of purposely naive narration and purposely misleading sentence structure, in which a verb like 'hinrichten' ('execute') follows only at the end of a mass of other information which does not seem to be leading to that word. Leo Horsky, the axis around which the anecdotes turn, 'felt no satisfaction at the end of the German doctor,' and could not understand 'the enthusiasm of the French ballet world, which had never forgotten their Jan' (p. 77). Gradually he takes on the stature of an almost silent reminder of things past, lets his ten men do their work in 1982 as they had in 1940–5, and waits for his patients to hiss out the last syllable of Auschwitz. In his capacity as masseur of the world, Leo Horsky works over the same bodies and the same types, from beautiful young women, who even in Auschwitz cannot resist the physical exhilaration conjured up by his 'wonderfingers' on their naked flesh, to the captains of Auschwitz and the captains of West German industry, whom he alone had seen transported into a peaceful physical trance, before they return to their respective arenas of business.

In his most compelling scenes, Steinke is capable of bringing unusual threads into the crazy-quilt pattern of his narrative; they function like the black verbs at the end of apparently innocent sentences. A darkness enters, produced by the same stylistic playfulness that has just been used in describing a somewhat humorous and harmless quirk of 1982; it moves on without apparent shift of tone to the most nihilistic theme of modern times:

> Horsky knew that when they used to mention the word 'genius' in Poland, it was time to start shaking. And today? Nineteen hundred and eighty two. Today every season has its genius. In other ways it's very similar, too, just think of the book of the season, the book of the month, the woman of the year, the best insight of last autumn, etc.
>
> Once Horsky squatted together with three rabbis right behind one of the crematorium ovens which had to be shut down for a moment to let it cool off. The three rabbis sat right in front of Horsky's nose and – put God on trial. They were going to pass judgment on God. They found him guilty.
>
> After that they prayed, in prayer God was in their midst again. (P. 59)

Much like Singer's narrator who offhandedly tells us about the nihilism of Harry Bendiner in 'Old Love,' this narrator chooses to comment on the superficiality of life in West Germany in the same tone as on the depth of spiritual despair into which the Jews of Europe were thrust by the events of the Second World War. This brief episode in the life of Leo Horsky can serve as a final commentary on the world of Sholom Aleichem's Anatevka and the sometimes almost desperate questioning by Tevye of his Jehovah. We do not know what language the rabbis speak while conducting their trial of Jehovah. In the Lodz ghetto, which maintained the most historically detailed chronicle of the events of ghetto life, much of the communication was carried out in the German of the Jews who had decided a generation before that this was the language that promised them assimilation into a liberating Western culture.

In the final circle, in Auschwitz, the assimilated German-speaking Jews of the West were transported to a meeting place with the Yiddish-speaking Jews of the East. And as it turned out it didn't matter at all whether those rabbis had a German-speaking, Polish-speaking, or Yiddish-speaking Jehovah or jury. It was not their language, their past, their financial status, their social position, their musical talents, or their connections that had brought them to Auschwitz, not even their religious beliefs or non-beliefs. The only thing that mattered was the percentage of Jewish ancestors in their genealogical table.[16]

In the end, that is what the rabbis are attempting to judge behind the crematoriums of Auschwitz. The ironic Yiddish plea to choose another people for awhile has been answered by a silence that ultimately overwhelms the entire chosen people and allows them to be selected for a bureaucratic list gathered together for only one purpose: the extermination of them all. The rabbis are faced with a situation that Tevye could not have foreseen, even at the moment he is told to abandon his house and move somewhere else. He had been chosen yet again as an object of extraordinarily prejudicial behavior by the Russian authorities, but he had not been chosen for mass extermination. If he had lived into the 1940s, his chances of surviving the Nazi occupation of his homeland would have been minimal.

It is the silence of God in the face of the murders of the millions of Tevyes of East Central Europe that the rabbis are judging behind the ovens. Their final meeting place is no longer the besieged synagogue, the holy temple (long since razed to the ground), but the briefly cooling furnaces of hell. They are briefly cooling because they are overheated from the amount of fire given off by the bodies of the chosen people. The final circle of hell for Dante is characterized by the absolute absence of heat, but hell for these rabbis is the all-devouring presence of a heat so extreme that the system of burning threatens to stop the functioning of the machinery.

In the one masterful novel written (in French) by the Ukrainian Jew Piotr Rawicz before his suicide, he chose an image of hallucinatory terror as a title, *Sang du Ciel* (*Blood from the Sky*, 1964), to suggest the fate of the Jews. But even this image offers more solicitude than do Steinke's cooling ovens and judging rabbis. Blood from the sky suggests a world in terrifying turmoil, a universe in which a battle to the death is taking place for control of the space formerly occupied by the spiritual authorities. It certainly also suggests a (perhaps temporary) total chaos until spiritual order can be restored. But Steinke's rabbis have gone through the blood from the sky and are squatting behind the ovens into which their entire world will pass from flesh to ash. Fire from the ovens hardly offers the possibility of a change in fortune for the squatting rabbis and their judgment is swift and blasphemous. God is guilty of having remained silent until the chosen people are no longer even present in order to be chosen. Joseph Roth's trials of Job placed upon the shoulders of Mendel Singer have a biblical example that ultimately suggests triumph at the end of adversity, a triumph fulfilled through the almost miraculous fate of Menuchim during Mendel's life. But Leo Horsky's trials suggest nothing more than the complete absence of any spiritual forerunners. A victory can be nothing more than survival for one more day because of his miraculous ten workmen. It is one more day in which he does his part in cremating the remains of the chosen people.

In the trial behind the ovens, Leo Horsky sits silently and observes. He does not take part in the rabbis' judgment, just as he does not wish to take part in the state's judgment afterwards. We are not given Leo Horsky's reaction to the judgment of 'guilty' placed upon his God by his spiritual advisers. Instead the story moves effortlessly on to a grotesque scene in Munich in which massaged doctors and lawyers play the role of the new gods. Leo Horsky lets his ten workmen soothe their bodies and says nothing. The tone of the narration suggests, however, that the narrator, like Horsky, cannot accept the stated idea that in the prayers of the rabbis behind the ovens of Auschwitz, God suddenly reappears in their midst. This narrator achieves this effect not by stating it, but by allowing his narrative flow to move from one God to another without comment. The new gods in their midst (and certainly the rabbis have not survived to experience them) are the elite of the society into which Leo Horsky has chosen to silently disappear, watching and observing, but hardly commenting and never seeking revenge. He becomes a silent witness to the absence of the old God in the new world, a witness who only points to the map on his wall, to 'the place of impossibilities, which he never spoke, which he had on a great map, which decorated the wall of his massage practice, with a fat nail, upon which a black flag hung, well marked' (p. 60).

In front of this black flag, the world of the new gods passes in review, and Leo Horsky lets his ten workmen work on. Ultimately, he, too, passes judgment on the spiritual powers, but unlike the rabbis, he does not weigh the pros and cons of guilt or innocence in the order of the world, nor does he then seek the presence of God in prayer as the rabbis did while the ovens were cooling down to working order. Leo Horsky passes silent judgment, and points at the map on the wall. The narrator of his story observes the world displayed on the map and finds that as 1981 passes on to 1982 not so very much has changed. 'The little Hitlers of Buenos Aires had recalled some islands back into the realm ("Heim ins Reich"), and London ... sent off its marine circus to the southwest in order to prepare a gauntlet for the freedom of the Falklanders. The game Battleship became the electronic hit of the year in Easter bunny baskets' (p. 152). The barbecue party of 1981 that opens the novel with the small talk of the Munich elite about Leo Horsky as they rotate the body of a sheep over glowing coals has become, in 1982, in honor of Easter, a more civilized feast. 'One had become more peace-oriented, and grilled spare ribs of lamb could be more delicately, somehow more non-violently snapped' (p. 153).

Like his hero, the narrator observes. Little Hitlers come and go. The victors of the Second World War play games with ships and lives. The massaged party-goers demonstrate their peacefulness by snapping ribs instead of grilling bodies, and somehow they are all related to the bodies that Leo Horsky massaged in order to survive forty years before, and to those that passed through his hands into the ovens. As for Horsky, he is content to accept the thanks of the murderers, whom he, like the judge at the mock trial of Max Schulz, refuses to sentence, and then to point at the map and wait for the sound of the hiss of the syllable 'schwitz.' Unlike the rabbis, who condemn and then rediscover the Jehovah who has gone too far in testing his chosen people, Leo Horsky is beyond judgment and beyond reconciliation. All he can do is bear witness with his map and his black flag to the 'age in which the impossible suffers from inflation' (p. 58). Leo Horsky as the final heir of Tevye is also the physical demonstration of the nihilistic end of a spiritual community numbering in the millions that within a decade had been reduced to thousands of numbed survivors.

There is no doubt that the story of the end of Tevye will be hard to tell in the German language for a long time to come. The questions of guilt and innocence, of knowledge and ignorance, of crime and (non)-punishment, are still an everyday topic of German society. An excellent submarine war film like *Das Boot* cannot be shown on German television without sparking a bitter debate about the amount of guilt that can be placed on the average German soldier or sailor under Nazi command; the answers range from 'they were at least the accomplices of the murderers' to 'they were engaged in the same struggle for survival as everyone who was forced to take part in the war.' If these soldiers had been involved with the Jewish population of Eastern Europe (for the Jewish question does not arise at all on a submarine) the debate would surely be raging even more in the aftermath.

Becker, Hilsenrath, and Steinke have shown, however, that it is possible to tell the story of the elimination of the Jews of Europe in the German language in a manner that demands critical input and reaction from the reader; their novels do not merely attempt to describe the horror the way it was (which in any case, as Appelfeld has said, cannot be done). It will always seem more bearable even in the most powerful visions of despair; it will always be better in words than it really was. Readers are forced to react to the quirks of Jacob, Ranek, Max, and Leo, are jolted into a conclusion demanded by the consciously cynical observations of the narrator, the conscious innocence of the narrator, the conscious manipulation of the narrator. As such they are forced, like Leo Horsky's patients, to look up from the massaging table, be reminded of the name behind the black flag, and, if they are then perceptive to their own reactions, to discover for themselves how they hissed out the syllable 'schwitz.'

Chapter Five

The Germans of Eastern Europe Pay the Price

The deathly silence and taboo, which refuses to admit the German-Jewish contribution to the development of Czech culture, is the gravedigger's spade for the European spirit in general.

Milan Uhde

When Leo Horsky staggered out of the gate that was marked 'Arbeit macht frei' ('Work makes free') to become the only prisoner to have survived the death camp from the first day to the last, he was about to enter a world from which his home culture had been almost totally eradicated during the relatively short period of his confinement. From the Baltic coast in the north to Bulgaria in the south, the Nazis had carried out the proposal of their leader to destroy the European Jews with an effective fury. In the heartland of Yiddish – central and eastern Poland, Lithuania, White Russia, Romania, and Ukraine – the result of only a few years of systematic murder was the virtual elimination of a language that had been spoken for centuries by a native population numbering in the millions. Only in the old territories of Romania, where the government for reasons of political exigency never deported its resident Jews, in Budapest, where planned deportations were stalled long enough to save the majority of the Jewish population, and in the unoccupied parts of the Soviet Union was there any significant remnant of the cultural and linguistic entity that had formed a trans-national bond through Eastern Europe for many centuries. Within a decade, Soviet anti-Semitic actions would deal another stunning blow to the last large European Yiddish-speaking population. A basically intact Jewish population was to be found only south of the Yiddish-speaking areas in Bulgaria, where almost all the Sephardic Jews had survived when the Nazi-allied government in Sofia did not carry out Nazi deportation orders. Bulgaria alone of the countries in the European war zone (if one excepts the tiny Jewish community of Finland) would have a larger Jewish population in the years after the war than it had had before.[1]

When the populations settled by the mid 1950s, there were almost twice as many Jews in Switzerland as in Sigmund Freud's Austria (19,000 versus 10,000), more Jews in Scandinavia than in Franz Kafka's Czechoslovakia (approximately 22,000 versus 19,000), and more in the Netherlands than in Edgar Hilsenrath's Germany (25,000 versus 23,000). In the Poland of Jurek Becker and Isaac Singer, the greatest slaughter had taken place. Of the population of 3.3 million before the war, there was left a numbed and scattered remnant, only slightly larger than that of the Jewish population of Belgium (45,000 versus 40,000), a number which has now been reduced to an estimated 4000–6000.[2] As far as Yiddish was concerned, a literature that had produced such major writers in this century as the Singer brothers was gone from its native realm. Although it is still possible to gather together an anthology of Yiddish writing from the postwar Soviet Union, tentative and depressing though it might be,[3] there are in today's Poland very few Yiddish speakers, not to mention writers, and they are virtually all old. Although the discussion continues with regard to the future prospects of the Yiddish language in a global sense, it now seems certain that no more Yiddish novels will arise out of the small towns of Poland or the ashes of Warsaw.

As Leo Horsky entered this strange new world, millions of Germans had already concluded that the consequences of this German expedition into Eastern Europe would not only include the violent onslaught of the advancing Red Army on the steadily retreating Wehrmacht, but indiscriminate revenge on the resident ethnic German populations as well, whether they had welcomed the Nazis or not. The panicked flight of millions attempting to keep ahead of the rapidly melting Eastern front was about to get under way. In the Baltic homeland of Aurel, two events had already occurred that had brought about a radical change in population structures with regard to German and Yiddish speakers in that area. These events were the expulsion of the Baltic Germans at the beginning of the war and the violent annihilation of the Jews during the war. As part of the Nazi-Soviet nonaggression pact of 1939, the remaining German ethnic population in the newly annexed Soviet Baltic states, as well as in other eastern areas of the Soviet Union, had been forced to move west into the German Empire, and Aurel's Baltic-German world, dealt a crippling blow by the events of the First World War, was thus eliminated by the Second World War.

Within four years, the Nazis had broken the pact, conquered the Baltic, exterminated the Jewish population, and declared their new territories to be 'judenrein,' 'free of Jews.' In reality, approximately 90 percent of the Baltic Jews were killed in the course of the war, the rest having escaped into the Soviet Union. Thus, these states, which by 1943 had lost first their German- and then their Yiddish-speaking populations, offered a pattern which would now be generally followed, although in reverse order, in the rest of East Central Europe.

The Nazis had systematically eliminated the Jews in these areas; now the time had come for revenge on the resident German population. Now the Germans were going to be driven 'Heim ins Reich' whether they wanted to go or not. For those who were not fleeing in panic and were intent on staying on in their homelands, despite the certainty of hostile governments, the agreements concluded by the victorious allies at the end of the war made it clear that this time the ethnic Germans would not be allowed to consider East Central Europe as a place for a homeland and that they were to be driven out of that area in what was supposed to be 'an orderly and humane manner.'[4] Because the space to be evacuated included such heavily German areas as the Sudetenland, the Danube Basin, East Prussia, Pomerania, Danzig, and Silesia, the very number of deportees involved virtually excluded the possibility of either order or humaneness.

This expulsion, which brought about the forced movements of an estimated 12–14 million East European Germans, has recently provided some major German-language writers with material for works of fiction. In the fictional use of historical catastrophe, these writings are reminiscent of the novels of the Holocaust. For the Germans of East Central Europe, virtually everything was lost: the fruits of lifelong labor, homeland, geographical linguistic space, and in many cases the lives of family and relatives as well. Questions of guilt and innocence cannot be avoided in any suggested comparison of the fates of the Jews and the Germans in Eastern Europe. The Jews were virtually destroyed through racist violence organized on an unprecedented scale by a brutal government determined to create an expanded land base for what it considered its superior race, and more than willing to eliminate 'inferior' groups occupying that land. In the case of the Jews (and the gypsies), this annihilation was done through mass murder; in the case of the Slavic peoples through expulsion or slave work camps, which often verged on death camps. The Germans of East Central Europe were driven out of their homelands by the very real threat of violent revenge by aggrieved peoples and by the agreements of those Allies who had defeated the Nazis, in particular at the demand of the Soviet Union, which had suffered by far the most casualties (an estimated 20 million) as the direct result of the German attempt to gain land in Eastern Europe. The Soviet Union was determined to create a sphere of influence that included the entire geographical space that had been conquered and occupied by the Nazis in East Central Europe, as well as eastern sections of the German Empire. This goal, in fact, had been virtually accomplished in early 1945 by the sweep of the Red Army across Eastern Europe from the Baltic to Hungary and into large parts of eastern Austria and Germany. This position would be more easily solidified if the irritant of a native German population were to be removed.

Thus, the expulsion of the Germans was rooted in the mixed soil of hatred and revenge on the one hand, and cold political reckoning on the other. The reason, therefore, why today's traveler through the Europe east of Austria and East Germany meets very few native German speakers is very different from the reason why the same traveler meets virtually no one who can speak Yiddish. As far as linguistic developments are concerned, however, the ultimate results are quite similar: taken together, they add up to the loss of virtually all the geographical space and almost all the speakers for one of these Germanic languages (Yiddish), and the loss of more than half the geographical space and a great majority of its speakers in the lost areas for the other (German). The German language could recover its numbers in the cramped area left to it in the west, and remains, after Russian, the European language with the most native speakers.[5] But Yiddish had no political entity to move to, and its future remains uncertain at best.

Postwar works of fiction dealing with the East European Germans and their expulsion automatically become part of the still raging debate over the proper stance of West Germany towards the lands formerly occupied by many millions of its citizens. As such, these works are a storehouse of childhood memories, as well as an emotional basis for a feeling of homeland that can be tested against life in the west. They also reflect a shimmering relationship between the past and the present, between a world that has been (apparently) lost forever and a land of exile, which has not (necessarily) been found to be all that was hoped for.

In von Vegesack's presentation of the fall of the Baltic Germans, a basic pattern becomes apparent that is also a crucial ingredient of the works of expulsion dealing with the end of the Second World War. In the first section there is the unfolding of the idyll of childhood, Blumbergshof; in the second, the narration of the growing threat of violence against that paradise; and in the third, the destruction of the garden and the panicked flight from it. The dangers lurking in such a presentation are evident. If the sacred and innocent dreamworld of childhood is depicted as the historical representation of a fundamentally healthy and good world, then the destroyers of that goodness may very well appear as the historical incarnations of disease and evil.

In the most idealized and sentimental of the novels of expulsion, the reader never leaves the garden, and the idyll of childhood is left intact or is threatened only at the end in order to conclude with a suggestion of loss and tragic alienation. These novels, which at least until recently have been the most commercially successful and popular 'Heimatromane' ('novels of the homeland'), disrupt the order of their garden only with the predictable problems of a rural or small-town population days away from the centers of European culture: problems of weather, natural catastrophes, love affairs, farming, child rearing. Noticeably absent from such novels are aspects of life such as relationships with the neighboring Slavic population and the position of the Jews. In most postwar German works describing the lost world of the Germans in Eastern Europe, the Jewish population often seems to be eerily absent from societies in which they certainly lived, if only often on the periphery. In the most popular novels about German Eastern Europe, the world of Blumbergshof remains the magnetic center of attention, and the suggestion that something was out of balance in the German idylls of Masuria, Pomerania, or Silesia is never brought to the surface to be tested.

One major consequence of this is that the German inhabitants who occupy the lands described inevitably become victims for an audience that is well aware of the fact that these lands are now in Poland or the Soviet Union or Czechoslovakia. Readers realize that the everyday people they have met in the writings have been forcibly and often violently driven from the charmed land they have gotten to know. For such works, therefore, the relationship between the land of exile and the former homeland is well established, even if it may not be clearly defined because the story is not carried over into the land of exile. The authors of such novels preferred and prefer to remain held by the beauty and fascination of the lost world of Blumbergshof or the East Prussian forest than to explore seriously the problems leading to and resulting from the expulsion from the remembered paradise. The potential guilt of those expelled or a weighing of the severe judgment passed upon them would mar the evoked landscape; the revenge is presented only under the given assumption that the expelled former inhabitants of the garden were the victims of the usurpers of the garden.

Things were, of course, more complicated than that, and it is the recognition of this complexity and the certainty of at least some German responsibility for their own fate in the Baltic that sets von Vegesack's novel apart from novels such as Hansgeorg Buchholtz's *Das Dorf unter der Düne* (The Village below the Dunes) or Ernst Wiechert's *Das einfache Leben* (The Simple Life), both of which were also first published in the 1930s, or numerous others of the postwar period. Von Vegesack was describing a world that, in effect, had already disappeared when he wrote about it, even though half the Germans had stayed behind in the newly founded Baltic republics. Any speculation about the future of the remaining Germans (which in the context of the novel is limited to the story of Aurel's brother, Reinhard, confined to a tiny patch of unproductive land) suggests in any case that Aurel's difficult decision to flee to the west was the reasonable one.[6] But in 1934 no one could imagine that only half a dozen years later the just-established government of Adolf Hitler would come to an agreement with the Latvians' neighbor to the East which ended the Latvian Republic and forced the removal of all the Reinhards who had attempted to hang on in it.

For the millions of ethnic Germans from East Central Europe and national Germans from East Prussia, Silesia, Pomerania, and other eastern parts of the empire who would be driven west, the attempt to find an appropriate narrative framework for such a vast and complex story as the destruction of their homeland would have to wait decades until the resettling process had reached a certain stability. In his novel *Levins Mühle* (1964; translated in 1970 as *Levin's Mill*), Johannes Bobrowski (1917–65), best known as one of the finest lyric poets of the postwar era, takes a first step by focusing precisely on the attitude of the East European Germans of the nineteenth century towards the outsiders – gypsies and Jews – who would later be mass-murdered by the Nazis. By telling the tale of his grandfather and the Jew Levin, and the fate that awaited Levin at the hands of the small-town Germans of the late nineteenth century, Bobrowski fills in the space so often left vacant in novels about German Eastern Europe: the precarious niche occupied by one of the millions of individual Jews who lived on the periphery of the German and Slavic settlements.

Bobrowski was born in Tilsit, now called Sowjetsk, directly on the East Prussian–Lithuanian border and was thus, in effect, the nearest 'German' neighbor of Aurel. As a student he went west 200 kilometers to Königsberg, now called Kaliningrad, where Ernst Wiechert was one of his teachers. He settled in East Berlin in the mid 1960s after service in the Wehrmacht and four years in Soviet prisoner-of-war camps. Bobrowski was aware that even for the so-called East Germans, the former eastern part of Germany had become an area better forgotten, a place in eastern Poland far beyond the Oder-Neisse border. Thus, his novel about the Germans in that area a century earlier begins with the presentation of geographical information for an audience that had chosen to forget about the roots from which the author came:

> Well then, the first sentence. The Drewitz is a tributary in Poland. There's the first sentence and right away I hear you say: so your grandfather was a Pole. And I reply: no he wasn't. And so, as you see, there's already room for mistakes and that's a poor start. Well then, a new first sentence. In the 1870s on the lower reaches of the Vistula, on one of its minor tributaries, there was a village populated predominantly by Germans. All right, that's the first sentence ... And I should have to say that the stoutest farmers were Germans, the Poles in the village were poorer, though certainly not so poor as in the outlying Polish timber villages.[7]

Bobrowski thus begins his tale of the old east with an insistence on almost pedantic geographical and sociological detail, which is clearly meant to jump historical time and space and to correct an impression among his readers that the linguistic line between Slavs and Germans had always been cleanly drawn. Bobrowski is presenting a warning that a misreading of the novel is inevitable if the reader does not understand that in the last century the area now known as Poland was occupied by other peoples as well. And the second piece of information is that there was a financial and social distinction apparent in village life based upon the ethnic background of the resident: Germans were richer than Poles.

On the very first page it becomes clear that Bobrowski's version of life among the Germans in East Central Europe will be more analytical and less idyllic than are the novels that refuse to leave the world of Blumbergshof. For Bobrowski, the problems which would eventually lead to the ability of a population to forget that Germans once lived in Poland begin with the economic realities of a settlement, like Blumbergshof, where the Germans were the ruling class. He sets his novel during the initial decade of the Second German Empire, the years in which his grandfather and his companions could for the first time consider themselves to be part of one of the dominant Western political and military powers, to whose ethnic group they belonged. Bobrowski is well aware of the historical significance of this date and allows the bullying superiority of the newly created 'Great German' population with regard to the Poles in general and the gypsies and Jews in particular to resonate across the decades from the Second Empire to the Third, to the Thousand Year Empire of Adolf Hitler. 'Their zeal for everything German is incomprehensibly great, as we see, and their zeal for everything great is German, this too we see: in short Germanically great' (*Levin's Mill*, 114).

Levin's Mill is the story of the thwarted attempt by the outsider Jews and gypsies to find a place in a society which has no intention of allowing them in. The insider Germans have a superior position which they understand to have been established by a natural order and confirmed by the new political constellation. The Poles can make their attempt to get in via the historically proved road of linguistic assimilation, a process that to some extent had already taken place. But in *Levin's Mill*, Bobrowski is mainly interested in the fate of the eternal outsiders who would be rounded up and eliminated in the course of the Third Reich. At the time of Bobrowski's grandfather, the actions of the combined German residents, as formulated in the Union of Malken of 1874 upon the establishment of the Second Reich, do not lead to transports, concentration camps, and executions. But they do involve the conspiracy of the God-fearing Christians to drive away by almost any other means the outsiders, who are perceived as a threat to religious, social, and financial harmony. Leo Levin, the Jew who comes from Polish-Russian Rozan and who is told to go back where he came from, is an eternal and unredeemable threat on all accounts:

> These Jews, he says, they nailed Jesus to the cross, with nails, eight inchers. He knows all about it. And now they are running around over the whole world, he says, marked like Cain as the murderers of Jesus.
>
> That's all so familiar now, that it seems like the truth. And that's the way he said it, the one who normally doesn't talk much, his voice was quite calm, without a trace of emotion. He knows his facts, he won't harm a single one of those Jews on that account, he won't anticipate the works of God. (Pp. 134–5)

In the Prussia of 1875 they do not yet anticipate God in passing irreversible judgment on those with the mark of Cain, but they do band together to make sure that there is no chance of the financial success of the outsiders in the community, and then they run them out of town. Levin's mill, built with great care and skill by the Polish Jew, offers successful competition to the mill of the narrator's grandfather, the richest man in town, and disappears after a meeting of the Union of Malken men, swept away when the river suddenly is allowed to pour through. 'And in the spring, one morning, all of a sudden Levin's mill was gone. Only the jetty was left and the two posts that held the chains' (p. 136). Mills are destroyed, gypsies are expelled from houses, sheds are burned, kangaroo courts are held, perjury is committed – the German community defends itself – and Bobrowski provides a preview of the world of seventy years later, when the Second German Reich had become the Third German Reich and the gypsies and the Jews were not merely told to go back where they came from. This time they were forcibly taken somewhere else from which very few returned. Bobrowski's witches' brew of prejudice and brutality, in which the pastor and the sole policeman are two of the major defenders of the rights of all things German, is a grotesque and only relatively harmless suggestion of things to come.

In Bobrowski's world, there is something rotten in the state of German Eastern Europe and the rottenness leaves a clearly traceable trail to the catastrophe of the Second World War. In his depiction of the assumed superiority of his own ancestors, an almost comic affectation turns into a dangerous threat as the combined forces of the insiders conspire against the outsiders. Bobrowski sets in motion the workings of a historical process he would personally witness in its final stages, both as a soldier in the German army on the Eastern front, parts of which were eliminating the outsiders with a fury, and then as a prisoner in the Soviet prisoner-of-war camps in which more than a third of the German prisoners died.[8] The destruction of Levin's mill by the German Union, which on its simplest level could be described as nothing more than the illegal removal of unwanted business competition, resonates in its deepest level down through seven decades to the days of the narrator-grandson who knows that all the mills of Levin have been washed away and the millers destroyed. For Bobrowski's narrator it is clear that the ruins of Levin's mill are to be found behind the town near the railway junction, which Leo Horsky never mentions by name, and that the remains of the ancestors of Levin and the gypsies can be found in the dust of the ovens behind which Horsky's rabbis debate the potential guilt of God.

In the end they are all called to the trial demanded by Levin, and, with the exception of the chaplain who refuses to lie, all the Germans commit perjury against the gypsies and the Jews. Levin leaves the pious Germans and returns to the hopeless poverty of Rozan with his gypsy woman, financially destroyed, sexually harassed, legally cheated and defamed, lucky (one feels) to have escaped without physical violence. He leaves behind only the mill-stones and the ruins of the footbridge:

> Then Feyerabend called out of the door: Where are you heading for? And Levin replies: I'll follow my nose. Will you be back? No. There they go, Leo Levin and Marie Habedank. Feyerabend calls after them: And the stones, are you leaving them here? Yes, they are leaving the stones. And the rest of the mill-jetty. That's all there is. Are they supposed to take the stones with them? Millstones? (Pp. 202–3)

Bobrowski ends his novel with the protest of the outsiders and the 'good' Germans, particularly chaplain Rogalla (who has the same family name as the protesting curator of Siegfried Lenz's *The Heritage*), and the artist Philippi, who provides the very last word on the topic of the relationship between Germans and outsiders on the eastern frontier. The grandfather, spending his retirement years reading anti-Semitic literature, has only one request of Philippi: 'Leave me in peace,' a request that Philippi, while clapping his hands right in front of the grandfather's nose, emphatically answers with 'No.' 'And we'll count this Philippian No. As our final sentence' (p. 230).

In view of the fate of those who said 'No' – Protestant chaplains, Catholic priests, artists, gypsies, or Jews – during the reign of the Third Reich, this final sentence and final word has an ominous historical ring to it. Bobrowski does not take his story into the twentieth century except in the sense that it is, he insists, not a local story about Prussia, but 'could have taken place in so many towns and in so many districts, and it was only intended to be narrated here' (p. 230).

Elsewhere Bobrowski suggests that the story could just as easily be set in Osterode, a town in West Germany, a name pulled apparently from a hat, but which suggests that the open wounds between ethnic groups and religions in Eastern Europe still exist beneath the surface of the apparently cured society of West Germany. Like Udo Steinke, Bobrowski allows his material suddenly to jump decades and spring across great distances in order to suggest that Philippi's final 'No' is still waiting to be heard and accepted by the rich millowners of the (German?) world.

In his second novel, *Litauische Claviere* (Lithuanian Pianos), written in a few short weeks before his death in 1965 at the age of only 48, Bobrowski brings his story into the time of the Third Reich and sets it in the area he knows so well, on the Lithuanian-German frontier. Once again Bobrowski is exploring the difficult relationship between the Germans and their neighbors in Eastern Europe, but this time there can be no suggestion that the story can take place in many places, that it would have been just as valid to set it in the Harz mountains. This time the framework is far more narrowly drawn and places within it the Germans and Lithuanians on a narrow frontier. The attempt of German and Lithuanian musicians to collaborate on an opera in the period just before the Nazi takeover of their jointly occupied land cannot escape the conflicts between two cultures and two languages, which can coexist only as long as the major language, German, does not attempt to take political advantage of its numerical superiority. In *Litauische Claviere*, it is clear that the inherent tendencies of the Great-German nationalists, who drive out Levin and the gypsies from Prussia, are going to make the continued collaboration of the Germans and Lithuanians of the Memelland, whether in music or everyday life, difficult, and finally impossible.

In neither of his novels, however, did Bobrowski attempt to handle the problem, which he and all his ethnic relatives had to face at the end of the war. Bobrowski was a soldier in a Soviet prison camp, and thus did not take part in the chaotic flight of the East Prussians and Memelland Germans to reach the last open ports of the Baltic before the Soviet troops. The treks of millions from Bobrowski's homeland would become a prominent example of the anarchy that ended centuries of German culture in Eastern Europe. Bobrowski was certainly, however, part of the situation that awaited his compatriots who had managed to survive. Upon his release from Soviet prisoner-of-war camp, he was not faced with the question of whether he should return to his homeland or move west. His homeland no longer existed. Tilsit was now a Soviet city one hundred kilometers east of the Polish-Russian frontier. All Germans had been driven out; the bill had been presented, not only to the German nationalists, whose destructive power we feel resonating between *Levin's Mill* and *Litauische Claviere*, but to all Germans, even those who had wanted to join Phillipi's call for a 'No' answer. There could be no 'No.' There were only ethnic realities, and Bobrowski drew the same conclusion as did Jurek Becker's father, and settled in the part of Berlin which belonged to East Germany. For other German writers of Eastern Europe, the story, which Bobrowski does not carry beyond the Lithuanian frontier, reaches its predictable climax in the agony of the expulsion and the terror-filled flight to the west.

Horst Bienek's recently completed tetralogy about the end of the German world of his birthplace, the Polish-German border city of Gleiwitz, moves from the first major event of the war, the Nazi-staged attack on their own radio transmitter in Gleiwitz, to the final one for much of the German population of Silesia, the firebomb destruction of Dresden. Bienek attempts to get at the roots of the German catastrophe and the terror of the expulsion by describing in minute detail the life of a small city that, like Bobrowski's Tilsit, marked the frontier between German and Slavic Europe. Like Bobrowski's Memelland, Silesia had been used as geographical punishment against the Germans at the end of the First World War, and following plebiscites with ambiguous results, had been divided between Poland and the Weimar Republic, leaving a brooding population of Poles and Germans on both sides.

As in *Die Baltische Tragödie* and *The Russian Dance of Death*, the Gleiwitz saga, consisting of four novels (1975–82, English translations 1984–8), *Die erste Polka* (*The First Polka*), *September Licht* (*September Light*), *Zeit ohne Glocken* (*Time Without Bells*) and *Erde und Feuer* (*Earth and Fire*), plus a volume of commentary *Beschreibung einer Provinz* (Description of a Province, 1983), begins in an idyll, a Blumbergshof of a small Silesian city, experienced by children who are in the midst of discovering the wonders of the world. Bienek builds his narrative structure by telling interconnecting tales about a cross section of the population, while constructing a nucleus around one family, whose fate the reader follows from the first day to the last. In the process, the wide-eyed children of the last day of peace are eliminated one by one by the violence of war. Like Leo Horsky in Auschwitz, the Piontek family is present for the duration of the catastrophe, from the opening salvo of the war at the radio transmitter, which the children accidently witness, to the firebombing of Dresden, which the survivors have reached with the fleeing German population of Silesia just in time to be incinerated by the British-American bombings of 13 February 1945.

Unlike Leo Horsky, however, Bienek is intent on telling us everything, and in four carefully chosen moments (31 August 1939 – the exploration of the childhood idyll at the moment of destruction; 4 September 1939 – the first realization of the destructive nature of war; Good Friday, 23 April 1943 – the transformation of the former paradise into a place of survival and destruction; Friday, 13 February 1945 – the annihilation of Dresden) he describes a society that almost unwittingly moves swiftly with its children from wonder to nightmare. Inexorably, overwhelming historical forces grind the individual and the peculiarities of his society into total submission. In the process Gleiwitz comes to stand as a microcosm of centuries-old German-Slavic relationships, which were coming to a violent end throughout Eastern Europe.

Bienek's prewar Gleiwitz is populated by Slavs and Germans who have worked out a modus operandi among themselves, a system functioning with reasonable success for centuries. Germans learn Polish, Poles learn German, family names become crossed and there is mutual benefit from cultural cross-pollination. Briefly we experience this old world, but after 31 August 1939 there are only ethnic distinctions drawn between rulers and ruled. In Gleiwitz the western Germans' demand for clear distinction between Aryan and non-Aryan causes great confusion as it becomes difficult to determine who is what. Germans forget they can speak Polish; Poles attempt to speak only German. Linguistic and ethnic boundaries are drawn, which had never been understood before, and the web of colorful carpeting is torn to shreds. A political order from the outside, which of course has its inside supporters and which gains absolute power with the invasion of Poland and the beginning of the war, brings the natural work of centuries to an end in the few days of *The First Polka*.

September Light illuminates the end of the former summer paradise for the children and introduces a figure who on a different narrative and historical level distinguishes Bienek's novel from others of its genre. In *Levin's Mill*, Bobrowski tells the story of the Jews among the Germans, but employs a buffer of two generations, and never attempts it in the context of the Holocaust. Bienek, in contrast, wants to tell the entire story of Gleiwitz, which includes the expulsion and extermination of the small Jewish population. Consequently, he faces the problem of how to deal with this segment without resorting to pathos, which he manages to keep out of the descriptions of other aspects of the annihilation of his homeland. There can be none of the jarring impact of the humor of Becker or the satire and irony of Hilsenrath and Steinke in this solidly and exactly described world.

Bienek's solution is to bring a figure into the complex narrative pattern that stands aside from the other characters and focuses the reader's attention on historical documents and literary history rather than melodrama. The converted German Jew, Arthur Silbergleit, leaves his loyal Christian German wife in Berlin and returns to Gleiwitz, the city of his birth, because he can think of nothing else to do, given the ever-worsening situation of the Jews in Berlin and the danger his Jewish background poses for his wife. The introduction of Arthur Silbergleit into the narrative, and with him the German-Jewish community of Gleiwitz, completes a pattern that is often left incomplete in narratives of this period, namely the place and fate of the assimilated Jews in the small cities and towns of 'German' East Central Europe. Bobrowski's Levin is clearly an outsider with whom the author sympathizes. But Arthur Silbergleit had been part of a community that would scarcely have been noticeable if it had not been for the Nazi race laws through which apparent insiders overnight became outsiders, and shortly thereafter statistics in Auschwitz. Arthur Silbergleit, however, was a real figure, a writer whose poems we get to read and whose stories provide the final commentary for Silbergleit and his companions on the train ride that ends in the place that Leo Horsky never names.

Thus Bienek's portrayal of Arthur Silbergleit serves a double purpose. First, it allows the introduction on a personal level of the story of the few Jews of Gleiwitz who are the first to realize that they have been expelled from the garden, but who still do not have an inkling that they will eventually be rounded up and slaughtered. On Good Friday 1943, in the year when the church bells were melted down for the war effort, Arthur Silbergleit carries the weight of all those who might have otherwise ended in the Jewish cemetery of Gleiwitz onto the transport trains to Auschwitz. Second, through the re-creation in fictional form of the last year of the real writer, Arthur Silbergleit, Bienek finds an extraordinarily effective method of bringing to life the tragedy of a writer such as Arthur Silbergleit.

Unlike the more experienced Sasha Granach, Arthur Silbergleit does not draw conclusions about the virulence of anti-Semitism in the Berlin of the 1930s. He mulls over the possibilities of emigration until they are taken out of his hands. Silbergleit cannot imagine that they are really talking about him, a writer who uses similar landscapes, images, rhythms and, of course, the same language as poets whose works are treated with reverence and pious humility. Bienek gives us both: the late romantic, brooding lyrics of the best-known poet of Silesia, Joseph von Eichendorff, which the good citizens of Gleiwitz like to recite, and then, in one of the last cultural events for the Jewish community of Gleiwitz, the poetry of Arthur Silbergleit, whose name was virtually erased with his works until dragged out of the hidden rubble of the war years by Bienek.

Here the author forces his readers to face the artistic as well as the physical destruction of a writer whose stylistic and geographical home was virtually the same as Eichendorff's, but whose blood was considered different. Silbergleit first reads off an early poem with clear echoes of the Eichendorff poem we have earlier heard recited. It has no Jewish reference points, as Silbergleit had never thought of himself as being a Jewish writer. He then follows it with his last works, prose parables drawn entirely from a Jewish tradition that had been forced upon him, and that ultimately provides him with artistic and creative strengths when the relation to Eichendorff has been physically removed.

Like Levin, Arthur Silbergleit eventually is driven off, but now it is in a cattle car to the east. Silbergleit's final piece of writing is not read at the meeting of the Jewish cultural society of Gleiwitz, but half-dreamed in the moments before the assembled Jews of Silesia are herded onto the transport train. Bienek uses this piece, *Der Leuchter* (The Candlestick), as the magnet that forces the readers to take note of what was done to the individual and to the culture of his homeland when they sent Arthur Silbergleit on the trains to the east. Buried in the wall behind the last pitiful ghetto residence in Gleiwitz are the manuscripts of *Der Leuchter* and the diaries of the final days, hidden because even the disbelieving Silbergleit ultimately fears that his books will never reach the supposed goal of the train, the ghetto in Riga, with passage to Sweden.

Beneath the wheels of Silbergleit's train an indescribable turn is made to the south, away from Sweden, and the wheels stop turning only when they reach the camps of Leo Horsky. Silbergleit's end comes not in Sweden but in the gas chambers on the Silesian plateau. By anchoring the story of the Holocaust in Gleiwitz with the weight of the real writer Arthur Silbergleit, Bienek manages to achieve what few other German writers have done. He captures the reader's imagination with the uncovering of the mystery of the disappearance of a fine writer, makes him listen to the writer's true voice, and forces him to consider at the end of the captivating narration of the story what was lost when that voice, and all that it represented, entered the trains for Auschwitz.

Bienek needs almost 1600 pages to tell his story, space enough to describe the end of both the Jews and the Germans. Arthur Silbergleit provides the counterpoint to the central story of the destruction of the Piontek family and the entire community of Gleiwitz during the war. By Good Friday 1943, the euphoria of the opening days, which in Gleiwitz were always tempered by skepticism about the geographical knowledge of the western Germans with regard to the spaces of Eastern Europe, has been staggered by the increasing evidence of German defeat on the Eastern front. By the time of the fourth book, the winter of 1945, the apocalypse is at hand. It means the catastrophic end of the world of the Germans of Gleiwitz and Upper Silesia only two years after the catastrophic end of the 1700 Jews of Gleiwitz. Now it was the Red Army, the imported slave laborers, and the resident non-German population who would demonstrate their ability to take revenge, this time on the Germans, who had provided 80 percent of the vote during the plebiscite of 1921.

In the fourth novel of the *Gleiwitz Suite*, *Erde und Feuer* (*Earth and Fire*), Bienek creates a mixture of fiction and history that places a German writer at the center of the annihilation of his culture. Bienek has Valeska Piontek reluctantly join the trek of Germans fleeing the approaching Red Army by any means of transportation possible. Trapped behind Soviet lines and blocked from proceeding by a retreating German army that overtakes and abandons its eastern population in a desperate attempt to reorganize itself on a new front further west, many of the Silesian Germans never make it through. They are killed or end in Siberian work camps; others who stay behind desperately try to reinterpret their activities of the past half-dozen years. All Nazi remembrances are burned, Polish names are retaken, the ability to speak Polish becomes a matter of life and death. But Valeska Piontek survives it all and manages to get through to Dresden, the unbombed 'western' German city the refugees are sure will offer them sanctuary, because, they presume, such an artistic treasure had already been chosen by the Allies as the next capital of Germany in place of destroyed Berlin. In the frozen splendor of Dresden, Valeska Piontek goes in search of her former student Ulla, and thus finds herself by chance, on 13 February 1945, the last day of the carnival, in the company of the grand old man of German and Silesian literature, Gerhart Hauptmann, who has journeyed to Dresden in search of sanatorium warmth.

In *Time Without Bells*, the Silesian-Jewish author Arthur Silbergleit, long forgotten and presumed lost, is sent to the gas chamber and into the fire of the ovens on Good Friday 1943. In *Earth and Fire*, the Silesian-German author Gerhart Hauptmann, winner of the Nobel Prize and most prominent German writer to remain in Nazi Germany, watches through the blown-out windows of his suburban hilltop sanatorium refuge the firebombing of Dresden, the event that remains the single most catastrophic act of destruction to a European city. In a desperate attempt to escape Slavic revenge, the Germans of Silesia staggered to Dresden, and were cremated by the British firebombing of a defenseless and militarily unimportant city. A final assault by American bombers followed on Ash Wednesday. Unlike

Silbergleit, Gerhart Hauptmann, in his hilltop retreat, survives the destruction of his city and his people, but it is a survival that he regrets. 'Once Hauptmann said to his wife: I longed for death, but it rejected me. Never have I so longed for death as that night. But I must suffer with my people and my people's suffering is not over.'[9]

Forty-five years after this catastrophe, the argument continues about the numbers of the victims, certainly in the scores of thousands with estimates of well over one hundred thousand, and about the question of justification and guilt, this time with an emphasis on the culpability of the Allies. In the novel Bienek remains silent. He does not follow his Gleiwitz world beyond Dresden, thus avoiding a commentary on the proper final stance of the Pionteks or Gerhart Hauptmann in relation to the land and the culture we have seen described in such detail. The last words of Hauptmann are heard differently by his son ('My Reich is through') and his wife ('The Reich is through').[10] The son's interpretation suggests the end of a cultural and spiritual world: the world of Silesia; the wife's suggests the end of the political monstrosity that had brought about the fiery destruction. Both were true.

In the novel, Bienek says nothing and allows his Silesian Germans to sit and watch the inferno that annihilated them. In articles, and in particular in the work of commentary to the novels, *Beschreibung einer Provinz*, Bienek makes clear his view of the situation in which the survivors in the west find themselves. For him Silesia is 'Heimat,' ('homeland'); he is even more than willing to agree that he has written a kind of 'Heimatroman,' but a critical one. It reflects a combination of love for the land of childhood memories and recognition of the cruelty of the historical truth in which Germans sent Arthur Silbergleit to the gas chambers and allowed their Slavic neighbors to be treated as slave labor. For Bienek there is no way back from these sad facts: 'But "Heimat" cannot be passed on through inheritance. It is in my head. There where I spent my childhood and my youth and first discovered the world, a third generation is already growing up, new, different childhoods being experienced and lived, a different language is being spoken. Childhood is "Heimat." In that sense I am an expellee (like all of us), when I was driven out of childhood and into adulthood.'[11]

But here we are already in the arena of political commentary, even if it is commentary about one of the major attempts at creative re-creation of the end of two worlds. Bienek's geographical space is limited – we move only from Gleiwitz as far as Dresden, although in its resonance it covers all of East Central Europe – and his time comes to a stop with Hauptmann observing the firebombing of Dresden. The novels that take the East Central European figures into the West and demand a reaction vis-à-vis the world of their childhoods are not able to spend so much time re-creating the world of that childhood or to journey in such detail through the labyrinth towards destruction. Siegfried Lenz and Christa Wolf, leading figures in the literatures of West and East Germany respectively, have recently made the attempt to find the path that allows Bienek's essayistic commentaries to find novelistic form.

In his two prose works set in his Masurian birthplace, Siegfried Lenz travels the distance between the Heimatroman, which is content to stay in the secure world of Blumbergshof, and the 'critical Heimat-roman' (suggested by Horst Bienek), which ends in the West. Lenz was born in Lyck in southeastern East Prussia, just west of the Polish border and somewhat to the east of Bobrowski's Tilsit. Today it is a Polish city approximately fifty kilometers from the Soviet border, but in Lenz's first prose work set here, *So zärtlich war Suleyken* (Suleyken Was So Gentle), published in 1955 within a decade of the expulsion of the Germans from East Prussia, there is no suggestion of the coming calamity or of the possible reasons for the violence and hatred of the final years of German East Prussia. Suleyken is the sunken world of German East Prussia, politically lost by the mid 1950s but still nostalgically alive in the memories of millions of refugees in the West, who were more than willing to have recalled for them a 'heile Welt' ('healthy world'). This was the world of Aurel's Blumbergshof two decades later and a few hundred kilometers to the southwest, on the edge of German political control.

In the world of Suleyken there is little resonance from the fate of the Levins or the Habedanks, the Jews and the gypsies whom Bobrow-ski so carefully set out on their journey to Auschwitz. Nor does it recall the end of the world of Aurel, whom von Vegesack so carefully had driven out of Blumbergshof and then out of his homeland. In the very title, Lenz gives notice that this will not be a 'critical Heimatroman' but a sentimental one, which is not to suggest that a sentimental Heimatroman cannot be an effective piece of literature. It does suggest, however, that a prose work that concentrates on the 'gentleness' of small-town life among the Germans of East Prussia is hardly going to approach the social, racial, and financial problems which Bobrowski finds in virtually the same town a half-century before and which surely had not disappeared in the meantime. It is simply a matter of choosing subjects that do not lead in the direction of critical social observation, and of allowing these characters to play roles in tales in which their eccentricity or stinginess might be an identifiable characteristic, but not their opinion about gypsies or Jews, and surely not the actions that might be taken by wealthy German businessmen against an upstart Jewish financial threat. Early in his career Lenz writes what he admits is a love story to his homeland:

> In southern East Prussia, between peat bogs and sandy wasteland, between hidden lakes and pine forest, we Masurians had our home – a mixture of Prussian and Polish elements, of Brandenburgian, Salzburgian, and Russian. The stories that I tell here are at the same time searches of the Masurian soil. They do not represent mournful songs of melancholy, on the contrary: these stories are whimsical declarations of love to my land, humorous homage to the people of Masuria. Of course they pass no binding judgment – it is *my land, my* village of Suleyken, which I have described.[12]

Ten years after being driven out, Lenz is still talking about *his* land, by which, of course, he means Masuria in East Prussia, declaring his love for it and homage to the people who populated it. *So zärtlich war Suleyken* remains a series of carefully constructed sketches of the beloved world of lost childhood; if it had not been written by Siegfried Lenz it would be remembered now only by the former inhabitants who would like to recall their homeland and their childhoods in a manner that Lenz succeeds in bringing to life in his stories. In short, it would be remembered only in connection with the many other tales of German Eastern Europe that may be harmless and very appealing in their evocation of a lost exotic world. But the stories certainly do not offer productive material for attempting to gain an understanding of why there are almost no Germans, no gypsies, and no Jews left in the lands so lovingly described. The effectiveness of *Suleyken* and other works like it is, surely, as Bienek suggests, to be found in the fact that the homeland of childhood no longer exists and the successful literary description of it immediately creates bridges of longing to the adults who have been forced to leave their childhoods in a foreign land. Here again there is a close relationship between German and Jewish contemporary attempts to conjure up the sunken world of Eastern Europe. Manes Sperber's remarks about his home could just as easily be Lenz's about Lyck or Bienek's about Gleiwitz:

> Perhaps my sense of being uprooted would never have developed if Hitler's victories had not led to that series of catastrophes which now seem as immediate as if twenty-seven years had not passed since his death. If the Jewish shtetls still existed today, they would belong, for me, only to a remote past. But since they were destroyed, so thoroughly wiped out that nothing of what they were or could have become can reach into the future, Zablotow now belongs to my present. It is at home in my memory.[13]

Sperber is describing the main reason for the enormous potential emotional response in both Yiddish and German evocations of life in East Central Europe, for in both cases the homeland remains only in the memory of its former inhabitants and can be brought back to life only through the words of writers who can translate that memory into effective prose. In *So zärtlich war Suleyken*, Lenz makes uncritical effective use of that memory bank. In his next novel about Masuria, *Heimatmuseum* (1978; translated in 1981 as *The Heritage*), written more than thirty years after the expulsion, this evocation of a memory bank is forced into a direction never suggested in the stories about Suleyken, in the direction of renunciation and permanent withdrawal from the concept of homeland. Here the writer who claimed in 1955 that Masuria was *his* land once again begins with a lingering and loving description of the land of his birth. But this time he shows the shadowy side of that world taking command during the Nazi period and follows through with the story of the falsification and misuse of memory in the Western world. Through reminiscences and flashbacks, retold tales and reexamined documents, Lenz has his narrator, Zygmunt Rogalla, recall in interview form (which surely is, stylistically, the weakness of the novel) his world that is no more. The narrative strength of this first section of the novel, the equivalent of Blumbergshof, lies in the extraordinary richness of tales and characters from a world that seems only distantly related to the landscape of northern West Germany. The discussions between the interviewer and Rogalla reveal only a language in common; even then, the dialect of Masuria is as difficult to understand for a West German as is Yiddish.

Lenz's Masuria of the early part of the twentieth century, a private culture filled with medicine men and eccentric family members, has as similar and remote a relationship to the contemporary Western world as does Sholom Aleichem's Ukraine or Granach's and Roth's East Galicia. It is a world of irrationality, sudden violence, and finally of brutal war, which sweeps across Masuria with the same devastating effect as it sweeps over Galicia and Ukraine. Ultimately, however, it remains beloved in the memory of the narrator because it is, on the one hand, lost forever, and, on the other, so completely different from the familiar claustrophobic world of the rebuilt West Germany that the refugees can recall it as an idealized rural paradise. It is also a world in which the relationship between the Germans and the Slavs plays a crucial role in determining the ultimate fate of both groups.

Lenz has chosen his title and his hero carefully; instead of the gentleness of Suleyken, the reader is confronted with that German phenomenon, the 'Heimatmuseum,' a museum found in many German communities in which the folkloric remains of the old culture are displayed. This museum is the crucial matter for the entire structure of the novel. It is in the first sentence of the novel, in which the museum curator Zygmunt Rogalla admits to the interviewer that he set the fire that burned the edifice to the ground. And on the last page he describes this act as 'my last freedom.'[14]

In between we are told the story of the world whose relics had been completely destroyed by the main figure even though he had risked his life to save the same relics during the panicked flight of the Masurians to the last open ports of the Baltic before the onslaught of the Red Army. Lenz structures his novel around recollections of the history of a family that included the specimen-collectors and curators in the old world. Their interest was in preserving the relics of all the peoples who populated a multicultural geographical locale, which like Bienek's Gleiwitz was characterized by a fertile mixture of German and Slavic elements. As in Vegesack and Bienek, Lenz's observer is a youth who this time sees the idyll of his childhood turn into the nightmare when Nazi functionaries demand a division of the relics of the culture into Aryan and non-Aryan, between 'true' and 'false' manifestations of a culture. The functionaries wish these items to be understood only in terms of racial policies. By having Zygmunt Rogalla become the only apprentice to the last of the great carpet weavers of Masuria, a semimythical figure who incorporates the entire history of a culture into the colors and patterns of her cloths, Lenz finds a particularly effective narrative line for a main theme, which is absent from the gentle world of Suleyken.

Rogalla's pattern for Masuria contains the dark threads in the apparently healthy world of the small-town Germans of Eastern Europe that Bobrowski also finds in the behavior of his Great Germans. Given the opportunity, they overwhelm the rest of the pattern during the Nazi years as the latent desire of part of the German population to denigrate their non-German neighbors is given free reign. The most striking aspect of *The Heritage* is, however, that the various characters who are given the opportunity to join the darkness or resist it journey on to the new world in the west and reflect there on their old world in the east. At the end of his story Aurel is on board a ship entering a western German harbor. We receive no information about his consequent relationship to Blumbergshof or a childhood homeland he seems to have abandoned. But Zygmunt Rogalla carries westward his memories of the magical childhood and of the secrets of the carpet weavers of Masuria, along with all physical relics of the culture assembled from the Lycknow Heimatmuseum that he had managed to transport onto the desperately filled boats carrying the lucky refugees to the safety of Western ports.

By moving his hero and the remaining relics of this ancient culture to the west, Lenz finds a narrative path to a confrontation with one of the major political problems of West Germany today. It is the relationship between the western state in which most East European

Germans finally settled, and the contemporary states occupying the land in which these peoples had lived for centuries. There, in the security and relative prosperity of the rebuilding West Germany of the 1950s and 1960s, Rogalla meets again the figures who had chosen a variety of roles in far-off Masuria during the period when the insecurities resulting from the First World War turned into the bullying of the Nazi period. Friends and enemies of the curator of the homeland museum reassemble in their new northern German homeland and gradually become an organized group, with newspapers and well-financed clubs. Their sole purpose becomes the propagandistic trumpeting of the opinion that 'Masuren ist (noch) *mein* Land' ('that Masuria is [still] *my* land'), to quote the young Lenz himself.

Zygmunt Rogalla, however, has come to know these characters in a Masuria in which the rise of the Nazis allowed the nuances and subtleties of racial prejudice in Bobrowski's 'Great Germans' to reach extremes. These prejudices clearly determined that these non-German neighbors, given the chance, would never voluntarily let the Great Germans return to *their* land. The united Great German community, dedicated to the protection of German interests, if necessary by the illegal and violent suppression of non-German competition, is given the opportunity to welcome the German troops, whose terrifying method of securing German hegemony in the east would eventually lead to the expulsion of the East European Germans. As in *Levin's Mill*, not all the Germans take part in the conspiracy; those who don't are immediately stamped as outsiders and clearly have no chance against the united front of the majority. Those who attempt to protect the minority are made outcasts in 1874 and are greatly endangered in 1940. Some of these 'resistance' figures (not exhibiting an active armed resistance, but rather a refusal to cooperate with the Nazis) survive it all and make it to the West, among them Zygmunt and his boyhood friend, Conny.

At the festive opening of Zygmunt's museum, they all meet again, in far off Schleswig-Holstein, with years in between, time enough for the disbelieving Zygmunt to witness the rebirth of an even more united league of Eastern Germans in West Germany. They sit and listen with open hostility to the speech of the government representative (and it is clearly the voice of Lenz and Bienek as well) in which the concrete reality of the Heimatmuseum is welcomed as 'an expression of justified longing' (p. 423). The Western government declares itself in agreement with this view 'that nothing was truly lost so long as it remained the object of our longing.' In that sense, the ' "land of dark forests and crystal lakes" was likewise not permanently lost,' (p. 423). However, political realities have changed things. ' "I know your lovely land," he said again; "now it is a neighboring country. We are not indifferent to it, but the true task that lies before us is this: to transform our longing for the old homeland into new neighborliness" ' (p. 425).

In the speeches by the former Masurians that follow, there is no further suggestion that the proper purpose of the Heimatmuseum is to serve as a receptacle of longing for a lost homeland that is now in the care of the others who had not been part of Great Germany. For Zygmunt it gradually becomes clear that his museum of multicultured Masuria is intended to be used as a museum of the Great Germans in the west. One by one they emerge from the mass, the figures we have met before: the good, the indifferent, and the bad Germans of Masuria; those who were sent to work camps and those who sent them, those who collected the Slavic cultural remains for the museum and those who demanded that they be removed from the museum. They all appear before Zygmunt's eyes and greet each other as old friends with a common goal. Finally there are even Doctor Anton Duddek, who survived the work camps with a paralysis of the face, and 'Reschat, the man with the golden oakleaves ... and his appearance scotched a number of rumors that had sprung up concerning his probable fate: for instance, that he had been caught by the British and upon the Poles' request sent to Warsaw for trial; that he had been in hiding disguised as a woodsman and had committed suicide upon being exposed; that he had escaped to South America and risen to new power and prosperity there' (p. 426).

They all reappear like ghosts from the past of Blumbergshof to lay their claim to the Heimatmuseum. Zygmunt observes the accidental meeting of victimizer and victim, quisling and prisoner, and awaits the violent reaction of Duddek to the unbelievable presence of the former Nazi overseer: 'Well, and then they did bump into each other and turn around. They recognized each other at once, just as if they had anticipated this moment countless times, and I would have expected anything but what occurred: their hands reached out, a smile gradually formed on both their faces, and then, as though their memories had retained nothing, they embraced, and for longer than was customary, too' (p. 427).

Thus they stand there united in the West, from Duddek to Reschat. In the end, Reschat is elected as the new chairman of the Heimatverein (Club of the Homeland), and Zygmunt burns down the museum. He understood it to be nothing more than an attempt to save the past from being forgotten, but others intend to use it in the present as proof of ownership of a land that was lost because of the brutality of those who now want to become the curators of memory. Lenz could have been writing about one of Steinke's embarrassing themes – namely the easy transformation of so many relatively small-time Nazi terrorists of the 1940s into prosperous citizens of the 1980s – but in *The Heritage* he is dealing specifically with the Western exiles and their former Eastern homes. His conclusion is that the exiles have not deserved to be allowed the luxury of museums of Suleyken, that the story of the East must be told with all the dark threads present, and with the terrible consequences of the war recognized. In the face of the presence of a virtually solid front of exiles that, despite a variety of experiences in the war, refused to remember anything but Suleyken and Blumbergshof, the only choice open to this true curator of memory is to destroy all the relics before they can be misused. Consequentially, Rogalla delivers a true report on the memoirs to Polish television before burning down his museum.

In this novel about the old world and its relation to the new, Lenz presented a controversial and ultimately political challenge to the powerful East European German clubs of West Germany ('Landsmannschaften'). They choose to worship the soil they often took with them from the east (two strange old women actually are seen stealing the sacred Masurian soil from the Heimatmuseum) often without considering the reasons they were driven from that soil in the first place. It was a book many did not like, as it demanded a different relationship to the former homeland, based now on nothing more than memories held sacred 'in the uncertain stillness of the no-man's-land' (p. 458). Bienek and Lenz meet at the point where the memories of childhood are allowed to blossom, but the realities of adulthood determine the course of contemporary behavior.

Christa Wolf, probably the best-known East German author, does not have to deal with the 'Landsmannschaften.' In East Germany there is no political movement that can suggest that Silesia or Masuria remain German forty-five years after the expulsion, or that other former homelands of East European Germans (Bobrowski's city of birth is now in the Soviet Union, Wolf's in Poland) still belong to them. For East Germany these places are now clearly the land of the Poles and the Soviets, and the former inhabitants will have to make do with forays into childhood memories. It is just such a journey that Christa Wolf makes in *Kindheitsmuster* (1977; confusingly translated as *A Model Childhood* [1980], it now appears as *Patterns of Childhood*), a novel dealing with another problem of exile that remains secondary to the plot of *The Heritage*. It might be said to be the main purpose of *The Heritage* as well, because it is meant to explain to the next generation what it was that actually happened out there in the former homelands that now speak another language and that have particularly strained relations with West Germany.

Like Lenz, Christa Wolf tells her story through the narrative structure of a journey. Like Max Frisch in *Montauk* (1975), Peter Handke in *Der kurze Brief zum langen Abschied* (*Short Letter, Long Goodbye* [1972]), or Ingmar Bergman in *Smultronstället* (*Wild Strawberries* [1957]), Wolf allows an actual journey in a car to serve as the narrative line that draws to it observations and reminiscences stretching far beyond the immediate environment of the traveled road. Handke and Frisch, like latter-day Kerouacs, travel west to the roads of North America to try to gain insights into their contemporary state of mind; Christa Wolf moves in precisely the opposite direction: from Berlin to 'the German city L, now Polish G.' This is Wolf's birthplace of Landsberg/Warthe, now the Polish city of Gorzow Lipsk, as far inside the western border of Poland as Lyck is inside the eastern. By making the journey from Berlin to her birthplace, Wolf follows a narrative path directly into the past, for the movement out of familiar postwar East Germany into the no-longer-familiar, linguistically alien city of her childhood, allowing the re-creation of an environment that briefly bloomed and was then utterly destroyed by the events of the war. Born in 1929, the author has the luxury of forming her novel out of an objective attempt to recall the lost world of Nelly Jordan – the fictional name she gives herself – for her daughter Lenka, who is along for the ride and who knows virtually nothing about the birthplace of her mother, and thus to try to explain how it could be that Landsberg became Gorzow Lipsk.

Other authors deliver detailed full versions of lost childhoods; Wolf gives us the struggle of the adult to attempt to reconstruct for the young the unbelievable story of the rise of the Nazis in provincial Eastern Europe. She is spurred on by the physical presence of the long-lost buildings and streets of childhood combined with the barrier of a resident population that cannot communicate, even with the best of will, with those who come seeking that childhood. Wolf makes her problems in trying to write about such ultimately inexplicable matters a main stylistic characteristic of her novel, a trait that continually forces the reader back into the world of the 1970s. Some critics might consider this a stylistic annoyance (like that of the interviewer in *The Heritage*), but it allows a fragmented puzzle of photos, letters, documents, and vague recollections gradually to come together into a portrayal of a world her daughter might vaguely be able to begin to understand. Nelly's childhood paradise, her Blumbergshof, is of shorter duration than those of Bienek's or Lenz's or von Vegesack's children. She allows cold statistics to begin the destruction almost before she has had the chance to explore it. In 1933, when she was four years old,

> of the 28,658 votes cast, 15,055 had already gone to the Nazis, but one didn't yet have the feeling that every single ballot was being checked ... and there were 3,944 unemployed in the town – a number which was to be reduced to 2,024 as early as October 15, 1933. But should one – can one – accept this alone as the explanation for the resounding success of the National Socialist Party on November 13 of the same year, when the town of L., with a voter participation of almost 100 percent and a negligible number of invalid ballots, had the most yes votes in the Ostmark district?[15]

Gradually it all begins to join together to become a unified picture of a small-city world in which the rise of fascist terror only slowly begins to work its way into everyday life. The father is asked by the newly elected functionary if it could possibly be true that he allows the wives of Communists to buy on credit. Rumors begin to be heard that the death of a Jewish citizen was not caused by heart failure but by physical pummeling. The Jewish child in the class is singled out by the teacher for special attention. The father refuses to respond to the functionary, Nelly refuses to let her memory run past the point where she, like the others, is supposed to give Itzig a punch on the way into class. Her attempt to conjure up for Lenka the world of Landsberg in the 1930s becomes the attempt to explain how it was possible that even the 'good' Germans, to whom her family belonged, could still be in Landsberg in the 1940s and have become a reluctant part of the war effort to turn Eastern Europe into a place of masters and slaves. Thus, *A Model Childhood* becomes one of the key works for an understanding of the total German catastrophe that followed in 1945. The expulsion of the supposed master race makes no distinction between good and bad Germans, although in the short run and on an individual basis this factor could determine life and death upon the arrival of the Soviet troops (indeed, the testimonials of the French prisoners of war in the father's control do save his life).

In her reminiscences of the end of East Prussia, Marion Gräfin Dönhoff records the place and dates of the participants as they reach the German Empire ahead of the Soviet army 'long before we ourselves had to join in. The first were the White Russian peasants with small horses and light wagons ... a few months later came the Lithuanians, then the Memel Germans, and finally the first East Prussians from the easternmost townships.'[16] By January 1945 it was time for the rest of East Prussia to join in a miserable hungering trek through a bitter winter in which week after week unending columns of starving refugees passed by the corpses of those who didn't make it. In the late spring of 1945 it is time for Christa Wolf's homeland. She puts on record the fate of the older generation:

For the old – for those who had babbled about death for years, just to hear the young contradict them – the time had come to keep silent; because what was going on now was their death, and they knew it. They aged years in weeks, and then died, not neatly one after the other, for a variety of reasons, but all at once, for one and the same reason, be it called typhoid, or hunger, or simply homesickness, which is a perfectly plausible pretext for dying. However, the real reason for their dying was that they had become totally superfluous, a burden to others, a burden whose weight sufficed to dispatch them from life to death. (*A Model Childhood*, 297)

For those who made it, the journey was not yet over: 'Charlotte Jordan was as old as you are now when she moved with her children and parents into a room at a hotel in the village of Grünheide near Nauen. She must have been absolutely certain of one thing: in the months ahead, there would be dying in great numbers. And she must have made up her mind: Not my children. I'll pull them through. That's what she did and nothing else' (p. 301).

Christa Wolf sets out in *A Model Childhood* to trace the patterns of her childhood that culminated in this disaster. She has no intention of suggesting to Lenka, or to her readers, that this was all an unjust act. On the contrary, the joined puzzle pieces of her memory force the conclusion that the behavior of the innumerable little Hitlers of East Central Europe was responsible for these treks. Unlike Lenz, she does not have to struggle towards the conclusion that the only proper response to the world of her childhood is that it is lost forever and that the friendly people inhabiting the buildings of her childhood, with whom she cannot communicate, are the proper and just owners of those buildings. She knows why Landsberg is now called Gorzow Lipsk and why Tilsit now appears on the maps as Sovjetsk. It is a conclusion that is a precondition to her decision to finally go through the irritating formalities necessary to visit the country of her birthplace. She does not have to burn down any museums; she merely has to visit the city from which the museum materials might have been assembled.

And yet, there is still an integral part of this novel, as well as those of Bienek and Lenz, that can hardly avoid suggesting bitterness at the mass expulsion based solely on ethnic background or at least an understanding of the reasons why the banished might feel that they have been unjustly treated. After all, the family of Nelly had been among those who were in opposition to the rise of fascism, and bowed to it only reluctantly and under the threat of a brutal force, which is depicted as all-consuming in the small city once it had gained control. Like the Pionteks of Gleiwitz and the Rogallas of Lycknow, the Jordans of Landsberg would have continued to live in complete ease with their non-German neighbors had it not been for the quixotic rise to power of a western government that put the local bullies into positions of power. And yet it is precisely these decent families whom we see decimated at the end of the reign of terror they had not asked for. Even in *A Model Childhood,* which is not interested in the topic of potential German victims, there are two full pages identifying the place and cause of death of the older family members. They have provided key puzzle pieces of childhood, and they are nothing more than average grandparents and uncles and aunts with all the quirks that go along with such relatives. In the end, though, Nelly recalls that they were driven to exhaustion, starved to death, and allowed to waste away and die:

> She, Nelly's other grandmother, died in June, 1945 near Bernau, of malnutrition, according to the death certificate, and that meant that she had starved to death. Nevertheless, she was given a grave that is still tended and on which a wreath is placed once a year.
>
> Things are different with the scattered graves of the three other grandparents. Whiskers Grandpa was the next to die, of typhoid, he was buried at the cemetery wall in the village of Bardikow in Mecklenburg. His grave is unmarked. Lutz claims to have identified it recently in the Bardikow cemetery by unmistakable signs. In Magdeburg, in a neglected grave, lies Auguste Menzel, his wife, Whiskers Grandma, from whom Nelly learned the meaning of self-denial and kindness. A simple attack of flu had been enough for her. Charlotte Jordan cut a gray strand of hair off the thin braid that rested on the shriveled body's right shoulder, and kept it God knows where.
>
> Heinersdorf Grandpa, Gottlieb Jordan, was the only one with a goal that kept him alive: he wanted to live to be eighty. He succeeded, although under difficult circumstances, in a hole-in-the-wall in a village of the Altmark. He then said: Now it's enough, and died. Nothing is known about the present condition of his grave. A color photo exists,

snapped by Aunt Trudy, his daughter, which shows Heinersdorf Grandpa's grave planted with flowers and surrounded by white gravel paths. The tombstone shows the epitaph he had chosen: Vengeance is mine, saith the Lord.

A blanket crocheted by Whiskers Grandma of good wool is the only object in the family's possession that recalls the grandparents' generation. Sometimes you think – Lutz and you – of the two stories that Whiskers Grandpa used to tell his grandchildren: the story of the snake and the story of the bear. Sometimes the taste of pudding reminds you of the blancmange with raspberry syrup that Nelly used to eat in summer at Heinersdorf Grandma's kitchen table. Sometimes someone will say: Lutz is so tall because he takes after his grandfather. Sometimes – but not for long anymore – Auguste Menzel's expression appears in one of her descendants. (P. 298)

Sometimes, one is tempted to add, Christa Wolf, in a novel that is attempting to explain political and historical realities to a younger generation, conjures up the lost world of a magic childhood in somewhat the same manner as does Ingmar Bergman in *Wild Strawberries*. There it is a strawberry patch, here it is the taste of pudding. For Christa Wolf the eerie evocation of the lost grandparents and the world they moved in so gracefully occurs only briefly; in Bergman it takes on the aura of reality and recalls the old man into the summers of his youth, from which he can draw conclusions about the winter of his life. Christa Wolf has no intention of allowing that to happen. The world of the grandparents that is recalled by the taste of pudding can influence the world of the struggling middle-aged author only insofar as it exists as one small piece of the puzzle that holds the pattern of the sunken world. And nevertheless, this one piece does exist, and in the flood of nostalgia that comes with the taste, an emotional bridge is constructed. It leads straight to the kitchens and fairy-tale-telling rooms of grandparents, whose unmarked, untended graves have just been described and whose entire earthly possessions have been reduced to the woolen blanket that has just been displayed.

In those fairy tales and in that woolen blanket we find the one thread that joins together all these novels from a German East Central Europe that is no more. For, although Christa Wolf would surely have nothing to do with the politics of the West German 'Landsmann-schaften' (who prefer the 'Heimatromane' that never leave Blumbergs-hof), she cannot write her novel about the catastrophic rise of fascism in the formerly German city of Landsberg/Warthe without recalling the graves of her family and the desolateness of the end of decent people who had filled her childhood with the magic of fairy tales and summer pudding. She cannot leave it out of the pattern of her childhood because it was undeniably there in her childhood, as it is undeniably there in Lycknow, Gleiwitz, and the Baltic manor of Blumbergshof. Everything changed afterwards with the breakdown of the Nazi offensive on the Eastern front, but the nostalgic bridge to the past, despite the dark sides of the social structure present in all these novels, cannot be avoided. The often violent and brutal mishandlings and deaths of people whose peaceful world has been evoked in the novels will continue for decades to come to make the story of the Germans in the east from 1939 to 1947 one full of hatred and brutality on virtually all sides.

All serious historians agree that the Nazi decimation of the Jewish population of Europe was an illegal act carried out with incomprehensible brutality. But it seems that more time will have to pass before a united judgment, East and West, can be drawn about the banishment of the Germans at the end of the war. The question of whether those unmarked graves and abandoned homesteads are the reminders of justifiable acts of revenge, or of the unjustifiable violent expulsion of unwanted natives, will remain a controversial question for years to come. In the meantime, they will surely provide rich and vivid material for those writers attempting to describe fictionally the end of the German world in East Central Europe. This dramatic fall was not as drastic and final as that of Yiddish Europe, but after forty-five years seems equally irreversible.

The Rogallas, the Pionteks, and the Jordans all became victims of the revenge of the East upon the West and received the full violence of the punishment. Overnight long-established families turned into charity cases dependent on the goodwill of western Germans who were themselves in a battle of survival, and by and large greeted the newcomers with less than open arms. To the present day, western

Germans tend to treat the 'Heimatvertriebenen' with the superior air of established family members who are bored to tears by unsolicited tales from their distant relatives about the injustices they have suffered. (There is now good reason to conclude that the massive immigrations of the 1990s will have a similar reaction.) To suggest in today's West Germany that there is something worthwhile to be garnered from the journals, newspapers, and books of the East European Germans, who are with great zeal documenting their histories, or that there should be some understanding of a historical perspective that maintains that a culture of seven centuries should not be considered extinct after forty-five years of exile is to run the risk of being labeled a 'revanchiste.'

Western Germans have found it very easy to forget that the lion's share of the punishment at the end of the Second World War was doled out to people like the East Prussians, the Silesians, and the Sudetenland Germans – not to mention the Volksdeutsche, many of whom were moved east rather than west and still live in Central Asia and Siberia. The postwar years were, of course, difficult everywhere, but within a decade, with the extraordinary financial help of a victorious enemy, West Germany was well on its way to becoming one of the most prosperous societies on earth. East Prussia, Pomerania, and Silesia were well on their way to becoming graveyards of memories for the former German inhabitants who were lucky enough to escape with their lives, as well as new homelands for Poles who themselves had often been displaced.

Only in Romania did Germans manage to maintain viable cultural centers in the decades after the war. In the 1970s, a Romanian-German literature of consequence arose there, with its center in Timisoara in the Banat, where in December 1989 the Romanian uprising began with a bloodbath. Powerful young writers such as Herta Müller (1953–), Richard Wagner (1952–), Rolf Bossert (1952–86), Horst Samson (1954–), and William Totok (1951–) joined Nikolaus Berwanger (1935–89) as names to be reckoned with in discussions of contemporary German-language fiction and poetry.

As long as they were publishing works like *Niederungen* (Müller in 1982) or *Hotel California 1* and *2* (Wagner in 1980, 1981) in Bucharest and Timisoara, it could not be said that the final word had been spoken about the literature of the Germans in Eastern Europe. But today, less than a decade after these publications, it seems that the brief flourishing of Romanian-German literature was a last hurrah that will be carried on only among the exiles in West Germany, where Müller and Wagner now live, where Bossert killed himself three weeks after immigrating, and where Niki Berwanger died early in 1989 after less than five difficult years in the West. The situation for the Germans of Romania has deteriorated so rapidly and so dramatically in the last decade, and the demand for emigration become so strong, even after a violent uprising, whose results remain unclear, that it now seems that one must conclude that the bell is tolling for the last viable German cultural community east of the German-language states.

It is a monumental journey from Latvia and the Volga River and Ukraine to west of Budapest and west of Prague, and the psychological journey is just as long from Gleiwitz and Landsberg and Lyck and Timisoara. Only the refugees are left to bemoan the lost worlds of German culture that not long ago flourished there, and they are largely ignored unless a political cause can be found. For Yiddish Europe, too, only the long-gone exiles can write their last reminiscences and their final stories, and then their world will be as deeply buried as is Blumbergshof. For forty-five years, the Polish government officially maintained that there was no German-speaking minority there; there is no need to make such a spurious announcement with regard to its former Yiddish-speaking minority. Wagner, Müller, and Berwanger allow us one more look at a now exotic world that was once the rural, small-city world of millions of Germans by focusing on a Romanian city that only seventy-five years ago still called itself 'Klein Wien' (Little Vienna). All indications are that the German world they described in powerful works only ten years ago will be almost completely gone within the next decade, as almost all the Romanian Germans take advantage of the newly won freedom to travel by immigrating to West Germany. At the moment, it seems reasonable to suggest that the last German trains from Eastern Europe are gathering at stations from Siberia to western Poland. The ones pulling away from the Timisoara station have on board the last German-language writers from a world that has provided the inspiration for some of the most powerful works ever written in that language. Their departure signals the end of an era. As the Romanian-German authors leave, they are heading west, away from the land of their birth and their poetry, with a certain reluctance and much sadness, and this story ends with a whimper, a strange muted finale to a tale full of fury.

Notes

Translations into English are by the author unless otherwise indicated. Original-language editions have been cited only if English translations are not available.

INTRODUCTION

1 The number of dead will never be known. In his map explaining the fate of the German population of Eastern Europe, Werner Hilgemann calculates more than 3 million deaths, but includes military casualties in his figures (p. 319). The archive of West Germany has specific documentation for more than 600,000 deaths of German civilians in Poland, Yugoslavia, and Czechoslovakia, but it also states that there are 2.2 million unsolved cases in all of Eastern Europe. However, the archive concludes that one cannot equate this number with the number of deaths related to crimes during the expulsion (see Hellmuth Auerbach in Wolfgang Benz, ed., *Die Vertreibung der Deutschen aus dem Osten*, 226).
2 See, for instance, the discussion by Elie Wiesel of works by William Styron and D.M. Thomas in Stephen Lewis, ed., *Art out of Agony*. Several of the interviews in this book touch upon this topic.
3 I am well aware of the difficulties in terminology in using terms like 'Eastern,' 'East Central,' and 'Central' Europe with regard to postwar

Europe, and have concluded that it is impossible to please everyone, even myself. For the purposes of this book, I have used the term 'Eastern Europe' in the conventional post-war sense of Europe under Soviet influence, while acknowledging that it is an inaccurate description of places like Warsaw, Prague, East Berlin, and Budapest, and will become even less useful during the 1990s. When it is necessary to make a clear distinction between the Soviet Union and the other 'East European' states, I locate them in 'East Central' Europe.

CHAPTER ONE   German and Yiddish: A Case of Awkward Family Relations

1 Harald Haarmann, *Soziologie und Politik der Sprachen Europas*, 17
2 By 1990, the implications of such mass immigration for West Germany has become a major topic of concern. With the opening of the East German border, 340,000 East Germans joined 350,000 ethnic Germans from Eastern Europe in 1989 to present a great challenge to West German housing, work, and social service programs. It is estimated that in 1990, at least 500,000 East German citizens will move west, and that as many as 2 million ethnic Germans may be planning to emigrate in the near future.
3 Wolfgang Benz, ed., *Die Vertreibung der Deutschen aus dem Osten*, 12
4 Ida Kaminska, *My Life, My Theater*, 25–6
5 For a fascinating and humorous account of the experiences of a Yiddish translator in the German Army in Russia from 1916 to 1918, see Sammy Groneman, *Hawdoloh und Zapfenstreich.*
6 See Magnus Magnusson, *Iceland Saga*, esp. 1–33.
7 Sol Gittleman, *From Shtetl to Suburbia*, 15–17
8 Glückel of Hameln, *The Life of Glückel of Hameln.* There is a more recent edition of a German translation: *Denkwürdigkeiten der Glückel von Hameln* (Darmstadt: Verlag Darmstädter Blätter 1979).
9 Otto Best, *Mameloschen Jiddisch – Eine Sprache und ihre Literatur*, 139
10 Aharon Appelfeld quoted in Stephen Lewis, *Art out of Agony*, 19. Subsequent references to this edition will appear in the text.
11 Immanuel Birnbaum, *Achtzig Jahre dabei gewesen*, 15
12 Best, 28–9
13 One of the ironies of contemporary German literature is that its latest winner of the Nobel Prize for Literature, Elias Canetti, is a native speaker of Ladino, which the Sephardic Jews took with them to Canetti's Bulgarian birthplace upon their expulsion from the Iberian peninsula in the late fifteenth century.

14 Leo Sievers, *Deutsche und Russen*, 126
15 Ibid., 196
16 Ibid., 199
17 Michael Freiherr von Kapri, *Buchenland*, 118
18 For a description of a futile contemporary attempt to seek out Jewish ancestral roots in Czernowitz, see Ruth Beckermann's contribution to Christoph Ransmayr, ed., *Im blinden Winkel*, 'Erdbeeren aus Czernowitz,' 79–100.
19 All population statistics are from Günther Stökl, *Osteuropa und die Deutschen*, 139–44.

CHAPTER TWO   The (relatively) Gentle Decline: Yiddish and the Modern World

1 Ezra Mendelsohn, *The Jews of East Central Europe between the World Wars*, 30
2 Martin Pollack, *Nach Galizien*, 19–20
3 For an excellent discussion of the historical background of the Pale of Settlement, and of the position of the Russian Jews at the time of the Tevye stories, see Hillel Halkin's introduction to Sholom Aleichem's *Tevye the Dairyman and the Railroad Stories*, ix–xli. It also includes a definitive explanation of the complicated history of the writing and publication of the Tevye stories. Rather than 'Sholem,' which is used in this edition, I have used the more common spelling, 'Sholom,' throughout.
4 David Roskies's exhaustive work on the Jewish response to catastrophe, *Against the Apocalypse*, contains a powerful description of the devastation caused by the First World War within the shtetl community, particularly in chapter 5, 'The Rape of the Shtetl.'
5 Jost Hermand, in his afterword to Franzos's *Der Pojaz*, 359. Subsequent references to this edition will appear in the text.
6 Manes Sperber, *God's Water Carriers*, 9
7 In the Hungarian-Jewish dramatist Julius Hay's memoirs, *Geboren 1900*, we meet the real actor Alexander Granach in Moscow and understand how different he is from the hero of *Da geht ein Mensch*.
8 Alexander Granach, *Da geht ein Mensch*, 7. Subsequent references to this edition will appear in the text.
9 Isaac Bashevis Singer, 'Old Love,' 433. The story is found in *The Collected Stories of Isaac Bashevis Singer*, 421–33.

CHAPTER THREE   Germans in a Russian War

1 Pollack, 72
2 Horst Bienek, *Beschreibung einer Provinz,* 12
3 Siegfried von Vegesack, *Die Baltische Tragödie,* 11. Subsequent references to this edition will appear in the text.
4 Georg von Rausch, *The Baltic States,* 14
5 Ibid., 23
6 For a historical overview of these areas, see Georg von Rausch, *The Baltic States,* Fred Koch, *The Volga Germans,* and Karl Stumpp, *Die Russlanddeutschen.*
7 Dietrich Neufeld, *A Russian Dance of Death,* 1–2. Subsequent references to this edition will appear in the text.

CHAPTER FOUR   Whatever Happened to Tevye?

1 The catalogue to this symposium, *Versunkene Welt,* edited by Joachim Riedl and published by the Jewish Welcoming Service, will remain one of the essential documents on this topic.
2 Uwe Magnus, 'Die Einschaltquoten und Sehbeteilungen,' in *Im Kreuzfeuer: der Fernsehfilm Holocaust,* eds. Peter Märthesheimer and Ivo Frenzel (Frankfurt: Fischer Taschenbuch Verlag, 1979), 223.
3 Ibid.
4 In *Tzili,* Appelfeld has his heroine, a young Jewish girl who has escaped capture, meet the survivors of the concentration camps. However, she never actually comes into contact with the camps themselves.
5 Manes Sperber, *Churban oder die unfassbare Gewissheit,* 63
6 Sperber, *God's Water Carriers,* 9
7 Interview with Joshua Sobol, 'Theater Heute,' August 1984, 7
8 Jurek Becker, *Jacob the Liar,* 13–14. Subsequent references to this edition will appear in the text.
9 *Der Nazi und der Friseur* would later go on to considerable public success in its paperback edition published by Fischer Verlag more than a decade after its first publication by Doubleday in English. Hilsenrath's difficulties with the German publishing industry also suggest how aware German publishers are of the explosive nature of literary works in German that venture into the taboo areas created by the Second World War.
10 Klaus Gruber, 'Pflegestätte einer zusammengeschmolzenen Kultur,' dpa-Brief, 7 June 1979, 2

11 Raul Hilberg, *The Destruction of the European Jews*, 485
12 Edgar Hilsenrath, *Night*, 28. Subsequent references to this edition will appear in the text.
13 Joseph Roth, *Job*, 239
14 Edgar Hilsenrath, *The Nazi and the Barber*, 337–8
15 Udo Steinke, *Horsky, Leo oder Die Dankbarkeit der Mörder*, 60–1. Subsequent references to this edition will appear in the text.
16 For a powerful description of the vicious brutality of this system, see Cordelia Edvardson's autobiographical novel *Bränt barn söker sig till elden* (Burned Child Seeks the Fire), which is available in German but not English translation. Edvardson, Middle East correspondent for *Svenska Dagbladet*, is the illegitimate daughter of the converted German-Jewish author Elisabeth Langgässer. The book describes, without pathos, how she ended up in Auschwitz, while her siblings were determined to have enough Aryan blood to be allowed to survive at home.

CHAPTER FIVE   The Germans of Eastern Europe Pay the Price

1 For a detailed examination of how it happened that in Bulgaria the Jewish population was larger after the war than before, see Frederick Chary's *The Bulgarian Jews and the Final Solution, 1940–1944*.
2 Werner Hilgemann, *Atlas zur deutschen Zeitgeschichte 1918–1968*, 331
3 *Ashes Out of Hope*, a selection of major Soviet-Yiddish writings from as late as the decade after the war, includes a very informative introduction by Irving Howe and Eliezer Greenberg (eds.), which emphasizes the tragic impact of the Stalinist purges on a Yiddish literature that had barely managed to survive the war.
4 Hilgemann, 334
5 Haarmann, 17
6 After the Second World War, von Vegesack wrote a novel, *Der letzte Akt* (The Last Act), about the further adventures of Aurel, in which he returns to the Baltic in order to visit his brother in 1939, just in time to experience the final expulsion order. Von Vegesack himself had not been in the Baltic since 1912, however, except for a brief 1939 visit, and the novel lacks the feeling of authenticity that characterizes *Die Baltische Tragödie*. It is also far less objective in its analysis of the reasons for ethnic conflicts between the Balts and the Germans.
7 Johannes Bobrowski, *Levin's Mill*, 5–6. Subsequent references to this edition will appear in the text.

8 For a discussion of the relative treatment of prisoners of war by Soviets and Nazis, see Heinrich Böll, 'Brief an meine Söhne,' *Die Zeit*, 15 March 1985, Extra, 13. According to Böll, 57.8 percent of Soviet prisoners of war died in German camps, a total of 3.3 million soldiers.

9 Horst Bienek, *Earth and Fire*, 245

10 This is not in the English translation, but is on p. 317 of the original *Erde und Feuer* (Munich: Carl Hanser Verlag 1982).

11 Horst Bienek, 'Schlesien, aber wo liegt es?' *Die Zeit*, 8 February 1985, 43

12 Siegfried Lenz, *So zärtlich war Suleyken*, 169–70

13 Sperber, *God's Water Carriers*, 99

14 Siegfried Lenz, *The Heritage*, 458. Subsequent references to this edition will appear in the text.

15 Christa Wolf, *A Model Childhood*, 37–8. Subsequent references to this edition will appear in the text.

16 Marion Gräfin Dönhoff, *Namen die keiner mehr nennt*, 14

Appendix
Information on Authors

Sholom Aleichem (1859–1916), b. Pereyaslav, Ukraine, Russia, d. New York

Jurek Becker (1937–), b. Lodz, Poland; now lives in West Berlin

Horst Bienek (1930–), b. Gleiwitz, Silesia, Germany (now Gliwice, Poland); lives in West Germany

Johannes Bobrowski (1917–65), b. Tilsit, Germany (now Sovjetsk, USSR), d. East Germany

Karl Emil Franzos (1848–1904), b. Chortkow, East Galicia, Austro-Hungary, d. Berlin

Alexander Granach (1891–1945), b. Werbowitz, East Galicia, Austro-Hungary, d. New York

Edgar Hilsenrath (1926–), b. Leipzig; lives in West Berlin

Siegfried Lenz (1926–), b. Lyck, Masuria, East Prussia (now Elk, Poland); lives in West Germany

Dietrich Neufeld (1886–1958), b. Orloff, Zagradovka, Ukraine, Russia, d. North America

Romanian-German writers *Nikolaus Berwanger* (1935–89), *Herta Müller* (1953–), *Richard Wagner* (1952–), all born near Timisoara, Romania; all moved to West Germany since 1984

Joseph Roth (1894–1939), b. Brody, East Galicia, Austro-Hungary, d. Paris

Isaac Bashevis Singer (1904–), b. Radyzmin, Poland; lives in New York

Udo Steinke (1942–), b. Lodz, Poland; lives in West Germany

Siegfried von Vegesack (1888–1974), b. Blumbergshof/Wolmar, Latvia, Russia, d. West Germany

Christa Wolf (1929–), b. Landsberg/Warthe, Germany (now Gorzow Wielkopolski, Poland); lives in East Berlin

Selected Bibliography

Aleichem, Sholem. *Tevye the Dairyman and the Railroad Stories*. Trans. from the Yiddish by Hillel Halkin. New York: Schocken Books 1987

Alexander, Edward. *The Resonance of Dust: Essays on Holocaust Literature and Jewish Fate*. Columbus: Ohio State University Press 1979

Anger, Per. *With Raoul Wallenberg in Budapest*. Trans. from the Swedish by David Mel Paul and Margareta Paul. New York: Holocaust Library 1981

Appelfeld, Aharon. *Tzili – The Story of a Life*. Trans. from the Hebrew by Dalya Bilu. New York: E.P. Dutton, Inc. 1973

– *The Age of Wonders*. Trans. from the Hebrew by Dalya Bilu. Boston: David R. Godine 1981

– *To the Land of the Cattails*. Trans. from the Hebrew by Jeffrey Green. New York: Weidenfeld and Nicolson 1986

Arendt, Hannah. *Rahel Varnhagen*. Munich: Piper 1959

– *Eichmann in Jerusalem*. New York: Viking Press 1970

Becker, Jurek. *Jacob the Liar*. Trans. from the German by Melvin Kornfeld. New York: Harcourt Brace Jovanovich 1975

Benz, Wolfgang, ed. *Die Vertreibung der Deutschen aus dem Osten*. Frankfurt: Fischer 1985

Berwanger, Nikolaus. *Die schönsten Gedichte*. Bucharest: Albatross Verlag 1984

– *Steingeflüster*. Hildesheim: Olms Presse 1983

Berwanger, Nikolaus, and Wilhelm Janesch. *Zwei Jahrzehnte im Rampen-licht-Illustrierte Chronik der Temeswarer Deutschen Staatsbühne.* Bucharest: Kriterion Verlag 1974

Best, Otto. *Mameloschen Jiddisch – Eine Sprache und ihre Literatur.* Frankfurt: Insel 1973

Bienek, Horst. *Beschreibung einer Provinz.* Munich: Carl Hanser Verlag 1983

– *The First Polka.* Trans. from the German by Ralph Read. San Francisco: Fjord 1984

– *September Light.* Trans. Ralph Read. San Francisco: Fjord 1987

– *Time without Bells.* Trans. Ralph Manheim. New York: Macmillan 1988.

– *Earth and Fire.* Trans. Ralph Manheim. New York: Macmillan 1988

Birnbaum, Immanuel. *Achtzig Jahre dabei gewesen.* Munich: Süddeutscher Verlag 1974

Bobrowski, Johannes. *Sarmatische Zeit.* Stuttgart: Deutsche Verlags-Anstalt 1961–2

– *Litauische Claviere.* Berlin: Wagenbach 1967

– *Levin's Mill.* Trans. from the German by Janet Cropper. London: Calder and Boyars 1970

Borowski, Tadeusz. *This Way for the Gas, Ladies and Gentlemen.* Trans. from the Polish by Barbara Vedder. New York: Viking Press 1967

Bosmajian, Hamida. *Metaphors of Evil.* Iowa City: University of Iowa Press 1979

Buchholtz, Hansgeorg. *Das Dorf unter der Düne.* Königsberg: Gräfe und Unzer 1933

Canetti, Elias. *The Tongue Set Free.* Trans. from the German by Joachim Neugroschel. New York: Seabury Press 1979

Chary, Frederick. *The Bulgarian Jews and the Final Solution, 1940–1944.* Pittsburgh: University of Pittsburgh Press 1972

Christiansen, Eric. *The Northern Crusades.* London: Macmillan Press 1980

Dawidowicz, Lucy. *The War against the Jews 1933–1945.* New York: Holt, Rinehart and Winston 1975

Dönhoff, Marion Gräfin. *Namen die keiner mehr nennt.* Düsseldorf: Eugen Diederichs Verlag 1962

Edvardson, Cordelia. *Bränt barn söker sig till elden.* Stockholm: Brombergs 1984. Trans. from the Swedish into German by Anna-Liese Kornitzky as *Gebranntes Kind sucht das Feuer.* Munich: Carl Hanser Verlag 1986

Ezrahi, Sidra. *By Words Alone.* Chicago: University of Chicago Press 1980

Filip, Ota. *Das Café an der Strasse zum Friedhof.* Trans. from the Czech by Josefine Spitzer. Frankfurt: Fischer 1968

Franzos, Karl Emil. *Der Pojaz*. Königstein: Athenäum 1979 (originally published in Stuttgart: Cotta 1905.)

Gilbert, Martin. *Atlas of the Holocaust*. London: Michael Joseph 1982
- *The Holocaust – The Jewish Tragedy*. London: William Collins 1986

Gittleman, Sol. *From Shtetl to Suburbia*. Boston: Beacon Press 1978

Glückel of Hameln. *The Life of Glückel of Hameln*. Trans. from the Yiddish by Beth-Zion Abrams. New York: Thomas Yoseloff 1963

Görz, H. *Die Molotschnaer Ansiedlung*. Steinbach, Man.: Echo Verlag 1950

Granach, Alexander. *Da geht ein Mensch: Roman eines Lebens*. Munich: Weisman Verlag 1984 (Abridged version originally published Stockholm: Neuer Weg 1945.) New edition to be published Piper Verlag: Munich 1990

Gronemann, Sammy. *Hawdoloh und Zapfenstreich*. Berlin: Jüdischer Verlag 1924

Grundmann, Herbert. *Wahlkönigtum, Territorialpolitik und Ostbewegung im 13. und 14. Jahrhundert*, vol. 5 of Gebhardt *Handbuch der deutschen Geschichte*. Munich: Deutscher Taschenbuch Verlag 1973

Haarmann, Harald. *Soziologie und Politik der Sprachen Europas*. Munich: Deutscher Taschenbuch Verlag 1975

Haffner, Sebastian. *Anmerkungen zu Hitler*. Munich: Kindler 1978
- *Der Teufelspakt: Die deutsch-russischen Beziehungen vom ersten zum zweiten Weltkrieg*. Zürich: Manessa Verlag 1988

Halecki, Oscar. *Die Geschichte Polens*. Frankfurt: Heinrich Scheffler 1963

Haumann, Heiko. *Geschichte der Ostjuden*. Munich: Deutscher Taschenbuch Verlag 1990

Hauser, Arnold. *Unterwegs*. Bucharest: Kriterion Verlag 1971

Hay, Julius. *Geboren 1900*. Munich: Langen Müller Verlag 1977

Hehn, Jürgen von. *Die Umsiedlung der baltischen Deutschen – Das letzte Kapitel baltisch-deutscher Geschichte*. Marburg: Johann-Gottfried-Herder-Institut 1982

Heym, Stefan. *The Wandering Jew*. Trans. from the German by Stefan Heym. New York: Holt, Rinehart and Winston 1984

Hilberg, Raul. *The Destruction of the European Jews*. Chicago: Quadrangle Books 1961

Hilgemann, Werner. *Atlas zur deutschen Zeitgeschichte 1918–1968*. Munich: Piper Verlag 1984

Hilsenrath, Edgar. *Night*. Trans. from the German by Michael Roloff. New York: Doubleday and Co. 1966
- *The Nazi and the Barber*. Trans. from the German by Andrew White. New York: Doubleday and Co. 1971. (This translation has also

appeared as *The Nazi Who Lived as a Jew*. New York: Manor Books 1977.)

– *Bronskys Geständnis*. Munich: Langen Müller 1980

– *Das Märchen vom letzten Gedanken*. Munich: Piper Verlag 1989. New editions of all Hilsenrath novels are planned by Piper in the early 1990s.

Howe, Irving. *World of Our Fathers*. New York: Harcourt Brace Jovanovich 1976

Howe, Irving, and Eliezer Greenburg. *Ashes out of Hope: Fiction by Soviet-Yiddish Writers*. New York: Schocken Books 1977

Howe, Irving, and Ruth Wisse, eds. *The Best of Sholom Aleichem*. Washington: New Republic Books 1979

Insdorf, Annette. *Indelible Shadows – Film and the Holocaust*. New York: Vintage 1983

Kaminska, Ida. *My Life, My Theater*. Trans. from the Yiddish by Curt Leviant. New York: Macmillan Publishing Co. 1973

Kapri, Michael Freiherr von. *Buchenland*. Stuttgart: Eigenverlag Landsmannschaft der Buchenlanddeutschen 1983

Keneally, Thomas. *Schindler's List*. New York: Simon and Schuster 1982

Klassen, Is.P. *Die Insel Chortitza*. Steinbach, Man.: Derksen 1979

Koch, Fred. *The Volga Germans*. University Park: Pennsylvania State University Press 1977

Kosinski, Leszek. *The Population of Europe*. London: Longman 1970

Kraeter, Dieter, and Hans Georg Schneege. *Die Deutschen in Osteuropa heute*. Bielefeld: Verlag Ernst und Werner Gieseking 1970

Krallert, Wilfried. *Atlas zur Geschichte der deutschen Ostsiedlung*. Bielefeld: Vernhagen und Klasing 1958

Krockow, Christian Graf von. *Die Reise nach Pommern – Bericht aus einem verschwiegenen Land*. Stuttgart: Deutsche Verlags-Anstalt 1985

Landmann, Salcia. *Abenteuer einer Sprache*. Munich: Deutscher Taschenbuch Verlag 1964

Langer, Lawrence. *The Holocaust and the Literary Imagination*. New Haven: Yale University Press 1975

– *Visions of Survival: The Holocaust and the Human Spirit*. Albany: State University of New York Press 1982

Lenz, Siegfried. *So zärtlich war Suleyken*. Hamburg: Hoffmann und Campe Verlag 1955

– *The Heritage*. Trans. from the German by Krishna Winston. London: Secker and Warburg 1981

Levi, Primo. *The Periodic Table*. Trans. from the Italian by Raymond Rosenthal. New York: Schocken Books 1984

Lewis, Stephen, ed. *Art out of Agony.* Toronto: CBC Enterprises 1984
Lind, Jakov. *Soul of Wood and Other Stories.* Trans. from the German by
Ralph Manheim. New York: Fawcett Crest 1966
Magnusson, Magnus. *Iceland Saga.* London: Bodley Head 1987
Magris, Claudio. *Weit von Wo – Verlorene Welt des Ostjudentums.* Trans.
from the Italian by Jutta Prasse. Vienna: Europa Verlag 1974
Marrus, Michael. *The Holocaust in History.* Hanover: Univ. Press of New
England 1987
Märthesheimer, Peter, and Ivo Frenzel, eds. *Der Fernsehfilm Holocaust:
Eine Nation ist betroffen.* Frankfurt: Fischer 1979
Mendelsohn, Ezra. *The Jews of East Central Europe between the World
Wars.* Bloomington: Indiana University Press 1983
Michel, Karl Markus, and Tilman Spengler. Kursbuch: *Die andere Hälfte
Europas,* vol. 81, Sept. 1985. Berlin: Rotbuch Verlag 1985
Milosz, Czeslaw. *The History of Polish Literature.* New York: Macmillan
1969
Miron, Dan. *A Traveler Disguised.* New York: Schocken Books 1973
Motzan, Peter, ed. *Der Herbst stöbert in den Blättern – Deutschsprachige
Lyrik aus Rumänien.* Berlin: Verlag Volk und Welt 1984
Müller, Herta. *Niederungen.* Berlin: Rotbuch Verlag 1984
– *Der Mensch ist ein grosser Fasan auf der Welt.* Berlin: Rotbuch Verlag
1986
Müller-Guttenbrunn, Adam. *Der grosse Schwabenzug.* Leipzig: Verlag L.
Staackmann 1914
Neufeld, Dietrich. *A Russian Dance of Death.* Trans. from the German
and edited by Al Reimer. Winnipeg: Hyperion Press 1977
Pollack, Martin. *Nach Galizien.* Vienna: Verlag Christian Brandstätter
1984
– *Des Lebens Lauf – Jüdische Familien-Bilder aus Zwischeneuropa.* Vienna:
Verlag Christian Brandstätter 1987
Pulzer, Peter. *The Rise of Political Anti-Semitism in Germany and Austria.*
London: Peter Halban 1988
Ransmayr, Christoph, ed. *Im blinden Winkel – Nachrichten aus Mitteleu-
ropa.* Vienna: Verlag Christian Brandstätter 1985. (See especially con-
tributions by Richard Swartz, Martin Pollack, Claudio Magris,
Christoph Ransmayr, and Ruth Beckermann.)
Rauch, Georg von. *The Baltic States.* Trans. from the German by Gerald
Onn. London: G. Hurst and Co. 1974
Rawicz, Piotr. *Blood from the Sky.* Trans. from the French by Peter Wiles.
New York: Harcourt, Brace and World 1964

Read, Anthony, and David Fisher. *The Deadly Embrace: Hitler, Stalin and the Nazi-Soviet Pact, 1939–1941.* New York: Norton 1988

Reich-Ranicki, Marcel. *Über Ruhestörer-Juden in der deutschen Literatur.* Munich: Piper 1973

Richler, Mordecai. *The Apprenticeship of Duddy Kravitz.* London: Andre Deutsch 1959

Riedl, Joachim, ed. *Versunkene Welt.* Vienna: Jewish Welcoming Service 1984

Rosenfeld, Alvin. *A Double Dying.* Bloomington: Indiana University Press 1980

Roskies, David. *Against the Apocalypse.* Cambridge: Harvard University Press 1984

Roth, Joseph. *Job: The Story of a Simple Man.* Trans. from the German by Dorothy Thompson. New York: Viking Press 1931

Schulz-Vobach, Klaus-Dieter. *Die Deutschen im Osten.* Hamburg: Hoffmann und Campe Verlag 1989

Serke, Jürgen. *Nach Hause – Eine Heimat-Kunde.* Cologne: Kiepenhauer and Witsch 1979

– *Böhmische Dörfer – Wanderungen durch eine verlassene literarische Landschaft.* Vienna: Zsolnay Verlag 1987

Seydel, Heinz, ed. *Welch Wort in die Kälte gerufen.* Berlin: Verlag der Nation 1968

Sievers, Leo. *Deutsche und Russen.* Hamburg: Stern-Buch 1980

Singer, Isaac Bashevis. *The Family Moskat.* Trans. from the Yiddish by A.H. Gross. New York: Farrar, Straus and Giroux 1950

– *The Magician of Lublin.* Trans. from the Yiddish by Elaine Gotlieb and Joseph Singer. New York: Farrar, Straus and Giroux 1960

– *The Collected Stories of Isaac Bashevis Singer.* Trans. by various translators from the Yiddish. New York: Farrar, Straus and Giroux 1982

Singer, Israel Joshua. *The Family Carnovsky.* Trans. by Joseph Singer. New York: Vanguard Press 1969

Sperber, Manes. *Than a Tear in the Sea.* Trans. from the German by Constantine Fitzgerald. New York: Bergen-Belsen Memorial Press 1967

– *Churban oder die unfassbare Gewissheit.* Vienna: Europa Verlag 1979

– *God's Water Carriers.* Trans. from the German by Joachim Neugroschel. New York: Holmes and Meier 1987

Steinke, Udo. *Horsky, Leo oder die Dankbarkeit der Mörder.* Frankfurt: Ullstein 1982

Stökl, Günther. *Osteuropa und die Deutschen.* Oldenburg: Gerhard Stalling Verlag 1967

Stumpp, Karl. *Die Russlanddeutschen*. Freilassing: Pannonia 1964

Swartz, Richard. 'Det låsta rummet. Den europeiska pluralismens under-gång,' ['The Locked Room. The Fall of European Pluralism']. *Du sköna gamla värld – den europeiska traditionens framtid*. Ed. Ingemar Karlsson. Stockholm: Sekretariatet för Framtidsstudier 1987

Torberg, Friedrich. *Die Tante Jolesch oder der Untergang des Abendlandes in Anekdoten*. Munich: Deutscher Taschenbuch Verlag 1975

Uhde, Milan. 'Wer das Gras auf den Gräbern mit Füssen tritt.' *Die Presse* (Vienna), 27/28 May 1989

Uhlhorn, Friedrich, and Walter Schlesinger. *Die deutschen Territorien*. Vol. 13 of Gebhardt *Handbuch der deutschen Geschichte*. Munich: Deutscher Taschenbuch Verlag 1974

Vegesack, Siegfried von. *Der letzte Akt*. Heilbronn: Eugen Salzer Verlag 1957

– *Die Baltische Tragödie*. Heilbronn: Eugen Salzer Verlag 1965 (Originally published by Salzer in 1935)

Wagner, Ernst. *Geschichte der Siebenbürger Sachsen*. Innsbuck: Wort und Welt 1982

Wagner, Richard. *Der Anfang einer Geschichte*. Cluj-Napoca: Dacia Verlag 1980

– *Hotel California 1*. Bucharest: Kriterion Verlag 1980

– *Hotel California 2*. Bucharest: Kriterion Verlag 1981

Weidenheim, Johannes. *Mensch was für eine Zeit oder eine Laus im deut-schen Pelz*. Munich: List Verlag 1968

Weiss, Peter. *De besegrade*. Stockholm: Bonniers 1948

– *The Investigation*. Trans. from the German by Jon Swan and Ulu Grosbard. New York: Atheneum 1966

Wiechert, Ernst. *Das einfache Leben*. Munich: Langen Müller 1939

Wisse, Ruth. *The Schlemiel as Modern Hero*. Chicago: University of Chicago Press 1971

Wistrich, Robert. *The Jews of Vienna in the Age of Franz Joseph*. London: Oxford University Press 1988

Wolf, Christa. *A Model Childhood* (in later additions it is titled *Patterns of Childhood*). Trans. from the German by Ursula Molinaro and Hedwig Rappott. New York: Farrar, Straus and Giroux 1980

Index